DICTATORSHIP, DEMOCRACY, AND GLOBALIZATION

DICTATORSHIP, DEMOCRACY, AND GLOBALIZATION

Argentina and the Cost of Paralysis, 1973–2001

KLAUS F. VEIGEL

The Pennsylvania State University Press
University Park, Pennsylvania

LIBRARY OF CONGRESS CATALOGING-IN-PUBLICATION DATA

Veigel, Klaus Friedrich, 1974– .
 Dictatorship, democracy, and globalization : Argentina and the cost of paralysis,
1973–2001 / Klaus F. Veigel.
  p.   cm.
Includes bibliographical references and index.
Summary: "Investigates the decline of the corporatist and inward-oriented postwar
 model of development during the 1970s and 1980s and the emergence of a new
 paradigm driven by the desire to participate in the process of globalization.
 Uses Argentina as a case study"—Provided by publisher.
 ISBN 978-0-271-03464-5 (cloth : alk. paper)
  1. Argentina—Economic conditions—1945–. 2. Argentina—Economic policy.
3. Debts, External—Argentina. 4. Argentina—Foreign economic relations.
5. Dictatorship—Argentina. 6. Democracy—Argentina. 7. Globalization—
Case studies.
I. Title.

HC175.V45 20
330.982'064—
2008047847

I DEDICATE THIS BOOK TO MY WIFE,

Gisela Garzón de la Roza

CONTENTS

FIGURES AND TABLES

AUTHOR'S NOTE AND ACKNOWLEDGMENTS

It would have been impossible to bring this book to fruition without the generous help and support from many people at Princeton University; in Buenos Aires, where I spent almost two years doing research and writing; and finally at Penn State University Press. First and foremost, I would like to thank Sandy Thatcher at Penn State University Press, who has been very supportive of my project and skillfully guided me through the revision process. I also greatly benefited from two anonymous reviewers' insightful comments on my manuscript. I would also like to thank Andrew B. Lewis, the copy editor of this book, whose attention to detail and thoughtful editorial suggestions were greatly appreciated.

This book has its origins in my graduate studies at Princeton University. My two academic advisers in the history department, Harold James and Jeremy Adelman, critically shaped my research and thinking about Argentine history, and I owe them a particular debt of gratitude. Harold James's writing on the international economy and economic crises has profoundly influenced my thinking on the subject. He has also been an inspiring teacher and mentor who gave me ample leeway to develop new ideas and explore new geographic regions. Jeremy Adelman introduced me to the history of Latin America, of which I had only the most basic knowledge when I first met him. Over the years, he displayed unwavering confidence that I could master not only the vast historiography but also make a contribution to the field. I am also grateful for the support and encouragement of Miguel Centeno of the Princeton Institute for International and Regional Affairs, whose sociological methodology proved inspiring. I would also like to thank Peter Kenen of the economics department, whose seminar on financial crises and the global economy during the fall semester of 2000 brought Argentina's predicament to my attention. Columbia University's Charles Calomiris explained during a guest lecture how Argentina had entered a debt trap that made economic collapse virtually inevitable. This inspired me to study Argentine economic history and to travel to Buenos Aires in June 2001 to conduct exploratory field research.

My first visit to Buenos Aires from June to August 2001 was a transformative experience. My initial goal had been to contribute to the understanding of

Argentina's long-term economic and political decline. My working assumption was that Argentina's reaction to the Great Depression was the turning point in Argentine economic history because it was then that the government had given up liberal free-trading attitudes and sound monetary management, which had made the country so successful during the Belle Époque.[1] While I carried out my research on economic policymaking in Argentina during the 1930s, a period known as the *década infame* (infamous decade), I witnessed Argentina slide into social and economic chaos in what Roberto Condés Conde would later describe as the worst crisis in the country's history.[2] This experience steered my research project in an entirely new direction. While strikes, demonstrations, and closed archives severely hampered my research on the Roca-Runciman Treaty, which was signed between Argentina and the United Kingdom in 1933, the heated public debate about the origins of the crisis and its culprits made it clear that the crisis had its most immediate origins in the struggle over how to respond to the onset of globalization since the 1970s and that there was still a lot to be learned about this critical period in the country's history.

Most of my research and writing took place in Buenos Aires, and I am grateful for the hospitality I received from the academic community. I owe particular debt of gratitude to Carlos Rodríguez for offering me a temporary home at the Universidad del CEMA, where I had my office space and could present my investigation at various research seminars. Among the professors at the Universidad del CEMA I would like to thank Mariana Conte Grand, Alejandro Corbacho, and Jorge Streb for their interest in my work and their helpful comments. I would also like to thank Jorge Schvarzer of the Universidad de Buenos Aires for his critical feedback and for the opportunity to present some of my research at a seminar in the economics department.

Primary research on the critical decades of the 1970s and 1980s was hampered by the sorry state of many archives and libraries in Argentina. Archives were difficult to access and generally incomplete; material on important periods has been lost or destroyed. Recordkeeping was not high on the agendas of governments whose main goal from week to week was survival. Moreover, governments that had violated property rights or left economic time bombs to their successors had every incentive to hide or destroy as much evidence of their administration as possible. Finally, thirty years of almost permanent economic crisis have left libraries and archives without the necessary resources to

1. Díaz Alejandro, *Essays;* Della Paolera and Taylor, *Straining at the Anchor.*
2. "Crisis, la peor de todas," *La Nación,* July 14, 2002.

catalogue and maintain their holdings. The fact that I still found a considerable amount of valuable material in archives and libraries in Buenos Aires needs to be attributed to the generous help of a large number of individuals. I would particularly like to thank Maria Mastrocesare and the late Enrique Gleizer at the Biblioteca del Congreso in Buenos Aires; Juan C. Foerster at the Tribunales de Commodoro Py in Buenos Aires, who helped me gain access to court documents from the case Alejandro Olmos vs. José Martínez de Hoz; and Daniel Scioli, vice president of Argentina, who personally intervened on my behalf to give me access to the archives of the Argentine Senate and Congress.

I supplemented documentary evidence with personal interviews in an effort to "read between the lines" of official documents and understand the intentions of political actors. Contacting and interviewing former politicians and technicians was easier than I had initially expected. I interviewed every living Argentine minister of the economy from the 1973–2001 period as well as many former ambassadors, central bank presidents, and ministers of labor, interior, economic coordination, and commerce. The most interesting conversations often took place with technicians, who had less of a personal stake in the history. I would like to thank Roberto Cortés Conde, Juan Carlos de Pablo, and Francisco Tropepi, who helped me to make first contacts with many politicians in Argentina.

Research on the international dimension of the Argentine crisis proved to be an easier endeavor. Tens of thousands of declassified documents from the State Department "Argentina Declassification Project" were invaluable. The State Department was also extremely responsive to my declassification requests under the Freedom of Information Act (FOIA) and granted me access to thousands of pages of previously closed documents from the U.S. Embassy in Buenos Aires, which had enjoyed unique access to sources inside every Argentine government. Intentions and actions of U.S. administrations can be understood using the presidential archives of Gerald Ford in Ann Arbor, Michigan; Jimmy Carter in Atlanta, Georgia; and Ronald Reagan in Simi Valley, California, as well as the personal papers of secretaries of the treasury William Simon and Donald Regan. The International Monetary Fund (IMF) was intensely involved in Argentina over the past three decades, as the abundant documentation of consultations shows. Most of the IMF documents have only recently been made available to the public in an effort to increase the transparency of the international organization and greatly enriched my understanding of the organization's influence on Argentine governments. I would particularly like to thank Jean G. Marcouyeux at the Archives of the International Monetary Fund,

Isabel Hagbrink and John Ferriter at the Inter-American Development Bank, Laura Kells of the Library of Congress, Mike Duggan at the Ronald Reagan Presidential Library, Donna Lehman at the Gerald Ford Presidential Library, James A. Yancey Jr. at the Jimmy Carter Library and Museum, Diane Shaw at the Special Collections Library of Lafayette College, Shelley Diamond at the Archives of JPMorganChase in New York, and Sarah Hartwell at the Rauner Library of Dartmouth College.

The research would have been impossible without generous financial support. In the first place, I would like to thank the Graduate School of Princeton University, the history department, and the Council on Regional Studies for the fellowship support I received during the five years of study. I received additional funds for my research trips and language training from the Center of International Studies at Princeton University and the MacArthur Foundation as well as from the Program in Latin American Studies (PLAS). PLAS also continued funding my research after my graduation when I worked as a lecturer at Princeton University. I am also grateful for financial support from the Dean's Fund for scholarly travel for the attendance of two conferences where I presented parts of my investigation.

Writing this book would have been impossible without extensive personal and academic support from family, friends, and colleagues in Princeton, Buenos Aires, and Germany. I would like to express my deep gratitude to Judy Hanson, Audrey Mainzer, and Tina Erdos of the history department and to Peter Johnson and the rest of the staff at Princeton University's Firestone Library for their relentless support. I would like to thank my friends, especially Kutlu Akalin, Ryan Jordan, Volker Menze, Clara Oberle, Ishita Pande, and Mitra Sharafi for including me in the "family" and instantly making me feel at home whenever I came to visit Princeton after months of research abroad. I am also indebted to Conor Healy, a close friend and my most important peer adviser, who read each of the chapters of the manuscript and always offered challenging and constructive criticism. In Argentina, I could also count on a large network of friends. I would like to especially thank Luis "Luigi" Nocetti, who always supported me and helped me contact some of the busiest politicians.

Finally, I would like to thank my family in Germany, my mother Ulrike Veigel, my father Frieder Veigel, and my brother Ulrich for their support during all the years away from home, and I am very grateful that they literally went out of their way to come and visit me in Argentina. This book is dedicated to my wife, Gisela Garzón de la Roza, whom I met on my first research trip to Argentina in the middle of the economic crisis of 2001. Our personal history is very much intertwined with the crisis of Argentina with which this book is concerned. She and her family helped me truly feel at home in Buenos Aires and to become much more than an outside observer. Her love and unrelenting faith in my ability to finish the book helped me through some of the hardest periods.

ABBREVIATIONS

PBIR	Banco de Intercambio Regional (an Argentine commercial bank)
BONEX	Bonos Externos (external bonds)
CAL	Comisión de Asesoramiento Legislativo (the legislative body of the military government)
CECI	Centre Européen de Coóperation Internationale (European Center for International Cooperation)
CEDES	Centro de Estudios de Estado y Sociedad (Center for the Study of State and Society)
CEPAL	Comisión Económica para América Latina y el Caribe (Economic Comission for Latin America and the Caribbean, U.N. agency)
CGT	Confederación General del Trabajo de la República Argentina (General Confederation of Labor)
CISEA	Centro de Investigaciones Sociales sobre el Estado y la Administración (Center for Social Research About the State and Public Administration)
GDP	Gross Domestic Product
IMF	International Monetary Fund
INDEC	Instituto Nacional de Estadística y Censos (Argentina's National Statistics Institute)
ISI	Import substituting industrialization
JP	Juventud Peronista (Peronist Youth)
LIBOR	London interbank offered rate
OPEC	Organization of the Petroleum Exporting Countries
OPIC	Overseas Private Investment Corporation
PJ	Partido Justicialista (Justicialist Party)
PRI	Partido Revolucionario Institucional (Institutional Revolutionary Party)
SELA	Sistema Económio Latinoamericano y del Caribe (Economic System for Latin America and the Caribbean)
UBS	Union Bank of Switzerland
UCR	Unión Cívica Radical (Radical Party)
UIA	Unión Industrial Argentina (Argentine Industrial Union)
YPF	Yacimientos Petrolíferos Fiscales ("Fiscal Petroleum Fields," Argentina's national petroleum company)

INTRODUCTION

The air was filled with tear gas and the smell of burning tires as Fernando De la Rúa and two bodyguards appeared on the roof of the Casa Rosada, the presidential palace in downtown Buenos Aires. Keeping their heads low, the three men ran toward the waiting presidential helicopter. Only minutes earlier, De la Rúa had resigned the presidency in the midst of the country's most severe economic crisis and following a week of violence that had left more than twenty people dead and hundreds wounded.[1] At 7:52 P.M., the helicopter lifted off into the dark clouds amid cheers from tens of thousands of angry protesters, who had gathered in front of the building on the Plaza de Mayo on this hot summer day, defying mounted police, armored vehicles, tear gas, and water cannons.[2] Two days later, provisional president Adolfo Rodríguez Saá declared the suspension of all debt payments. Lawmakers cheered the largest sovereign debt default in history by rising to their feet and chanting "Argentina, Argentina."[3]

1. "En helicóptero, como Isabel, y entre el llanto de sus ministros," *Clarín*, December 21, 2001.
2. "Represión en Plaza de Mayo: una batalla con cinco muertos," *Clarín*, December 21, 2001.
3. "Argentina to Suspend Debt Payment: Stage Appears Set for Historic Default," *Washington Post*, December 23, 2001.

The images of a legally elected president escaping from the roof of the Casa Rosada were fraught with symbolism. Throughout the twentieth century, the Plaza de Mayo had been the center of Argentine political life. Populist politicians, popular uprisings, peaceful protesters, and military coups had all attempted to claim the public space in front of the government house for themselves and their causes. Juan Domingo Perón held rallies that attracted hundreds of thousands of his followers to the square during the late 1940s and early 1950s and again after his return from exile in the early 1970s. His opponents were keenly aware of the symbolic importance of controlling the Plaza de Mayo. In June 1954, a military uprising following Perón's excommunication from the Catholic Church resulted in hundreds of deaths as navy fighters bombed Plaza de Mayo in order to disperse a pro-Perón demonstration.[4] During the late 1970s and early 1980s, the Plaza de Mayo again became highly contested. In defiance of the repressive military government the Madres de la Plaza de Mayo protested every Thursday against the disappearances of their children.[5] In early 1982, the plaza also became the site of the first large-scale demonstration against the military dictatorship and for a return to democracy. Shortly thereafter, the military managed to rally its supporters to the square as well. Following the invasion of the Falkland/Malvinas Islands in the South Atlantic in April 1982, hundreds of thousands of Argentines filled the Plaza de Mayo to cheer the dictator Leopoldo Galtieri.

The Casa Rosada itself is emblematic of Argentina's former prosperity, long economic decline, and the superficial nature of its economic success during the 1990s. The presidential palace was inaugurated at the zenith of the Belle Époque, the export-driven economic boom at the end of the nineteenth century. By the late 1980s, it was in urgent need of renovation, renovation that was repeatedly postponed because of the notorious emptiness of the public coffers. In 1997, President Carlos Menem finally decided to apply only a cosmetic makeover to the venerable building. The front of the building facing the Plaza de Mayo—the perspective most frequently depicted on postcards—was painted in the original bright pink.[6] Behind this shiny façade, the building continued to crumble. This structural instability made it impossible for the presidential helicopter to set down completely on the roof of the building on the fateful December evening in 2001.

4. "Argentine Rebels Rise, Raid Capital, but Perón Reports Revolt Crushed," *New York Times,* June 17, 1955.
5. Bouvard, *Revolutionizing Motherhood.*
6. "Demoran arreglos en la Casa Rosada," *Clarín,* August 30, 1998.

Explanations of the unparalleled crisis have largely focused on corruption and economic policymaking during the heady 1990s and the alleged incompetence of the hapless president Fernando De la Rúa.[7] Critics of the policy of economic liberalization pursued during the presidency of Carlos Menem argue that Argentina had become another victim of "neoliberalism," which had been actively promoted by the U.S. government and the International Monetary Fund (IMF) under the "Washington Consensus."[8] Others insist that Argentina had failed to implement neoliberal economic reform with enough determination.[9] They argue that Carlos Menem and his successor Fernando De la Rúa had been unable or unwilling to control public spending and had been forced to borrow from abroad to continue to govern. Foreign debt combined with the fixed exchange rate of the Convertibility Program made Argentina vulnerable to the sudden reversal of financial flows.[10] If the IMF was at fault, proponents of this view argue, it was not because they had imposed "orthodoxy" but rather because they had failed to do so consistently.[11]

This focus on the 1990s misses important long-term developments in Argentina. Twenty-five years before De la Rúa's unscheduled departure, another president was whisked off the roof of the Casa Rosada. At 12:49 A.M. on March 24, 1976, an air force helicopter with Isabel Perón on board rose into the night skies over Buenos Aires. The military coup had just begun, and the military would arrest the president shortly thereafter at the Aeroparque, the city's domestic airport.[12] This time, the Plaza de Mayo was not filled with protesters; the trade unions had not responded to calls for a general strike to defend the embattled constitutional government. While patriotic military marches blared out of the radio, the military started rounding up and arresting opposition leaders around the country.[13]

This study focuses on the quarter century between Isabel Perón's and Fernando De la Rúa's hasty departures from the roof of the Casa Rosada. It argues that these two departures were not just the results of cyclical political and economic instability.[14] Rather, both were part of an epic struggle over the very model

7. Blustein, *And the Money Kept Rolling In (and Out)*.

8. Arceo, "Hegemonía norteamericana"; Oxhorn and Ducatenzeiler, *What Kind of Democracy?*

9. Perry and Serven, "Argentina's Macroeconomic Collapse"; Teijeiro, "Una vez más, la política fiscal."

10. Guidotti, Sturzenegger, and Villar, "On the Consequences of Sudden Stops."

11. Mussa, *Argentina and the Fund*.

12. "A treinta años de la noche más larga," *Clarín*, March 24, 2006.

13. Telegram, Buenos Aires to State Department, "Coup in Argentina: SITREP No. 3," March 24, 1976, U.S. Department of State, Argentina Declassification Project.

14. Gerchunoff and Llach, *El ciclo de la ilusión y el desencanto*, 9.

of economic and political order. The military coup that ousted Isabel Perón marked the end of the corporatist and inward-oriented model, which had dominated Argentina since the 1940s, and the troubled emergence of a new paradigm driven by the desire to participate in the worldwide economic integration, now commonly known as "globalization." De la Rúa's resignation was closely linked to the failure of this new model to solve the long-standing problems of the country. Both departures highlight the conflictual nature of policymaking in Argentina, where veto players—such as the military, trade unions, provincial governors, and even rival politicians within the ruling party—can paralyze the country and bring down the government without offering a viable alternative.

The Argentine postwar social and economic order had its origins in the experience of depression and war, when the country had turned its back on the world in the face of the economic crisis and the exclusion from its traditional export markets. In response, Argentina adopted inward-oriented economic policies aimed at building a modern industrial country and moved toward a corporatist polity with strong and combative trade unions and a growing public sector. This strategy initially bore fruit. During the 1950s and 1960s, the economy grew almost as fast as during the last decade before World War I and substantially faster than during the interwar years.[15]

The combination of corporatism and inward-oriented economic development laid the foundations for continued economic and political instability. Import-substitution industrialization failed to eliminate the country's dependence on imports because modernization required ever larger investments in advanced technology not available domestically. At the same time, the domestic industry—sheltered from international markets by high tariffs—became less and less competitive and therefore less and less able to generate much-needed foreign exchange. The consequence was continued economic instability as balance of payment crises led to "stop-go" cycles with periods of sharp downturn alternating with periods of rapid economic expansion.[16] By the late 1960s and early 1970s, economists and politicians in Argentina had reached a broad consensus about the nature of the economic impasse; however, they found solutions much more difficult to agree upon and even harder to implement.[17]

This internal struggle coincided with a severe worldwide economic and political crisis. The 1970s saw the end of the postwar social consensus throughout the Western world. This loss of consensus threatened the political stability

15. Sourrouille, Kosacoff, and Lucángeli, *Transnacionalización*, 54.
16. Díaz Alejandro, "Stop-Go Cycles"; Taylor, "On the Costs of Inward-Looking Development."
17. Sourrouille, Kosacoff, and Lucángeli, *Transnacionalización*, 60.

to which governments had grown accustomed in previous decades. Social and political unrest rocked capitalist countries from Japan to Europe and throughout the Americas during this critical historical juncture. The situation in Argentina was especially dramatic. Excluded from power for almost two decades, the Peronist movement had become increasingly radicalized and violent. The military and right-wing organizations regarded all left-wing militancy as part of a communist campaign to infiltrate the country and responded with repression and violence using counterinsurgency tactics they had learned from the United States. The result was a vicious circle of increasing political violence in the early 1970s that left hundreds dead.[18]

The 1970s were also a period of crisis and transformation for the world economy. The postwar economic order was based on nation states with strong welfare systems. They protected themselves from the vagaries of world financial markets through capital controls and fixed exchange rates and relied on the financial, political, and military strength of the United States in times of crisis. During the late 1960s and early 1970s, both layers of protection started to fall apart simultaneously. Capital market liberalization during the late 1960s allowed for larger global capital flows and destabilized the system of fixed exchange rates. Following the devaluations of the dollar in 1971 and 1973 and stunned by the twin humiliations of the withdrawal from Vietnam and President Nixon's Watergate Scandal, the United States was experiencing an unprecedented crisis of confidence. The oil shocks, which rattled the world in 1973, added to the sense of gloom. By mid-1974, the world economy was in the throes of rampant inflation, economic growth was decelerating, and a massive disequilibrium emerged in international payments.

How developing countries would react to this new international environment was far from preordained. Their choices were to deepen their economic integration with the West or to attempt to break free from it. The first option offered the opportunity to finally overcome the problem of exchange bottlenecks and achieve what W. W. Rostow called "takeoff into self-sustained growth."[19] As capital markets expanded, foreign loans offered a seemingly painless way of overcoming the structural impediments to industrialization that had held them back during the postwar decades. However, this required both political stability at home and support from the United States and international financial institutions abroad, preconditions democratic governments often found difficult to

---

18. Lewis, *Guerrillas and Generals.*
19. Rostow, *Stages of Economic Growth.*

fulfill during this turbulent period. The second option, proposed by critics of the existing international economic system, was based on the assumption that the crisis of the capitalist center presented an excellent opportunity for peripheral countries to break out of their economic and political "dependency" by reducing economic ties to the West.[20]

Over the course of the 1970s, Argentina attempted both these strategies and failed, despite the fact that its near self-sufficiency in energy production placed it in a significantly better position than most Latin American countries to cope with the new global economic environment. Yet Argentina not only endured the bloodiest dictatorship in Latin America with between twelve and thirty thousand dead and disappeared; it turned in the worst economic performance by far of any major Latin American country. While Brazil enjoyed a long economic boom starting in the late 1960s, the "Brazilian miracle," and Chile enjoyed strong growth driven by foreign borrowing in the second half of the 1970s, in the early 1980s the Argentine military dictatorship had nothing to show for high inflation and staggering foreign debt. To make matters worse, Argentina's sufferings continued during the international debt crisis of the "lost decade" of the 1980s. Between 1970 and 1990, Argentina's per capita income fell by almost a quarter, while Brazil's doubled and Chile's rose by nearly half (see fig. 1).

Why did Chile and Brazil perform much better than Argentina despite having been faced with similar political, social, and economic problems in the 1970s and despite having also been governed by military dictatorships over a long period of time? This study argues that Argentina's dramatic political, social, and economic disintegration was caused by political paralysis over how to respond to the challenges of a rapidly changing global environment during the critical decades of the 1970s and 1980s. When the postwar consensus crumbled, no new strategy could muster enough support to replace it. The reason for this was another legacy of depression and postwar economic growth, namely the emergence of two new centers of power in Argentina: the Peronist trade unions and the armed forces.

The power of the Peronist trade unions dates back to 1943 when Juan Domingo Perón became minister of labor in the military government of Pedro Ramírez Pablo. Only two years later, the trade unions won a showdown with the military government. On October 9, 1945, Perón's opponents in the military government forced him to resign and imprisoned him on Martín García Island

---

20. Frank, *Capitalism and Underdevelopment in Latin America*, 7.

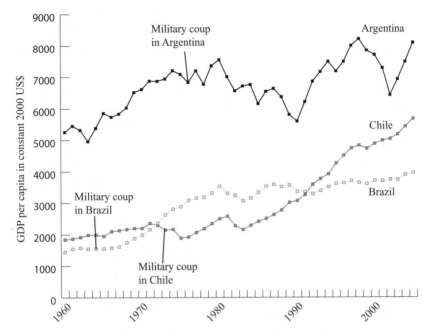

Fig. 1   Economic performance of Argentina, Brazil, and Chile, 1960–2004

in the Rio de la Plata delta. However, they were obliged to release him shortly thereafter when his supporters staged mass protests. With this political victory, the Peronist trade unions established themselves firmly as a political power to be reckoned with. Neither repression under military dictatorships nor trade union reform under democratic rule succeeded in eliminating them as a power over the course of the subsequent half-century.

The military became an active participant in politics because of the Great Depression. In September 1930 Hipólito Yrigoyen, the first Argentine president elected by broad popular suffrage in 1916, also became the first to fall to a military coup.[21] Over the course of the next half-century, the military intervened directly or indirectly in the political process during every major economic downturn or political crisis. When tanks rattled through the streets of Buenos Aires on March 24, 1976, this was a familiar sight. The cia described the unfolding events as a part of a political cycle in which "the military intervenes to take power from an ineffectual civilian government, only to give it back when they

21. Torres, *La década infame.*

cannot govern effectively either."[22] While this prediction that the dictatorship would return power to civilians after failing to solve the problems itself ultimately proved to be correct, the military government of 1976–83 marked a clear departure from its predecessors. It was not only more repressive and violent than any previous military regime in Argentina; it was also more revolutionary.

Military coups in Argentina had often proclaimed themselves to be revolutionary. The anti-Peronist coup in 1955 called itself the Revolución Libertadora, the "liberating Revolution," and the coup that overthrew Arturo Illia in 1966 proclaimed the "Revolución Argentina." However, neither of the two military coups had revolutionary implications. They aimed merely at keeping Juan Domingo Perón and his followers from power while continuing to pursue an inward-oriented development project within a corporatist political framework. The leaders of the Proceso de Reorganización Nacional, the "Process of National Reorganization," by contrast, believed that they had to abandon the postwar economic model in order to break out of the cycle of political instability and eliminate Peronism as a political force. They hoped to achieve these goals with the help of brutal repression on the one hand and economic opening and liberalization on the other.[23]

In Brazil, the military had played a similar role during the postwar decades. They saw themselves as the incarnation of their country's corporatist national project, which encompassed a strong political as well as economic component. The military repeatedly intervened in the political process when it felt that democratically elected governments threatened their vision of the country's future greatness. At the same time, the military had become tightly intertwined with the country's industrialization and modernization project and controlled a large share of heavy industry. Unlike the Argentine coup in 1976, the Brazilian coup of 1964 did not represent a break with the military's corporatist past, and the two decades of military rule that followed did not see any drive toward economic liberalization or privatization. In fact, the "Brazilian miracle" was not built on free-market economics but on a new form of authoritarian developmentalism that created important incentives for entrepreneurial activity and encouraged foreign borrowing to create a self-sufficient industrial base.[24]

Chile's military coup and economic policies, by contrast, strongly resembled

---

22. Central Intelligence Agency, Directorate of Intelligence, Office of Political Research, "Whither Argentina: New Political System or More of the Same?" February 1976, Declassified Documents of the National Security Council, 4.

23. Azpiazu, Basualdo, and Khavisse, *El nuevo poder económico*, 186.

24. Coes, *Macroeconomic Crises*; Flecha de Lima, "Liberalism Versus Nationalism."

Argentina's. Only three years apart, both coups were motivated by a growing sense of "ungovernability" and a "crisis of the state" among important sectors of society.[25] Both juntas, that of Augusto Pinochet in Chile and of Jorge Rafael Videla in Argentina, persecuted political opponents and real or imagined "subversives" with unprecedented brutality and imposed economic policies inspired by an anti-Keynesian free-market ideology championed by economists at the University of Chicago.[26] Not surprisingly, both countries experienced an exploding foreign debt, growing income inequality, and the destruction of a large part of the industrial sector that had emerged since the 1940s as a response to government incentives to substitute imports.[27]

The difference between the two countries lay in the political dynamics of economic reform. In Argentina, important sectors of the military establishment remained skeptical of the free market creed espoused by the Videla's minister of the economy José Martínez de Hoz and resisted any economic reforms that threatened their economic power. At the same time, they were unable to return to a corporatist model, which the Brazilian military continued to promote. When Argentina started to face serious economic difficulties in 1981, the military was no longer able to hide the deep division between the corporatist and the neoliberal factions. Within two years, the military changed the course of economic policy no fewer than five times, wavering between renewed interventionism and more vigorous economic liberalization. The economic consequences were disastrous; indeed, the military government achieved the precise opposite of what it had intended—and promised. When the military government departed in late 1983, not only had they failed to achieve sustainable growth, the economy was as closed as it had been seven years earlier and state control was still ubiquitous. In addition, the military government had burdened the country with more than US$45 billion in foreign debt. Instead of overcoming the stop-go cycles and creating sustainable economic growth, the military government had burdened the country with a high external debt that created a permanent exchange bottleneck during the 1980s that suffocated growth completely. The inept and arbitrary economic management of the military dictatorship left Argentina burdened with two additional long-term liabilities. By association with its authoritarian right-wing agenda it had delegitimized liberal reform and integration into the world economy. This perception could only be overcome

25. Schamis, "Reconceptualizing Latin American Authoritarianism in the 1970s," 202.
26. Valdés, *Pinochet's Economists*.
27. Gatica, *Deindustrialization in Chile*.

with great difficulty during the 1990s and is now—after the failure of the Menem experiment—again conventional wisdom in Argentina. At the same time, the repeated experience with arbitrary confiscatory policies during the military dictatorship prepared the ground for an unprecedented degree of corruption, which haunted Argentina through the 1990s and into the early twenty-first century. The military's disastrous failure in the political, military, and economic realms also eliminated the armed forces as a major political player, thus strengthening the Peronist party, the Partido Justicialista (Justicialist Party, or PJ), and the very trade unions it had sought to eliminate. Following the return to democracy, the Unión Cívica Radical (Radical Party, or UCR) would be unable to govern effectively in the face of Peronist opposition, and both Radical presidents—Raúl Alfonsín and Fernando De la Rúa—resigned prematurely amid economic and political chaos and massive popular mobilization.

In Chile, by contrast, the military had been neither a major political force nor a pillar of the country's developmentalist project during the postwar decades. When the military coup overthrew Salvador Allende's government on September 11, 1973, Pinochet was able to establish himself as undisputed leader in part by exploiting the Chilean military's professionalism.[28] Pinochet's one-man rule was in turn an essential precondition for the creation of a new hegemonic order based on free trade and free-market economics because it shielded civilian technocrats from pressure to reverse their policies in time of crisis.[29] The difference between Chile and Argentina became particularly pronounced when the lending boom of the 1970s came to a sudden halt in 1981/82. Both countries experienced a severe currency and banking crisis, which led to a steep recession and rising unemployment. However, while the Argentine military abandoned the market-oriented reform project and ultimately withdrew to the barracks amid growing political turmoil, Pinochet remained firmly in power, moderating some of his economic policies but not giving up the neoliberal agenda.[30] When Pinochet finally surrendered the presidency in 1990, the new economic consensus was already so engrained and appeared so successful that subsequent civilian leaders, including the socialist presidents Ricardo Lagos and Michelle Bachelet, left the basic tenets of Pinochet's economic model unchallenged.[31]

28. Arriagada Herrera, *Pinochet*, 38.
29. Valenzuela, "Military in Power."
30. Silva, "Capitalist Coalitions," 559.
31. Scott Mainwaring, "Democracy in Brazil and the Southern Cone"; Tulchin and Varas, *From Dictatorship to Democracy*.

International actors such as the U.S. government, the IMF, and large multinational banks played a major role in the unfolding events. However, extensive research using recently declassified documents and personal interviews with many of the protagonists show that at no time were they in the position to "impose" an economic or political model as many Argentine observers assert.[32] The reason for this is that Argentina was never a high priority in the U.S. foreign policy agenda (except during the brief South Atlantic conflict in early 1982). Unlike the case of Brazil in 1964 and Chile in 1973, the U.S. government and the CIA did not actively participate in the preparations for the military coup that ousted Maria Estela Martínez de Perón on March 24, 1976, even though the CIA and the State Department were aware of the military's intentions and broadly approved of them.[33] Subsequent U.S. administrations wavered between support of and opposition to the Argentine military government. The incoming Carter administration sharply opposed the Argentine dictatorship for their human rights abuses. The economic pressure they tried to apply, however, was of almost no consequence. Ronald Reagan initially embraced Leopoldo Galtieri for his staunch anticommunism and his support of U.S. intervention in Central America. However, he dropped his ally in favor of the "Iron Lady" Margaret Thatcher when Galtieri invaded the Falkland/Malvinas Islands and rejected Reagan's personal plea to withdraw. After the return to democracy, Reagan embraced the newly elected president Raúl Alfonsín, and James Baker, secretary of the treasury during Reagan's second term, enjoyed a very close working relationship with his Argentine counterpart Juan V. Sourrouille. However, the United States was unable to convince the Alfonsín administration to adopt an orthodox, "liberal" economic policy, and the Argentine authorities never managed to convince the Reagan administration to extend a helping hand in their quest for a substantial debt reduction.

The U.S. government also tried to exert influence on Argentina through the IMF. However, evidence from the period under investigation reveals that the Treasury of the United States was unable to dominate the IMF completely. In critical moments, the IMF asserted its autonomy. Two episodes are noteworthy. While the Carter administration tried to apply economic pressure on the military dictatorship starting in 1977, the IMF consistently maintained its strong working relationship, thus undermining the U.S. efforts. In 1988, Secretary of

32. Galasso, *De la Banca Baring al FMI;* Minsburg and Antognazi, *Los guardianes del dinero;* Tenembaum, *Enemigos.*
33. Davis, *Brotherhood of Arms;* Kornbluh, *Pinochet File;* Parker, *Brazil and the Quiet Intervention;* Sigmund, *United States and Democracy in Chile;* Skidmore, *Politics of Military Rule in Brazil.*

the Treasury James Baker applied considerable pressure on the World Bank and the IMF to continue supporting the Alfonsín administration's faltering Austral Plan. The World Bank gave in, but the IMF did not, which led to a painful rift between the two sister institutions.[34]

Nor was the IMF as powerful as some observers have suggested. It became a critical actor only during moments of crisis when the Argentine government desperately needed financial help. Even then, the IMF was far from able to "impose" austerity measures on the country. Rather, Argentina successfully used open threats of default and pleas for special help to a democracy under attack as bargaining tools in negotiations with the IMF.[35] More important than the concessions the IMF granted Argentina in the negotiations was the inability of the IMF to oblige the authorities to live up to the promises they had made. When this happened, the IMF could only declare the country in breach of the agreement and cut additional financing.

Developments in the wake of the crisis of 2001 offer some reason to assume that the fundamental political paralysis that has hindered Argentina's integration into the world economy has been broken. Néstor Kirchner has enjoyed a firm hold on power since 2003 and has been able to consolidate a new political and economic consensus based on state intervention in the economy, an undervalued peso, and the rejection of neoliberalism and free trade. The short-term results of the new economic policies have been impressive. Between 2003 and 2007, the Argentine economy grew at a faster rate than in any period since World War I. The rapid expansion has coincided with a large fiscal surplus, a competitive exchange rate, and the first meaningful reduction of the external debt since the beginning of its accumulation in the 1970s. This has led some analysts to believe that Kirchner has finally found the "holy grail" of economic policy, namely a recipe for sustainable, noninflationary economic development.[36]

This faith in Kirchner and his economic policy closely resembles the admiration Carlos Menem and Domingo Cavallo received in the mid-1990s when the Convertibility Plan seemed to be propelling the country into a bright future. Not unlike the previous economic miracle, Kirchner's economic success could quickly falter if external circumstances change and internal conflicts resurface. Since 2003, the external environment has been extremely favorable for Argentina. Liquidity in world financial markets is unusually high. This has helped

34. Kapur, Lewis, and Webb, *World Bank.*
35. Stiles, "Argentina's Bargaining with the IMF."
36. Ministerio de Economía y Producción, *Evolución Reciente de la Economía Argentina y Perspectivas de Sostenibilidad.*

reduce interest rates on Argentine sovereign bonds to record-low levels—despite its recent default on a large part of its obligations.[37] Prices for Argentine agricultural exports are extremely high because of the growing demand from China and India.[38] This has led to an agricultural boom, which has also helped eliminate Argentina's chronic fiscal deficit because export taxes on agricultural products are the federal government's third-largest source of revenue (after sales and income taxes).[39] In the rest of the economy, rapid growth has contributed to a significant reduction of unemployment and poverty. Nevertheless, not all is well. The destruction of property rights and widespread price controls in the wake of the crisis curtailed necessary investments in plants and infrastructure. Many companies operate at or close to their capacity, and shortages, especially of gas and electricity, have become a common occurrence throughout the country. Prices also continue to rise rapidly even though the National Statistics Institute (Instituto Nacional de Estadística y Censos, or INDEC) attempts to conceal it.[40] Only time will tell whether Néstor Kirchner or his wife and successor Cristina Fernández de Kirchner will be able to manage the economy once external conditions turn less favorable and sectoral interests begin to conflict.[41]

37. "El riesgo país bajó un punto básico a 205 unidades," INFOBAE, February 2, 2007.

38. For a detailed statistics of Argentine exports, see Polonsky, "Estructura del comercio exterior argentino del año 2006."

39. According to the statistics of the Argentine Ministry of the Economy for the first half of 2008, available at http://www.mecon.gov.ar/sip/basehome/pormes.htm (accessed August 25, 2008).

40. "Escándalo en el Indec: denuncian que borraron datos de inflación," El Cronista, May 4, 2007.

41. "Mrs Kirchner Steps Forward," Economist, July 5, 2007.

1 THE CRISIS OF THE 1970S AND THE SEARCH FOR A NEW ECONOMIC ORDER

The 1970s were a watershed in twentieth-century economic history. With the breakdown of the Bretton Woods System and the oil shocks of 1973 and 1979, the postwar economic order came to end; and after almost a decade of adjustment a new and more tightly integrated world economy slowly took its place, a process now commonly referred to as "globalization." Industrial and developing countries alike were caught off guard by these developments and wavered in their response to them. In the United States, Richard Nixon and Gerald Ford proposed more state intervention in the economy as a remedy to the crisis. A new consensus in favor of economic liberalization emerged only slowly in the industrialized countries during the late 1970s and early 1980s.

The changing international political and economic environment of the mid-1970s contributed decisively to the spreading of a new kind of military dictatorship throughout Latin America. While the 1970s were a turbulent decade in the entire Western world, the uncertainty and rapid social and political changes had even more explosive consequences in increasingly polarized and politically mobilized Latin American countries. The search for a new political and economic model in response to the changing international economic environment often resulted in a violent showdown between two uncompromising ideological camps. On the one side stood populist or leftist movements seeking to end Latin America's dependency on trade with and investments from the industrial North. On the other side were conservatives who saw the easy availability of capital on international markets as an opportunity to realize ambitious projects and grow rapidly at a time when industrial countries languished. The latter needed the support of the military because access to international capital markets required economic stability, which military dictatorships found easier to guarantee than democratically elected governments.

The postwar economic order was a direct response to lessons learned from the experience of the Great Depression and World War II. The system of fixed but adjustable exchange rates established at the Bretton Woods Conference sought to avoid the rigidity and deflationary tendencies of the interwar gold-exchange system on the one hand and the destructive consequences of unilateral devaluations and trade restrictions during the Great Depression on the other. Restrictions on international capital flows were intended to eliminate destabilizing currency speculation and give member countries political freedom to pursue active fiscal and monetary policies. Self-professed Keynesian economists argued that the state had to play a vital role in the economy in order to avoid a repetition of the economic collapse of the 1930s.[1] These lessons were largely unquestioned during the immediate postwar period. The evidence from the failure of the market to regulate itself during the Depression and the success of government-sponsored programs during Roosevelt's New Deal and World War II was simply too overwhelming. Consequently, during the postwar years state bureaucracies grew faster than ever before, and state participation in the economy reached new heights.[2]

Developing countries also learned important lessons from war, depression, and the new currents of economic theory. The crisis of the 1930s discredited economic liberalism and after the war pushed Latin American countries toward an economic and political regime of "state capitalism."[3] The combination of a corporatist system of interest representation and state-led, inward-oriented economic policies created a tight interdependency of state and civil society. Corporatism acknowledged political mass participation while trying to control it by channeling political activities into a limited number of recognized functional

1. Winch, "Keynes, Keynesianism, and State Intervention," 107.
2. Shonfield, *Modern Capitalism*, 64.
3. Malloy, "Authoritarianism and Corporatism in Latin America," 11.

interest groups, which could negotiate with each other and the government. The state—under both civilian and military governments—appropriated the role as a mediator between different interest groups and at the same time assumed responsibility for economic growth and prosperity. Consequently, the state grew more and more powerful but governments less and less stable. Economic crises threatened the very legitimacy of the government and often resulted in unscheduled and often unconstitutional regime changes.[4]

The breakdown of international trade during the Depression and World War II also cautioned developing countries against relying on international cooperation for future growth. During the Depression, many countries closed their markets to imports from developing countries or levied hefty tariffs on their products. During the war, peripheral countries were unable to purchase necessary capital and consumer goods because the belligerents needed everything they produced for the war effort.[5] The widely shared assumption among economists that trade would play an increasingly marginal role in the postwar world reinforced the skepticism toward the prospect of trade-led growth. They reasoned that growth and industrialization in the periphery would reduce the need to exchange raw materials for finished goods, the predominant form of exchange during the nineteenth century.[6] Economic theorists in the periphery even went a step further, explaining that international trade of traditional Latin American export goods not only failed to offer a sustainable path to economic development but rather channeled the benefits of productivity growth to consumers in the industrial North instead of raising levels of prosperity in the South. The reasons for this unequal relationship between center and periphery was to be found in an unlimited supply of labor, which kept wages close to subsistence levels as W. Arthur Lewis explained or a long-term decline in the terms of trade as Hans Walter Singer and Raúl Prebisch argued.[7] This new economic paradigm, endorsed by the United Nations Economic Commission for Latin America (CEPAL), convinced governments in most Latin American countries to apply a policy of import-substituting industrialization (ISI), which consisted of incentives for domestic industrial production and protection against foreign competition.[8]

4. Ibid., 4; Lewis and Torrents, *Argentina in the Crisis Years*, 494.

5. Díaz Alejandro, "Latin America in the 1930s."

6. James, *End of Globalization*, 106.

7. Lewis, "Economic Development"; Prebisch, *Towards a Dynamic Development Policy*; Singer, "Distribution of Gains."

8. Hirschman, "Political Economy of Import-Substituting Industrialization."

Keynesian economic policies have often been credited for the success of industrial countries during the postwar decades, while the application of ISI has served as explanation for the economic failure of Latin American during the same period.[9] Both assertions are misleading. The two countries most eager to introduce Keynesian economic measures were also the least successful in relative terms, namely the United Kingdom and the United States. Germany and Japan, by contrast, pursued rather orthodox fiscal and monetary policies during the 1950s and 1960s.[10] Economic development in Latin America during the postwar decade was better than observers have made it out to be. Growth rates during the 1950s and 1960s were considerably higher than during the first half of the twentieth century and in many countries even higher than during the boom years of the late nineteenth century, the Belle Époque. However, they fell short of expectations because of even higher rates of growth in industrialized and East Asian countries.[11] Latin America development only entered into crisis in the 1970s when the postwar economic order started to disintegrate and countries started to look for new recipes for growth and development.

What happened in the early 1970s to cause such a permanent disruption of the postwar economic order? The stability associated with the industrialized North was based on the international economic order of the Bretton Woods System and faith in the financial and political strength of the United States. Both disappeared simultaneously in the early 1970s. The crisis the United States lived through in the early 1970s was not only economic but also political, military, and moral. The U.S. withdrawal from Vietnam following the peace talks in Paris in January 1973 showed American military weakness in the face of communist advances. When even this cease-fire failed to hold and Saigon fell to the North Vietnamese in April 1975, the military morale and the international standing of the United States reached a new low. In the domestic arena, the United States had also seemingly lost the moral high ground. Richard Nixon's ignominious resignation in June 1974 shattered confidence in the American political class and heightened the sense of moral and political decay. Some scholars started to liken the United States to the Roman Empire before its fall.[12] In 1975, the Trilateral Commission in a report written by Samuel Huntington even talked

9. Taylor, "On the Costs of Inward-Looking Development."

10. Shonfield, *Modern Capitalism*, 64.

11. For a discussion of reasons for the postwar boom in Europe, Japan, and the United States, see Eichengreen, "Institutions and Economic Growth"; Kindleberger, *Europe's Postwar Growth;* Lewis, *Evolution of the International Economic Order;* and Olson, *Rise and Decline of Nations.*

12. Grant, *Fall of the Roman Empire.*

about a "crisis of democracy" caused by an excess of democratic participation in government.[13]

The countries of Latin America were all keenly aware of the hegemonic crisis but they differed sharply in their responses to the new situation. The Peronist government in Buenos Aires concluded in a strategy paper titled "Análisis de la situación estratégica regional y mundial" (Analysis of the Global and Regional Strategic Situation) that the world was approaching a new equilibrium with a stronger Soviet Union and a permanently weakened North America. Argentina should use the opportunity to break out of its dependent relationship with the United States.[14] The briefing papers for Brazil's military dictator Ernesto Geisel showed that his advisers had a different reaction. While they agreed with the Argentine perception that the United States was severely weakened following the debacle in Vietnam and Richard Nixon's Watergate scandal, they cautioned him not to underestimate the United States. They argued that the United States might have renounced its "omnipotence," but not its power. Brazil should use this transition to strengthen its ties with the United States while at the same time asserting a stronger and more egalitarian position.[15] When some Latin American countries—most notably Mexico and Venezuela—tried to organize a Latin American Economic System (SELA) in an effort to weaken the influence of the United States in the region, Brazil was strongly opposed to the "disastrous articulation of Latin American resentments against the United States" and used every possible means to block it.[16]

A series of events in the Middle East compounded the sense of insecurity that characterized the 1970s. Terrorist attacks, such as against the Israeli Olympic team in Munich in 1972 and the hijackings of airplanes, became increasingly frequent, and tensions between Israel and its Arab neighbors continued to escalate. The 1973 Yom Kippur War between Israel on one side and Egypt and Syria,

13. Crozier, Huntington, and Watanuki, *Crisis of Democracy.*
14. Subsistema Relaciones Internacionales, "Análisis de la situación estratégica regional y mundial," Marzo 1975, 4, legajo: Carpetas Especiales 1975, Organismos Internacionales, caja: América Central (política), Archivos del Ministerio de Relaciones Exteriores y Culto de la República Argentina.
15. Golbery pelo Presidente Geisel, "política externa americana," Secreto, Brasília, 20 de março de 1974, folder: EG pr 1974.03.18, box: EG pr 1974.03.28 F-1464–1484, Ministerio de Fazenda, Arquivo Ernesto Geisel.
16. Telegrama, BRASEMB Montevidéu para Exteriores, "Particular para o Senhor Ministro de Estado," Secreto-Exclusivo-Urgentissimo, 22/7/75, AAS mre ai 1974.06.07, Dossiê Integração Econômica, Subserie Assuntos Interamericanos, Arquivo Azeredo da Silveira; Telegrama, BRASEMB Panamá, "Comemoração do Sesquicentenario do Congresso Anfictionico. Cancelamento da Reunião de Presidentes," Confidencial, 29/3/76, AAS mre ai 1974.06.07, Dossiê Integração Econômica, Subserie Assuntos Interamericanos, Arquivo Azeredo da Silveira.

aided by other Arab nations, on the other showed the fragility of the world political and economic order. Even though Israel won the war quickly, Arab nations realized after their military defeat that the dependence of the West on their oil exports placed a potent economic weapon in their hands. In early October 1973, the Organization of Petroleum Exporting Countries (OPEC) threatened sanctions against the United States if they rearmed Israel. The mere threat of the embargo led to a sharp rise in prices as some European countries and Canada started to curtail exports of oil products to the United States in anticipation of shortages.[17] On October 17, 1973, Saudi Arabia's King Faisal enacted the oil embargo against the United States and the Netherlands. The terms of the embargo explicitly forbade the transshipment of crude or refined derivatives by other countries. The result was that the price of crude oil rose sharply, first to US$5.1 per barrel for Saudi Arabian light crude, only to double the price again to US$11.6, effective January 1, 1974.[18]

The oil shock of late 1973 has often been described as an unanticipated event that suddenly raised the issue of scarcity of natural resources. In fact, oil prices had been rising relatively rapidly even before the Arab embargo. Oil prices rose almost 70 percent from US$1.8 per barrel to more than US$3 between January 1971 and October 1973, and in late 1971 *Foreign Affairs* worried about the dependency of industrial economies on a small number of oil exporters.[19] In May 1973, internal documents from the Nixon White House show intense preoccupation with gasoline shortages.[20] In June 1973, William Simon, deputy secretary of the treasury and chair of the Oil Policy Committee, received a report warning of an impending "world crude oil shortage building by the middle of the 1970s."[21] Nevertheless, the oil shock added a sense of urgency and even panic to the latent fear of "scarcity." The quadrupling of oil prices sent shock waves around the world. By mid-1974, the world economy was in the throes of rampant inflation,

17. Memorandum, William A. Johnson to William E. Simon, "Curtailment in Oil Shipments to the United States," October 10, 1973, folder 22: Oil Policy Committee-Internal Correspondence and Memoranda, 1973, drawer 16: Oil Policy Committee—Philanthropy and Tax Policy, Series III A: Subject Files (Deputy Secretary), William Simon Papers.

18. De Vries, *International Monetary Fund*, 306.

19. Levy, "Oil Power."

20. Memorandum, W. Richard Howard to the President, "Gasoline Shortage," May 31, 1973, folder 20: Oil Policy Committee-Internal Correspondence and Memoranda, 1973, drawer 16: Oil Policy Committee—Philanthropy and Tax Policy, Series III A: Subject Files (Deputy Secretary), William Simon Papers.

21. Memorandum, Assoc. Director, Office of Oil and Gas, U.S. Department of the Interior, to William E. Simon, "Reporting on International Developments," June 20, 1973, drawer 16: Oil Policy Committee—Philanthropy and Tax Policy, Series III A: Subject Files (Deputy Secretary), William Simon Papers.

economic growth was decelerating, and a massive disequilibrium emerged in international payments. In its 1974 annual report, the IMF characterized the situation as "perhaps the most complex and serious set of economic problems to confront national governments and the international community since the end of World War II."[22] Real gross national product in industrial countries as a group, which had risen steadily by at least 6 percent per year in 1972–73, fell by an average annual rate of 4 percent in the second half of 1974 and the first half of 1975. Substantial declines in production took place in nearly all major industrial countries, and unemployment reached levels not experienced since the 1930s.[23] Worldwide inflation, which had already started rising sharply before the price spikes in late 1973, now reached new highs with almost 10 percent in the United States in 1974 and 1975 and more than 20 percent in Japan and the United Kingdom.

How would politicians and the public react to the new challenge? Many "Third World" countries perceived the actions of OPEC as a model for them to imitate in order to reverse the postwar trend of declining terms of trade and redistribute income from industrial countries to themselves. This tendency was supported by various declarations at a special session of the United Nations General Assembly, which called for a "New International Economic Order."[24] Partisans of the "scarcity" approach believed that the day of reckoning had come and the oil crisis was another unmistakable sign that the world economy had reached its natural limits.[25] The Trilateral Commission, which followed this reasoning and would later gain large influence on the Carter administration, therefore argued for the acceptance of the reduction in standards of living and radical efforts to conserve energy and reduce wasteful consumption.[26]

The Nixon White House assumed a third (and contradictory) position. On the one hand, it questioned the legitimacy of the recent price increases. The United States adopted the official position that "consuming nations should not accept the indefinite continuation of the current level of oil prices." It argued that the world needed to resolve the "root cause" of the present economic problems, namely high oil prices. Arguing in favor of a free play of market forces, the report concluded, "None of these problems would be plaguing us today if the world oil market were free from manipulation by the governments of the

22. *IMF Annual Report,* 1974, 1.
23. De Vries, *International Monetary Fund,* 389.
24. James, *International Monetary Cooperation Since Bretton Woods,* 313.
25. Meadows and the Club of Rome, *Limits to Growth.*
26. Campbell, de Carmoy, and Kondo, *Energy.*

oil producing states."[27] On the other hand, Nixon enacted a series of highly interventionist measures. As early as October 11, 1973, Nixon urged Congress to create a Department of Energy and Natural Resources and to allocate more resources to the development of alternative sources of energy. In early November, Nixon proposed far-reaching emergency energy legislation and enacted nationwide fuel rationing not only for government agencies but also for private homes and gas stations.[28] On November 25, 1973, he announced what became known as "Project Independence," a plan for the United States to achieve energy self-sufficiency by the end of the 1970s: "Let me conclude by restating our overall objective. It can be summed up in one word that best characterizes this Nation and its essential nature. That word is 'independence.' From the beginning 200 years ago, throughout its history, America has made great sacrifices of blood and also of treasure to achieve and maintain its independence. In the last third of this century, our independence will depend on maintaining and achieving self-sufficiency in energy."[29]

Besides the technical difficulties "Project Independence" faced,[30] it had the obvious drawback that it needed too much time to solve the immediate crises of rising inflation and large worldwide imbalances of current accounts. In each area, the U.S. government believed it had to intervene actively in order to avoid a disaster.

In the domestic arena, President Gerald Ford declared the fight against inflation to be the highest priority. Ford called on academics and practitioners alike to "draw up . . . a battle plan against a common enemy, inflation. Inflation is our domestic enemy number 1."[31] However, anti-inflationary measures remained

27. Issue: The High Price of Oil Established and Maintained by the OPEC Cartel, folder 20: International Monetary Fund (World Bank Annual Meeting—Issues: 1974 [Sept. 30]), drawer 31: Income Maintenance Program—International Monetary Fund, Series IV: Briefing Books, William Simon Papers.

28. Chronology of Past Energy Actions by President Nixon, prepared by Edward H. Koenig, U.S. Treasury Department, November 29, 1973, folder 22: FEO-Correspondence—White House, 1973–1974, Series III A: Subject Files (Deputy Secretary), William Simon Papers.

29. "Project Independence: A Proposed Program for U.S. Energy Self-Sufficiency by 1980," staff paper by the Office of Policy Analysis and Evaluation, Federal Energy Office, Washington, D.C., February 5, 1974, folder 48: FEO-Project Independence, 1974, drawer 13: Federal Energy Office, Series III A: Subject Files (Deputy Secretary), William Simon Papers.

30. Federal Energy Office, Office of the Assistant Administrator for Economic and Data Analysis and Strategic Planning, "United States Energy Self-Sufficiency: An Assessment of Technological Potential," February 6, 1974, folder 49: FEO-Project Independence, 1974, drawer 13: Federal Energy Office, Series III A: Subject Files (Deputy Secretary), William Simon Papers.

31. "Opening Remarks of the President," September 5, 1974, box B 117: White House Conference on Inflation (2), Gerald R. Ford Presidential Library.

halfhearted because Ford was afraid of deepening the recession. This fear was fueled by an exhaustive study by one of the leading experts on inflation at the time, Arthur Okun, an economist at Yale University. He argued that a permanent reduction of basic inflation by one or two points would increase unemployment by as much as three and a half percentage points and lead to output losses of as much as US$200 billion. Okun concluded, "To pay $200 billion for a point or even two points of reduced inflation must be judged unreasonable—indeed absurd—by economists who hold the standard view that anticipated (that is, correctly predicted) inflation imposed no major social welfare costs."[32] Ford therefore proposed something akin to a heterodox stabilization program, which included price controls on petroleum products and close cooperation between all sectors of society to break the inflationary dynamics. One of the means he employed was the "Inflation Fighter Program." Manufacturers were to pledge not to raise prices for six months. As reward, these companies would receive an "IF" pennant to fly over their plant. Retailers and consumers would be encouraged to purchase only from companies with the "IF" pennant.[33]

The second major problem of the post–oil shock world economy was how to deal with massive imbalances in the balance of payments, which resulted from higher outlays for petroleum products by importing countries as well as sharply higher revenues of exporters. An analyst of the Federal Reserve Bank of New York warned in an internal report in April 1974 that industrial countries as a group "could see their 1973 current account surplus transformed into a current account deficit of as much as $35–40 billion. The oil importing less developed countries, for their part, faced a 1974 current account deficit of $15–20 billion."[34] However, not all developing countries were affected by the crisis in the same way. Exporters of petroleum, such as Venezuela and—with some delay—Mexico, benefited directly from higher oil prices. Other countries, like Argentina, were largely energy self-sufficient but benefited from the simultaneous rise of other commodity prices. Countries without sizable domestic oil production were hit hardest. Brazil, for example, imported 70 percent of its oil, of which almost 90 percent came from the Gulf region. A special Brazilian

32. Arthur M. Okun, "Efficient Disinflationary Policies," presentation at AEA meetings, 12/28/77, box K 26: Okun, Arthur M., Arthur F. Burns Papers.

33. Memorandum, Paul Theis to William Seidman, "Inflation Fighter Program," September 26, 1974, folder 27: White House—Memoranda to and from L. William Seidman, 1974, drawer 27: Transition—Zero-Base Budgeting, William Simon Papers.

34. Report, Peter Fousek, Federal Reserve Bank of New York, "The Jump in Oil Prices and the World Economy," April 2, 1974, box B 86: Oil, April 1974, Arthur F. Burns Papers.

envoy to the Gulf warned in January 1974 that the impact of higher oil prices would be "enormous" because the import bill for oil products would more than triple between 1973 and 1974 and reach more than half of the total export receipts.[35]

How to maintain economic growth in developing countries soon became the main preoccupation of policymakers and multinational financial institutions. Contrary to what leaders of industrial countries practiced at home, they urged developing countries not to try to eliminate their current account deficits through recessionary adjustment but rather to finance them with the help of new loans. In early March 1974, only five months after the price hike in the crude oil sector had destabilized the world economy, the president of the World Bank, Robert McNamara, explained that the high growth goals set for the "Second Development Decade" were unlikely to be attained. The only possible solution to the dilemma would be generous lending to facilitate the transition. He estimated that even under the most optimistic projections developing countries would need an additional yearly capital inflow of US$ 10–12 billion for the rest of the decade to achieve modest rates of growth.[36]

Who would provide these countries with loans? Analysts were initially skeptical that international financial markets would be able to achieve this goal without active intervention by governments or multinational financial institutions. In June 1974, the IMF agreed on the first "Oil Facility" with a volume of more than US$3.6 billion, which OPEC countries funded. It offered subsidized loans covering the additional costs of oil imports. Although theoretically open to every member country of the IMF, by informal agreement only developing countries (and Italy) borrowed from it.[37] However, financial markets soon proved to be more than eager to handle the so-called petrodollar recycling because it was such a profitable venture for international banks. A paper prepared for the special study on economic change showed that five out of the largest ten U.S. banks earned more than half their income from international operations by the mid-1970s. With shares of 82 and 80 percent, Citicorp and Bankers Trust were

35. Observações de Ordem Geral Formuladas Pelo Chefe da Missão Especial, Paulo Nogueira Batista, PNB ad 1973.110.05, pasta I, Atividades Diplomáticas, Dossiê Subsecretária de assuntos econômicos, Fundação Getulio Vargas, Rio de Janeiro.

36. International Bank for Reconstruction and Development, memorandum to the Executive Directors, "Interim Report on the Additional External Capital Requirements of Developing Countries to Deal with the Effects of the Increased Prices of Oil and Other Commodities," March 5, 1974, box B 86: Oil, March 1974, Arthur F. Burns Papers.

37. "Problems of Developing Countries," box B 87: Oil: Ditchley Conference on Oil Surpluses, January 31–February 2, 1975, Arthur F. Burns Papers.

the two banks most heavily dependent on profits from international lending.[38] International bankers enjoyed more luxury and prestige than ever before; Walter Wriston, chair of Citicorp, boasted publicly "Round here, it's Jakarta that pays the check."[39] Within the short span of six years between 1973 and 1979, bank lending to Latin American countries increased five-fold from US$30 billion to more than US$160 billion.

At first, the U.S. Treasury and international financial institutions openly encouraged large-scale lending. They argued that increasing lending to developing countries was the only sound strategy to keep the world economy growing. A Treasury report dated June 28, 1974, stated: "Rising debt need not be harmful to the LDC [less developed countries]. [It] offers the borrowing countries an opportunity to develop their economies at a rate above that which could be attained solely on the basis of available domestic resources."[40] Joseph Saxe of the World Bank even argued that "long-term prospects for many of the developing countries are brighter than the older industrial economies. . . . In short, Brazil could be a better loan risk over the long run than Belgium."[41]

Only at the end of 1976 did the international financial community start to warn of the potentially incalculable consequences of a prolonged crisis for the world financial architecture. In November 1976, an internal memorandum of the Federal Reserve, titled "An Analysis of Threats to the International Financial System," argued that continued high oil prices or, even more, a further price hike would impose unbearable burdens on weaker countries. In order to balance their accounts, they would be faced with an impossible choice between a sharply recessionary policy on the one hand and devaluation, capital controls, and import restrictions on the other. "International financial markets would be plunged into turmoil," it warned prophetically.[42] The Federal Reserve Board circulated a paper worrying about developing countries' ability to pay their rising debt and the potential consequences for the U.S. banking system, which was the most important lender. It noted that U.S. banks were particularly exposed

38. Paper Prepared for the Special Study on Economic Change of the Joint Economic Committee of the U.S. Congress, Robert L. Sammons, "International Debt: Its Growth and Significance," January 31, 1979, box 5, Robert Ash Wallace Collection, Jimmy Carter Library.

39. Walter Wriston, interview by *Fortune* magazine, March 1975; quoted in Miller, *Citicorp*, 108.

40. Memorandum, Richard Elliot Benedick to Henry F. Lee, "Treasury Study on Debt Rescheduling," June 28, 1974, U.S. Council of Economic Advisers: Records, 1974–1977, box 161: Laney Subject, Debt Rescheduling (2), Gerald R. Ford Presidential Library.

41. Draft, Discussion with Joseph Saxe, IBRD, on the external debt problem of developing countries, November 29, 1977, box 3, Robert Ash Wallace Collection, Jimmy Carter Library.

42. "An Analysis of Threats to the International Financial System," November 13, 1976, box B 64: International Finance General, November 1976, Arthur F. Burns Papers.

in Latin America, which had absorbed three-quarters of U.S. foreign lending of almost US$43 billion.[43] The report concluded that a cessation of payments of a large group of borrowers could be dangerous for the U.S. banking system.[44] However, the Federal Reserve played down the probability of this event, explaining, "The vast majority of U.S. bank claims on the LDCs are to the middle-income countries whose economies are tied strongly to the industrial countries on which they depend both for imports and as a market for their exports."[45]

While the immediate economic fallout from the oil shocks differed widely from country to country, the feeling that an economic paradigm had ended was almost universal. The crisis shook the foundations of the postwar economic consensus, which had rested on trust in the state's ability to manage the economy and avoid deep recessions. This loss of faith in the state occurred rapidly and transcended ideological and party lines. While Richard Nixon stated in 1971, "I am now a Keynesian in economics,"[46] by 1977 a study on economic change commissioned by Jimmy Carter concluded that economic policy needed to adapt to the new circumstances and break with the Keynesian past. It specifically called for reducing state intervention in the economy.[47] The breakdown of the postwar consensus also threatened the political stability to which countries had grown accustomed during the postwar decades. Social and political unrest rocked capitalist countries from Japan to Europe and the Americas during the late 1960s and early 1970s.

In Latin America, the transition was even more traumatic. The corporatist social and political order came under attack from both the Left and the Right. The populist and Marxist movements, which had become increasingly mobilized and radicalized in the wake of the Cuban Revolution, called for a break out of "dependency," believing that the momentary weakness of the United States created an opportunity to do just that. The democratic election of the Marxist Salvador Allende in Chile in 1970 aroused hopes among popular sectors that this change could actually materialize. It also instilled fear among conservative

43. Office Correspondence, Henry S. Terrell to Vice-Chairman Gardner, "Paper on U.S. Bank Lending to LDCs," November 8, 1976, Box B64: International Finance, November 1976, Arthur F. Burns Papers.

44. Office Correspondence, Ted Truman to Chairman Burns, "Impact of deferral of interest payments by LDC borrowers on the income of major U.S. banks," November 29, 1976, box B 64: International Finance, November 1976, Arthur F. Burns Papers.

45. Office Correspondence, Henry S. Terrell to Vice-Chairman Gardner, "Paper on U.S. Bank Lending to LDCs," November 8, 1976 (see note 43).

46. "Economy: Nixon's Program—I am now a Keynesian," New York Times, January 10, 1971.

47. Study, "Joint Economic Committee: Special Study on Economic Change," undated, Development of SSEC, box 2, Robert Ash Wallace Collection, Jimmy Carter Library.

sectors, who believed that Latin American countries needed to move in exactly the opposite direction.[48] They called for an end to import-substituting industrialization and the adoption of an outward-oriented model of economic development and tighter economic integration with the West. They also held that the moment was propitious because the ready availability of petrodollars in the wake of the oil shock allowed Latin American governments to access private international financial markets on a large scale for the first time since the Great Depression.[49]

Argentina and Brazil exemplify two different responses to the new international environment. Brazil, ruled by a military government since the coup that deposed João Goulart in 1964, chose to continue the pro-business economic policies pursued during the years of the "Brazilian Miracle."[50] When the oil shock hit in late 1973, Brazilian finance minister Mário Henrique Simonsen's first priority was to avoid any negative impact on domestic economic growth. His measures included renewed efforts at import-substituting industrialization in order to reduce dependency on imports in the long run. At the same time, Brazil borrowed heavily on international financial markets to soften the blow to the economy in the short run.[51] Brazil also sought better relations with Arab countries while at the same time maintaining close ties to the United States as part of a "responsible pragmatism" in its foreign policy.[52]

Argentina, by contrast, initially chose to confront the United States, refused to participate in the international petrodollar recycling, and withdrew from world markets. This decision was driven almost exclusively by domestic political considerations. While the oil shock rattled the entire Western world, Argentina experienced its own political earthquake with the return of Juan Domingo Perón from eighteen years of exile. In June 1966, the Argentine military had toppled the democratically elected government of Arturo Illía. Despite the violent suppression of opposition, after almost seven years in power the military had failed to create political and economic stability. Rising popular unrest opened up political space for the return of the now old and frail Juan Domingo Perón, who skillfully used the increasing polarization of society to portray himself as the only person who could save the country from civil war.[53] During his

48. Drake, *Labor Movements and Dictatorships*, 6.
49. Ffrench-Davis and Tironi, "El nuevo escenario económico internacional."
50. Fishlow, "Flying Down to Rio."
51. Perspectivas—Dezembro 1974, 29, EG pr. 1974.03.28, F-1760–1790, Ministério de Fazenda, Arquivo Ernesto Geisel.
52. Pinheiro, "O pragmatismo responsável."
53. O'Donnell, *Bureaucratic Authoritarianism*, 311.

exile, Perón was able to balance both sides of the Peronist movement. On the one hand, he praised the radical Peronist youth movement, which openly endorsed violent tactics, as "marvelous youth," while on the other he promised the leaders of the traditional labor unions a restoration of their power and a pacification of the country.[54] The fragility of Perón's political base became apparent upon his return to Buenos Aires. On his arrival in June 1973, rival Peronist factions opened fire at each other while waiting for their *líder* on the highway to the international airport of Ezeiza.[55]

Perón saw the critical transformation of the 1970s through the ideological lens of the immediate postwar period when he had first been in power.[56] His rhetoric was strongly nationalistic. He promised to lead Argentina to economic and political greatness ("Argentina Potencia").[57] The economic policy, which followed during the next two years, was classic populist economic policymaking. Perón's domestic policy was firmly based on the concept of the "corporatist state." He argued that an "organized community" could avoid labor unrest and at the same time extract concessions from businesses. The state would assume a more prominent role in stimulating growth and fostering employment.[58] The foreign policy rested on the assumption that the United States was in decline and American-style capitalism was in crisis. This led him to the conclusion that the time was right for developing countries to break out of "dependency" and gain "national autonomy."[59]

The Peronist ideas crystallized around two important elements: the "Acta de Compromiso Nacional" (Act of National Commitment), which contained the "El Pacto Social" (the Social Pact) as its most important element, and the "Plan Trienal Para la Reconstrucción y Liberación Nacional" (Three-year Plan for National Reconstruction and Liberation).[60] The Social Pact, a plan for recovery designed by José Ber Gelbard, Peron's minister of the economy, offered a seemingly easy way out of the difficult situation of slow growth, high inflation, and falling real wages that was plaguing Argentina around the time of Perón's return.

54. Lewis, *Crisis of Argentine Capitalism*, 419.

55. Verbitsky, *Ezeiza*, 13.

56. Gerchunoff and Llach, *El ciclo de la ilusión y el desencanto*, 335.

57. Torre, *Los sindicatos en el gobierno*, 152.

58. Juan Domingo Perón, "Modelo Argentino para el proyecto nacional," in *Obras completas*, 27:373.

59. Subsistema Relaciones Internacionales, "Análisis de la situación estratégica regional y mundial" (see note 14).

60. "Acta de compromiso nacional del 20 de mayo, dada a conocer en el Congreso durante el mensaje al pueblo del presidente Héctor Cámpora" (Buenos Aires: Dirección Nacional de Prensa, 8 junio 1973).

It froze wages and prices at a predetermined level. Subsequent adjustments and distributional conflicts would be handled within an institutional framework with the state as mediator. This would eliminate, the theory went, spiraling inflation while gradually shifting income toward the popular sectors.[61] The ultimate goal was to give labor a share of the national income comparable to what it had had at the end of the previous Peronist experience in 1955, 47.7 percent.[62] The three-year plan laid out an ambitious long-term growth strategy. The Argentine economy was supposed to grow at an annual rate of 8 percent with the help of higher government spending, increased private investment through artificially low interest rates, and improved productivity from existing capital stocks. The optimistic forecasts rested on the assumption that the economy had large unused production capacities and that increasing demand could actually lower unit costs by fully exploiting economies of scale and that income redistribution toward the popular sectors would increase demand and thus improve the overall performance of the economy.[63]

Many observers were skeptical of the program's chances of success. The Latin American Economic Report argued that Gelbard was being overly optimistic when he predicted that the rate of economic growth would rise to 7.5 percent in 1977 and 8 percent in 1978, and referred to his Social Pact as the "if-everything-goes-as-well-as-possible" program.[64] Before his visit to the Argentine embassy in February 1974, Federal Reserve Chairman Arthur Burns was briefed not to discuss Argentine economic policies at all but rather to commend the authorities for cracking down on terrorists.[65] Still, domestic and foreign businesses initially felt that the program was the only viable way to avert a revolutionary movement or a full-blown civil war—following the motto: "Better a lower profit rate than the People's Revolutionary Army."[66] Contrary to gloomy predictions, the program was successful over the short term. Inflation reached record lows in mid-1974 while economic growth soared to almost 8 percent. Carlos Leyba, undersecretary of the economy during this period, remembered that many observers believed that an "Argentine miracle" had occurred because the Social Pact achieved full employment, price stability, and a current account surplus at

61. Torre, *Los sindicatos en el gobierno*, 148.
62. Ayres, "Social Pact," 475.
63. Epstein, "Recent Stabilization Programs in Argentina," 993.
64. "Argentine Three Year Plan," *Latin American Economic Report*, February 8, 1974.
65. Memorandum, Reed J. Irvine to Chairman Burns, "Suggested Remarks at Argentine Dinner," February 13, 1974, box C 10: Irvine, Reed, 1973–1975, Arthur F. Burns Papers.
66. Ayres, "Social Pact," 496.

a time when most countries were experiencing the opposite, namely rising unemployment, high inflation, and current account deficits.[67]

This success was partly due to favorable external factors. Argentina was lucky in the "commodity lottery" of the early 1970s.[68] Being largely autarkic in petroleum production, the initial price increase in crude oil affected Argentina little. At the same time, it benefited from rising commodity prices, which contributed to an export boom. Exports rose from under US$1 billion to almost US$2 billion between the first half of 1972 and the first half of 1974, while imports only slowly caught up with rising exports.[69] The other reason for the initial success was more questionable. Sharply increasing government outlays and public employment while simultaneously repressing inflation, the Peronist economic program bought short-term growth at the price of severe long-term problems. With public spending and government employment soaring at double-digit rates, the budget deficit was soon out of control, exceeding 10 percent of GDP in 1975.[70] Such large fiscal deficits needed to be financed either by borrowing on financial markets or—in the absence of access to credit—with the "printing press," which led to higher inflation. While the Social Pact initially succeeded in repressing this inflation, this was clearly an unsustainable strategy and prices were bound to rise eventually. The short-term economic success was therefore little more than a bubble, which burst as soon as confidence in its sustainability dissipated.

The second element of the Peronist national project was its attempt to break out of "dependency," an unequal relationship with industrial countries that was perceived as pernicious for the country. Long-term trends in the world, such as rapid population growth, seemingly strengthened the economic outlook for Argentina, which offered plenty of natural resources for a world that was literally starving for its products.[71] Perón concluded that breaking out of "dependency" could not be achieved in isolation but rather required cooperation among Third World countries. He proclaimed that "the year 2000 will find us united or dominated."[72] To implement this new strategy, Argentina began to develop closer economic and political ties with Arab, African, and Eastern European

67. Carlos Raúl Leyba, in Di Tella and Braun, *Argentina, 1946–83*, 122.
68. Taylor, "On the Costs of Inward-Looking Development."
69. Fishlow, "Latin American Adjustment," 62.
70. Di Tella, *Argentina Under Perón*.
71. Subsistema Relaciones Internacionales, "Análisis de la situación estratégica regional y mundial," 26 (see note 14).
72. Perón, "Modelo Argentino," 346 (see note 59).

countries. In early 1974, José López Rega, Perón's personal envoy, struck a deal with Mu'ammar Gadhafi, the revolutionary leader of Libya. In exchange for three million tons of Libyan oil, Argentina sold Libya goods that included a vehicle assembly plant, Ika-Renault Jeeps, and an oil refinery.[73] In May 1974, José Ber Gelbard and Raúl Lastiri led a delegation to the Soviet Union, Poland, Czechoslovakia, and Hungary in an attempt to improve economic ties.[74] In May 1973 Argentina became the third Latin American country to reestablish diplomatic relations with Cuba since the revolution. This was followed by efforts at improving bilateral trade. The Peronist government extended annual loans of US$200 million to Cuba in exchange for purchases of light machinery and motor vehicles from Argentine factories. What made this trade deal particularly explosive for U.S.-Argentine relations was the fact that the exporting companies were subsidiaries of U.S. automobile manufacturers, especially Chrysler, Ford, and General Motors.[75] By 1974, Argentina had made major inroads into markets of the Soviet Union, Cuba, and the Middle East with exports rising sharply from less than US$50 million in 1972 to more than US$600 million in 1975.[76]

A second element of the "Third World" strategy was the reduction of the influence of multinational corporations in the Argentine economy. For this purpose, Congress passed a series of laws that explicitly favored Argentine-owned companies over foreign-owned ones. The Foreign Investment Law of 1973 banned foreigners from buying a majority stake in any company doing business in Argentina and prohibited investment in areas deemed important for national security.[77] In 1974, the Argentine government also started the process of nationalization of a number of foreign-owned banks, among them subsidiaries of Chase, Morgan, and First National City Bank, and other foreign-owned enterprises such as Deltec Swift.[78] Despite the radical rhetoric of the Peronist government, discrimination against and nationalizations of foreign companies were much more limited than during the late 1940s and early 1950s when Perón had first been in power.[79]

73. "Libyan Oil for Argentina," *Latin American Economic Report,* February 22, 1974.
74. Rapoport, *Historia,* 781.
75. Henry Kissinger to William Simon, "Financing of Argentine Motor Vehicle Exports to Cuba," July 22, 1974, folder 42: VIP Letters Kis–Kz, drawer 8: Secretary of the Treasury, series 1: General Correspondence, William Simon Papers.
76. Source: IMF Direction of Trade Database (accessed May 1, 2005).
77. Lewis, *Crisis of Argentine Capitalism,* 422.
78. Memorandum, ARA/ECP Gerald R. Olsen, "Current Economic Trends for 22 Latin American Countries," March 15, 1974, Latin America and Caribbean (3), Office of Editorial Staff, Charles McCall, Director of the Research Office: Files, 1974–1977, Gerald R. Ford Presidential Library.
79. Gerchunoff and Llach, *El ciclo de la ilusión y el desencanto,* 339.

Nevertheless, the confrontation with the West contributed to a growing economic isolation of the country. The U.S. government and the CIA watched these developments with growing unease. In mid-August 1974, an internal White House memorandum warned explicitly of the tendency of Latin American countries to drift toward a "Third World" position. It called for the protection of "our backyard" from infiltration and stressed the importance of protecting U.S. economic interests in Latin America, a major supplier of raw materials to the United States.[80] Foreign direct investment completely dried up in 1974 and 1975, and Argentina failed to share in the great lending boom to Latin American countries. While international banks extended almost US$40 billion in new loans to Latin America between 1972 and 1975, Argentina received less than US$1 billion over the same period. The Argentine government reasoned that this was a small price to pay, since it required little external financing and was seeking to discourage U.S. investment in Argentina in an effort to reduce its economic influence in the country anyway.

The international isolation coincided with and was reinforced by growing political and economic problems at home. Already during the first half of 1974, the corporatist regime started to show its weaknesses as the Peronist government progressively lost its ability to coerce the support of organized interests. In June 1974, the CIA warned of growing politically inspired violence, which Perón had been unable to quell.[81] As kidnappings and assassinations of business leaders spread, many foreign companies started to move their executives and their families out of the country. In March 1974, *U.S. News & World Report* called Argentina the "Land of the 'Vanishing American.'"[82] The political violence was only a symptom of the growing radicalization of the Peronist base, which had grown disaffected by Perón's failure to implement their oft-contradictory visions of Argentine society and its place in the world. Tensions rose even further when the Social Pact started to run into difficulties in early 1974.[83]

80. Memorandum, George S. Springsteen to Brent Scowcroft, "Issues Briefing Paper: U.S. Latin American Relations: The Future of the New Dialogue," August 19, 1974, Organization of American States—Latin America—General (1), National Security Adviser—Presidential Country Files for Latin America, box 2: Gerald R. Ford Presidential Library; Central Intelligence Agency, "Juan Domingo Perón, President of Argentina," June 28, 1974, Declassified Documents of the National Security Council.

81. Central Intelligence Agency, "Juan Domingo Perón, President of Argentina," June 28, 1974, Declassified Documents of the National Security Council.

82. "Why Argentina Is Becoming 'Land of the Vanishing American,'" *U.S. News & World Report,* March 11, 1974.

83. Gerchunoff and Llach, *El ciclo de la ilusión y el desencanto,* 344; Robben, *Political Violence and Trauma in Argentina,* 342.

Public confidence was essential to the success of the Social Pact. Once the population started to lose faith in the viability of the program, every actor had strong incentives to cheat on the price or wage controls, causing the other side to call for adjustments. In the face of growing shortages in the regulated market and rising labor unrest, the official guidelines set out by the Social Pact became increasingly meaningless. This created additional incentives to renege on the commitments.[84] Soon, repressed inflation began to surface, and the peso became increasingly overvalued. The loss of confidence was reflected in the black market premium on the exchange rate, which soared from 15 to more than 40 percent above the official rate between March and June 1974 alone.[85]

Over time, disaffection with the Social Pact became almost universal. The Left—led by the Peronist Youth (Juventud Peronista, or JP) and the Montoneros—were disappointed because they had hoped that Perón would enact a much more forceful program of redistribution of income and nationalization of private property—something akin to what Salvador Allende had attempted in neighboring Chile only two years earlier. Employers complained about unrealistically low prices. Trade unions grew restive because wages were not rising as fast as they had hoped. The political nature of the crisis was highlighted when Perón threatened to resign in June 1974 if the country did not support his government.[86]

With the death of the *líder* in July 1974, political and economic disintegration accelerated dramatically. During the following months, the internal fighting between the left, the right, and the center of the Peronist movement intensified as the economy started to crumble; inflation rose sharply, and smuggling and black market transactions became an increasingly important part of daily life. The economic policies adopted in late 1974 and early 1975 reflected this struggle for ideological and political hegemony within the Peronist movement. The leading contenders were José Ber Gelbard, the original architect of the Social Pact, and his sharpest rival, Alfredo Gómez Morales, the president of the Central Bank and part of the conservative wing of the Peronist movement. Gelbard still had the upper hand in September when Alfredo Gómez Morales resigned in protest over the plan to float a US$500 million bond issue, which he claimed would only encourage capital flight.[87] Shortly thereafter, the former president

---

84. Torre, *Los sindicatos en el gobierno*, 149.
85. Epstein, "Recent Stabilization Programs in Argentina," 994.
86. "Argentina: Don't Go!" *Latin American Weekly Report*, June 21, 1974.
87. "Argentina: Nationalist Myths and Realities," *Latin American Weekly Report*, September 6, 1974.

of the Central Bank publicly proclaimed that the whole price policy was in crisis and needed to be completely overhauled.[88] In late October, the situation changed radically when Isabel Perón shifted her support away from Gelbard to Gómez Morales. José Ber Gelbard had to resign; Gómez Morales was appointed in his place.[89] The new minister of the economy promised to impose fiscal austerity and to control inflation; however, he lacked the political power to implement a new direction in economic policymaking.[90]

The underlying problem was a lack of political leadership. Isabel Perón, whose only qualification for office was her marriage to the late Juan Domingo Perón, lacked both political skill and institutional support within the Peronist movement. Her most important ally was José López Rega, Juan Domingo Perón's private secretary during the previous eight years and minister of social welfare since May 1973. López Rega belonged to the right wing of the Peronist movement and had been linked to paramilitary death squads—known as the AAA—who had abducted and killed many left-wing labor leaders and members of the Peronist Montonero movement.[91] His influence over Perón and his wife Isabel had long aroused suspicion not only among Peronists. Wild rumors about his spiritualist practices circulated. He was therefore often referred to as "Rasputin" or "el brujo" (the sorcerer).[92] With Perón's death, López Rega's became the presidential secretary in charge of Isabel Perón's agenda and finances, which further increased his influence. However, the intense opposition to him by most sectors of the Peronist movement and society soon made him a liability for her.[93]

Because of the political weakness of Isabel Perón's government, Gómez Morales's new policies only created additional problems instead of solving the existing ones. He relaxed price controls in an effort to reduce economic distortions. At the same time, however, he insisted on a fixed exchange rate in order to avoid a new boost of inflation driven by higher import prices.[94] This led to an increasingly overvalued peso. The higher black market premium people were willing to pay for the dollar clearly reflected the perceived overvaluation of the peso at the official exchange rate and expectations of an impending

88. Sturzenegger, "Description of a Populist Experience," 101.

89. "Argentina: Exit Gelbard," *Intelligence Research Ltd., Latin America*, October 25, 1974.

90. "Argentina: History Repeats Itself," *Latin American Weekly Report*, November 29, 1974.

91. Telegram, Buenos Aires to State Department, "Former Triple A Member Talking to Congressional Committee," February 6, 1976, State Argentina Declassification Project (1975–84).

92. Larraquy et al., *López Rega*.

93. Central Intelligence Agency, "Biographic Handbook: Argentina," February 1975, folder 59, box 3: Argentina: Correspondence U—Argentina: Rogers' Visit, Robert Hill Papers.

94. Di Tella, "Argentina's Economy," 222.

devaluation. The overvaluation of the peso had the predictable consequence that imports rose sharply in the second half of 1974 and the current account turned negative. At the same time, black market operations increased dramatically. In October 1974, the Latin America Economic Report noted that "two major sources of black money are freely admitted here as a fact of life: Smuggling and invoice-juggling to get around the price freeze.... Last year's entire soy bean crop was smuggled out of the country despite its considerable bulk—well over 150,000 tons."[95] The black market premium, which rose from less than 50 in June to over 100 percent in December, reflected the rapid disintegration of public trust in the Peronist economic policies.[96]

With rising inflation and a sharp drop in foreign exchange reserves, economic policy reached an impasse in mid-1975. The *Economist* reported from Buenos Aires that coffee was disappearing from the market and that "housewives scour the streets in search of cooking oil, rice and many other staples, or queue to buy whatever is available before the price goes up. Shopkeepers are posting 'in mourning' signs to avoid having to open up and sell goods at half the price they expect to get in a hyperinflationary while. And industrial workers are staging protest strikes up and down the country because they say a 45 percent wage increase is not enough."[97]

Isabel Perón also found herself with her back against the wall politically. With support from her own party rapidly evaporating, she called for presidential elections in October 1976.[98] It was under these circumstances that she decided to abandon the Peronist paradigm. Her decision was moot, however; she had lost too much support among her constituency to take the country in a new direction.

Within a period of only two years, the Peronist government went from euphoria to sharp recession with near hyperinflation. What had gone wrong with the populist stabilization program? The main reason for the failure of Gelbard's Social Pact was the flawed design of the economic strategy. Gelbard had promised everything to everybody: high growth, rising wages, no unemployment, and no inflation. However, by the first half of 1974, Argentina had run into important bottlenecks with shortages, growing black markets, and increasing dissatisfaction. While growing internal conflicts and increasing violence further

95. "Argentine Laundry," *Latin American Economic Report,* October 18, 1974.
96. Banco Central de la República Argentina, *Memoria anual,* 1976.
97. "Argentina—Boom to Bust," *Economist,* June 21, 1975.
98. Celestino Rodrigo, interview, in De Pablo and Alemann, *La economía que yo hice,* 2:82.

undermined the fragile economic program, the Social Pact would probably have failed even if Argentina had not been a conflict society.[99] During the months following the death of Perón, however, the infighting within the Peronist movement became a decisive destabilizing factor. The government of Perón's widow, Isabel Perón, unsuccessfully tried to move to the right, abandon the Social Pact, and seek improved relations with the United States. Yet she lacked the leadership skills to impose her measures on the conflictual Argentine polity. Amid rising political violence and with the economy spiraling out of control, Argentina entered one of the darkest chapters of its history.

---

99. Mallon and Sourrouille, *Economic Policymaking in a Conflict Society.*

2 GLOBAL MARKETS AND THE MILITARY COUP

On March 24, 1976, tanks rattled through the streets of Buenos Aires. The radio played military marches while teams of men in uniform or civilian clothes rounded up known or suspected political enemies across the country. The next seven years would cost Argentina thousands of innocent lives and leave the country impoverished and traumatized. The same day the military toppled the civilian government in Buenos Aires, José Alfredo Martínez de Hoz, a successful lawyer and executive with extensive international experience, received a telegram while on safari in Kenya. He was to return to Buenos Aires immediately. The new military junta needed him to help pull the economy back from the brink of collapse.[1] Only three months later, Martínez de Hoz was at the pinnacle of his personal and professional success. David Rockefeller had invited him to stay at the Rockefeller estate and to speak at the prestigious River Club in New York City. Over an elaborate dinner of cold striped bass in sauce gribiche with a macedoine of vegetables, the new Argentine minister of the economy explained his economic policy

---

1. José A. Martínez de Hoz, interview, Buenos Aires, April 28, 2005 (all unpublished interviews were conducted by the author).

to some of the most prominent representatives of the U.S. business and financial community.[2] The trip was a resounding success. On the day of the dinner,
a bank consortium under the leadership of Chase Manhattan, David Rockefeller's bank, granted Argentina a US$950 million loan to cover its balance of
payments deficit. This contributed critically to overcoming the immediate economic crisis and restoring confidence in Argentina.[3]

The military coup on March 24, 1976, was part of a larger trend toward right-
wing authoritarian governments across Latin America in the 1970s. These military dictatorships differed sharply from the military governments of earlier
decades not only in their brutality but also in their economic policies. Rather
than deepen import-substituting industrialization as Guillermo O'Donnell had
argued,these new juntas implemented outward-oriented policies that often resulted in a substantial deindustrialization of the countries in question.[4] This
was to a large degree a function of the new international environment in which
gaining investors' confidence had become increasingly important. Since democratic governments were often unable to create political and economic stability,
they found it much more difficult to tap into international financial markets
than military dictatorships. The U.S. government and the IMF played an enabling
role in this development. They insisted on political and economic stability as a
precondition for aid and abandoned democratic governments if they were unable
to deliver it. Neither the United States nor the IMF directly encouraged the coup
plotters in Argentina; however, the leaders of the junta used this insistence on
political stability as a precondition for aid as justification for taking power and
the subsequent aid itself as proof that Washington endorsed their actions.

While the Western world slowly recovered from the economic crisis that had
followed the oil shock of 1973, Argentina began to slide into a crisis of its own
making in 1975. The Peronist government had come to power in 1973 based on
a coalition between the anticapitalist Left on the one hand and trade unions
and industrialists with vested interests in the maintenance of the corporatist

2. Invitation to Dinner in honor of His Excellency Dr. José Alfredo Martínez de Hoz, Minister
of Finance of Argentina, Host: Mr. David Rockefeller, Chairman of the Board, The Chase Manhattan Bank, N.A., Friday June 18, 1976, The River Club, New York City, DINNER I /H /O Minister
of Finance—ARGENTINA JOSE MARTÍNEZ DE HOZ 6/18/76, David Rockefeller Collection.

3. Memorandum, Jose R. Leon to David Rockefeller, "Banco Argentino de Comercio," June 18,
1976, DINNER I/H/O Minister of Finance—ARGENTINA JOSE MARTÍNEZ DE HOZ 6/18/76, David
Rockefeller Collection.

4. O'Donnell, "Reflections on the Patterns of Change"; Schamis, "Reconceptualizing Latin American Authoritarianism in the 1970s."

model of development on the other. From exile, Juan Domingo Perón had been able to cater to both sides of the Peronist movement. From the Casa Rosada, however, he found it much more difficult to hold this coalition together.[5] His death in July 1974 accelerated the political and economic disintegration of the movement. Perón himself had been unable to make the economic stabilization program work; his widow Isabel, a former nightclub dancer, was utterly incapable of succeeding where he had failed.[6]

Listening to the advice of the right wing of the Justicialist Party, Isabel Perón became convinced that a radical change in economic policy was necessary. In mid-1975, she selected the conservative Celestino Rodrigo to serve as the new minister of the economy. Rodrigo promised to stabilize the faltering economy, open the country to international investors, and promote agricultural exports with the help of an economic shock program. The program included a sharp devaluation of the peso, high interest rates, and a relaxation of capital controls in order to encourage savings and foreign investments. Rodrigo demanded major sacrifices from the Peronist base by calling for wage restraint in the face of rapidly rising prices especially of public services.[7]

The initial reactions from capital markets were positive. In late June 1975, Argentina signed a letter of intent with the First National City Bank for two syndicated loans worth US$250 million.[8] However, Isabel Perón underestimated the opposition of important sectors of the Peronist movement to any departure from traditional policies. The powerful trade unions saw the economic measures as a declaration of war. They complained that the sharp reduction of real wages and the favorable treatment of agricultural exporters and foreign investors contradicted the core values of Peronism. As a result, they mobilized for general strikes and a full confrontation with the president and her economic team. On July 11, Isabel Perón gave in to labor's demands. Rodrigo and one of her closest confidants, Minister of Welfare José López Rega, were forced to resign while she was obliged to increase wages as much as, in some cases, 150 percent.[9] These events became known as the *Rodrigazo* and marked the beginning of the implosion of the Peronist government.[10]

Isabel Perón attempted to return to a more traditional populist economic

5. O'Donnell, *Bureaucratic Authoritarianism*, 311.
6. Pedro Andrieu, interview, Buenos Aires, June 12, 2004.
7. Celestino Rodrigo, interview, in De Pablo and Alemann, *La economía que yo hice*, 2:90–92.
8. *Boletín Semanal del Ministerio de Economía*, June 27, 1975.
9. Economist Intelligence Unit, "Quarterly Report Argentina," no. 3, 1975, 4.
10. Restivo and Dellatorre, *El Rodrigazo*, 11.

policy under the new minister of the economy Antonio Cafiero, but she had lost all remaining credibility and political support.[11] She had antagonized the trade unions, which were no longer willing to hold back on their wage demands. Employers, disillusioned by the failure of the orthodox program, openly reneged on their commitments under the Social Pact and increased prices sharply to match higher costs. A new and fierce struggle over the distribution of income set in—a struggle her husband had explicitly sought to avoid. Monthly inflation jumped from less than 10 percent to more than 35 percent in July and August, setting off a new vicious circle of rising inflation and ballooning fiscal deficits. At the same time, the economy collapsed, falling from an annualized growth rate of more than 6 percent at the beginning of 1975 to a contraction at the same rate by the end of the year.[12]

The growing political crisis in Buenos Aires compounded the economic crisis. Following the *Rodrigazo,* Isabel Perón lost a series of internal power struggles. Congress elected Ítalo Luder, her political rival within the Justicialist Party, provisional president of the Senate—and next in line for presidential succession—while her ally Raúl Alberto Lastiri was banned from the Chamber of Deputies. She also failed to maintain support among the military. Pro-Peronist generals—including Jorge Raúl Carcagno, Alberto Numa Laplane, and Leandro Anaya—were forced to retire and were replaced by the hard-line anti-Peronists under the leadership of the future coup plotter Jorge Rafael Videla.[13] The political vacuum became evident when Isabel Perón asked for a "leave of absence" from her presidential duties purportedly because of health problems on September 13, 1975.[14]

The Peronist movement was deeply divided, and Isabel Perón enjoyed little support among the party leadership. Ítalo Luder, who became provisional president during her leave, tried to oust her and assume the presidency himself. Even though he failed and Isabel Perón returned to office in late October, he continued to plot against her. In a confidential conversation at the U.S. Embassy, he told the ambassador that Isabel Perón was "simply not physically or mentally capable of ruling the country." Luder argued that the "simplest solution

11. Di Tella and Justo, *Perón-Perón,* 216.

12. Ramos, "Economics of Hyperstagflation."

13. Telegram, Buenos Aires to State Department, "Analysis of Political Situation Wake of Military Crisis," September 10, 1975, State Argentina Declassification Project (1975–84).

14. "Remite Copia del Mensaje No 2524 en el que comunica que la excelentisima señora presidente de la Nación, Dona Maria Estela Martínez de Perón, ha resuelto tomar un periodo de descanso y que queda en ejercicio del poder ejecutivo el señor presidente provisorio del Senado Dr. Italo Argentino Luder," Cámara de Diputados, Poder Ejecutivo, No 104, Periodo Legislativo 1975, Archivos de la Cámara de Diputados.

would be to have [the] military issue [an] ultimatum demanding her resignation and then put her on a plane to join López Rega in Madrid." However, he preferred "less abrupt means" of removing her, which could best be achieved if she resigned voluntarily.[15]

Isabel Perón's political standing was further undermined by a series of scandals and corruption charges against her. The clandestine settlement of a debt owed by her late husband's estate with a check drawn on a major Peronist charity Cruzada Justicialista triggered the "Check Scandal," which led to a rupture of the Peronist block and Isabel Perón's loss of control in Congress.[16] The same charity was also involved in a major municipal land scandal. In addition to that, it was alleged that the Ministry of Social Welfare had made over three thousand payouts directly to Isabel Perón, López Rega, and other members of her circle. These allegations led to renewed calls for her impeachment.[17]

In addition to the domestic economic and political crises, external imbalances loomed dark over the Peronist administration. While Argentina's total external indebtedness amounted to only US$9–10 billion in early 1976, a large part of this debt matured simultaneously and needed to be refinanced. Argentina also faced a large and growing current account deficit caused by the misaligned exchange rate, rampant contraband trade, and the European Economic Community's banning of Argentine beef imports.[18] By September 1975, Argentina desperately needed new foreign loans to avert a balance of payment crisis. They approached international banks and multinational financial institutions and even took the unusual step of asking the U.S. government for a loan of US$600 million.[19] However, the spiraling political and economic crisis made international observers hesitant to help the embattled government. Despite his combative rhetoric, the United States had welcomed Perón's return because they saw him as a source of stability in the Southern Cone. As late as April 1975 the White House still believed there was no viable alternative to the Peronist government.[20] Starting with the *Rodrigazo,* however, that perception changed radically.

15. Telegram, Buenos Aires to State Department, "Sen. Luder's Views on Situation," November 6, 1975, FOIA Released Documents.

16. Rapoport, *Historia,* 670.

17. Telegram, Buenos Aires to State Department, "Scandal now a Major Political Issue," November 4, 1975, FOIA Released Documents.

18. Compensatory Financing Purchase, March 18, 1976, EBS/76/140, Archives of the International Monetary Fund (henceforth "IMF Archives").

19. Memorandum of Conversation, Antonio Cafiero et al., September 2, 1975, National Security Advisers—NSC Latin American Affairs Staff: Files, box 1: Argentina—Economic, Social, Gerald R. Ford Presidential Library.

20. Memorandum, Stephen Low to Jon Howe, "Attached Talker for the Vice President's Meeting

Indeed, that very government now seemed to be the main source of instability in the country. The question of whether to aid such a weak government was one of the defining issues of U.S. Argentina policy in late 1975. The U.S. Embassy in Buenos Aires stressed the political benefits Washington could reap from supporting "a middle-of-the-road constitutional government under most difficult circumstances."[21] The National Security Council (NSC), by contrast, argued that Argentina's economic and political collapse was inevitable, given the growing public hostility and the labor sector's unwillingness to accept austerity measures. They therefore opposed any aid, arguing that "until Argentina implements a sound and sustainable economic policy, a bail-out only postpones the day of reckoning."[22] The White House finally sided with the NSC and denied Argentina's request.

The IMF was also hesitant to support the Peronist government when it applied for loans under the Oil Facility. These loan requests faced two problems. First, Argentina did not suffer particularly from the oil price hike because it was largely self-sufficient in its oil production. It was therefore unclear whether it technically qualified for these special loans.[23] Second, the Oil Facility of 1975 was also subject to "first credit tranche conditionality." Argentina needed to present an economic program and abide by some additional conditions, known as the Rome Communiqué, which included a pledge not to impose trade restrictions on its neighbors. Argentina was reluctant to comply with these conditions. The new minister of the economy had recently implemented emergency tariffs against Chile, Uruguay, and Paraguay and was loath to abolish them. He also resisted the idea of inviting an IMF mission to Argentina. Peronists had always opposed the IMF as an agent of the United States, and Antonio Cafiero feared that the presence of an IMF mission would further incite tensions between

with the American Ambassador to Argentina, Robert C. Hill," April 3, 1975, National Security Advisers—NSC Latin American Affairs Staff: Files, box 14: Vice President (2), Gerald R. Ford Presidential Library.

21. Telegram, American Embassy in Buenos Aires to Secretary of State, "Embassy Views on USG Support for Argentine Financial Requests," September 1975, National Security Adviser—Presidential Country Files for Latin America, box 2: Organization of American States—Latin America—Argentina—State Department Telegrams to SECSTATE—EXDIS, Gerald R. Ford Presidential Library.

22. Briefing Paper for Mr. William Seidman, "Your Meeting with Argentina Minister of Economy, Antonio Cafiero, Tuesday, September 2, 3:00 pm," September 2, 1975, National Security Advisers—NSC Latin American Affairs Staff: Files, box 1: Argentina—Economic, Social, Gerald R. Ford Presidential Library.

23. Memorandum, the Secretary to Members of the Executive Board, "Argentina—Purchase Under the Oil Facility," October 20, 1975, EBS/75/376, IMF Archives.

the left and the right wings of the movement.[24] Argentina and the IMF finally reached a face-saving compromise on October 20, which allowed for the release of US$90 million.[25]

Negotiations with the IMF were even more difficult when Argentina applied for additional loans under the Compensatory Financing Facility. These loans were normally granted almost automatically if the country could prove an unexpected shortfall in exports and "cooperated" with the IMF. The conflict boiled down to the question of what "cooperation" meant. Was the sharing of information enough, or did Argentina need to heed the IMF's advice in order to prove that they were "cooperating"? The IMF wavered between the two meanings of the word. In early October 1975, Jorge del Canto from the Western Hemisphere Department of the IMF stressed the apparent unwillingness of the Argentine government to cooperate with the IMF in finding a solution to its balance of payments problems. However, he argued in an internal memorandum to the managing director that a loan would be the only way to "establish some sort of working relationship" through which the IMF could gain some influence over future economic policies.[26] This reasoning initially failed to convince the managing director and the executive directors of the IMF, who refused to grant the loan. Two months later, however, the IMF lowered its expectations and agreed to a loan of US$129 million. Del Canto noted that Argentina was only cooperating with the IMF in the sense of keeping them informed. However, he argued, "Cooperation does not require proof of complete success in carrying out policies."[27]

The difficulties in procuring financing from official sources during the second half of 1975 underscored the fragility of the Peronist government and its inability to inspire confidence abroad. The IMF and the U.S. government had made it clear that political stabilization was a precondition for further financial support. However, all attempts to secure this financial support actually further destabilized the government because they divided its ranks and alienated its base. The president of the Central Bank, Emilio Mondelli, believed that a formal stand-by agreement with the IMF would bolster confidence in the government and help overcome the immediate crisis. The minister of the economy,

24. Antonio Cafiero, interview, Buenos Aires, June 24, 2004.
25. Christian Brachet, interview, Washington, D.C., April 14, 2004.
26. Memorandum, Jorge del Canto to the Managing Director, "Argentina—Negotiations on Use of the Oil Facility," October 3, 1975, IMF Archives.
27. Memorandum, Jorge del Canto to the Managing Director, "Argentina," December 17, 1975, IMF Archives.

however, feared such an agreement could be perceived as betraying Peronist principles of opposition to IMF intervention.[28] With the economy spiraling out of control and the military waiting in the wings to stage a coup, Isabel Perón decided to side with Mondelli in a last-ditch effort to win IMF approval in early February 1976. While the exact background of the reshuffle in the economic team remains unclear, the documentary evidence indicates that Antonio Cafiero sent two letters to the managing director of the IMF through Eduardo Zaldu-endo, vice president of the Argentine Central Bank, who was visiting Washington on February 2, 1976. The first requested a full Article VIII Consultation to visit Argentina at the earliest possible moment, and the second expressed the intention of drawing on the first credit tranche. Both were unprecedented steps for a Peronist government and contradicted its earlier anti-IMF rhetoric. However, the same evening of February 2, Antonio Cafiero resigned, and the Argentine executive director to the IMF ordered all the communication to the managing director to be held until further notice.[29]

Negotiations resumed shortly thereafter under the leadership of the new economic team led by Emilio Mondelli, who faced an increasingly hopeless task. Cafiero's departure cost Isabel Perón the support of organized labor. From that point on, she and Mondelli had to confront their constant opposition at a time when they needed all the political support they could get in order to implement the ambitious emergency plan Mondelli unveiled on February 3, 1976. This plan was supposed to cut public sector expenditure, increase fiscal revenues, and reduce inflation drastically without the use of price controls. At the same time, it was to stimulate the economy and improve the foreign trade position.[30] Internal IMF documents show the growing frustration of IMF staff with the Argentine government. The mission that visited Buenos Aires in February described the situation as tragic: even though the minister of the economy and the president of the Central Bank fully cooperated with the IMF and diagnosed the economic problems almost exactly as the IMF had, they lacked the political support necessary to implement any solutions. Key elements of the proposed agreement were blocked in the cabinet. In response, Minister of the Economy Mondelli openly threatened to resign if his stabilization plan was not put into place.[31]

28. Antonio Cafiero, interview, Buenos Aires, June 24, 2004.
29. Memorandum, Jorge del Canto to the Acting Managing Director, "Argentina—Mission" February 4, 1976, IMF Archives.
30. Interview with Emilio Mondelli, in De Pablo and Alemann, *La economía que yo hice*, 194.
31. Memorandum, Jack Guenther to Managing Director, Acting Managing Director, March 1, 1976, IMF Archives.

On March 6, Mondelli declared the country to be in a state of "economic emergency," implying the need to impose a social truce for 180 days.[32] It was widely perceived as a final effort to placate the IMF mission in Argentina so that they would help the embattled government with a desperately needed loan. While Eduardo Zalduendo, now the president of the Argentine Central Bank, tried to convince the IMF in Washington that the new program was sustainable and deserved international support, Mondelli pleaded for support of his strategy at home. He acknowledged that the strategy might be tough on "the working man, but he should know that if it is not put into effect by his government, it will be imposed by others, and not precisely with his welfare in mind."[33]

Mondelli was trapped in an impossible situation. The economy disintegrated as businesses refused to invest and international banks turned down loan requests because of the political and economic uncertainty, while at the same time the powerful trade unions called for strikes to raise their wages, which had been drastically eroded by ever higher rates of inflation. Stabilization would have required primarily a change in people's expectations with respect to the future course of the country; however, in early March 1976, it was an open secret that Isabel Perón's days were numbered and none of her proposed measures would be implemented. The military had already completed their preparations for the eventual coup and were not going to back down. Mondelli had unsuccessfully tried to negotiate a common economic strategy with the military leadership in great secrecy.[34] The open threat of a coup created incentives to speculate against the success of the Peronist government's program. Knowing that the military government would most likely implement a more business-friendly economic program, businesses postponed investments, hoarded goods in expectation of higher margins after a change of government, and asked their trading partners to delay payments for exports hoping for more favorable exchange rates.

The last-minute attempts to resolve the political and economic deadlock only showed the hopelessness of the situation. Congress had tried but failed to muster the majority needed to impeach Isabel Perón, and there was a growing perception that she would actually rather be ousted by a military coup rather than replaced constitutionally.[35] Ricardo Balbín, president of the opposition

32. "El estado económico impone una tregua social, dijo Mondelli," *La Nación,* March 6, 1976.
33. "Argentina Plays It Again: The IMF Calls the Tune," *Latin America Economic Report,* March 12 1976.
34. This was reported to me by one of Mondelli's assessors who preferred to remain anonymous.
35. Telegram, Buenos Aires to State Department, "Position of UCR in Face of National Crisis," March 16, 1976, FOIA Released Documents.

UCR, vented his frustration when he told reporters on February 19, "The government may not want a coup but it seems to be doing everything in its power to bring one about."[36] At the same time, the negotiations with the IMF, instead of solving the economic crisis, deepened the political divisions within the Peronist movement. The main obstacle to the approval of US$48 million in oil facilities was the lack of fiscal discipline.[37] Mondelli's efforts to push a fiscal package through Congress with the argument that it was essential in order to obtain new loans from the IMF was received with outrage by Peronist representatives, who accused Mondelli of selling out to the IMF by giving it authority over Argentina's economic policy.[38] On March 11, 1976, del Canto concluded that the IMF could not proceed with Argentina's request for the final tranche of the Oil Facility because Argentina had failed to comply with the previous program. He especially criticized the Argentine authorities for failing to bring the "disastrous fiscal situation" under control. However, he indicated that the payments of US$130 million under the Compensatory Financing Facility could still go forward.[39] On March 18, 1976, the IMF staff recommended that the Executive Board approve the release of US$130 million under the Compensatory Financing Facility but not the additional US$48 million under the Oil Facility.[40] The Argentine Central Bank requested the disbursement on Monday, March 22, to be deposited in their account at the Federal Reserve Bank of New York.[41] However, this came too late to help the struggling Peronist government. When the deposit was finally made on March 30, 1976, the military government had already taken power in Buenos Aires and publicly took credit for the achievement.[42]

Internal IMF documents show that they were expecting a military coup and

36. Telegram, Buenos Aires to State Department, "Key Meeting Produces No Solutions," February 24, 1976, FOIA Released Documents.

37. Memorandum, Jorge del Canto to Managing Director, Acting Managing Director, March 10, 1976, IMF Archives.

38. Ferreira y Asmar: "Dar intervención al tribunal de cuentas de la nación para que determine la responsabilidad administrativa que pueda caber en las actuaciones promovidas por el poder ejecutivo para obtener del Fondo Monetario Internacional la segunda etapa de la asistencia financiera en las denominadas 'facilidades petroleras,'" Cámara de Diputados, No 3259, Periodo Legislativo 1975, Archivos de la Cámara de Diputados.

39. Memorandum, Jorge del Canto to the Acting Managing Director, "Argentina—Use of the Final Tranche Under the Oil Facility Decision for 1975," March 11, 1976, IMF Archives.

40. Memorandum, the Secretary to the Members of the Executive Board, "Argentina—Use of Fund Resources—Compensatory Financing, 1976," March 18, 1976, EBS/76/140, IMF Archives.

41. Telegram, Banco Central de la Rep. Argentina to International Monetary Fund, Washington, "Attn: Treasury," March 22, 1976, EBS/76/140, Supplement 1, IMF Archives.

42. "Dispónese de un préstamo del FMI," La Nación, March 27, 1976.

decided to delay negotiations with the Peronist government as long as possible.[43] The United States also anticipated the military coup, a development it saw with a combination of fatalism and relief. The CIA argued in February 1976 that the situation in Argentina was a "familiar political cycle" where the authority of an elected civilian government disappeared in the face of its inability to solve the country's problems, which were both of its own making and a legacy of forty years of failed policies. They predicted that Isabel Perón would be toppled by a "divided and reluctant armed forces," which would return power to a civilian government as soon as they saw that they could not solve the country's problems either.[44] The State Department did not share this pessimistic outlook. It held that a military government would lead to improved relations between the two countries and could yield positive economic results. In an internal memorandum to Secretary of State Henry Kissinger, William Rogers noted that the new government would probably move fast to "restore Argentina's standing with the international financial community, including the resolution of the investment cases involving U.S. firms." Consequently, he continued, "recognition of the new regime would not present a problem."[45]

On March 16, Admiral Emilio Massera, one of the future members of the military junta, spoke privately with U.S. Ambassador Robert Hill. Massera directly announced the military's plans explaining "that it is no secret that military might have to step into [the] political vacuum very soon." The conversation showed that the Argentine military was primarily concerned with its image abroad. Massera asked the ambassador for assistance "as a friend" because the military was worried that human rights abuses might create negative publicity around the world, which could jeopardize the efforts to create confidence in the new authorities. He promised, "Argentine military intervention if it comes will not follow the lines of the Pinochet takeover in Chile" but will try to "avoid human rights problems." He inquired whether the ambassador could help the new junta find "one or two reputable public relations firms in the U.S. which might handle the problem for a future military government."[46] While the U.S.

43. Memorandum, Jorge del Canto to the Acting Managing Director, "Argentina—Mission," February 4, 1976, IMF Archives.

44. Central Intelligence Agency, Directorate of Intelligence, Office of Political Research, "Whither Argentina: New Political System or More of the Same?" February 1976, 4, Declassified Documents of the National Security Council.

45. Memorandum, ARA, William D. Rogers to the Secretary, "Possible Coup in Argentina," February 13, 1976, FOIA Released Documents.

46. Telegram, Buenos Aires to State, "Ambassador's Conversation with Admiral Massera," March 16, 1976, FOIA Released Documents.

government gave tacit support to the coup plotters, it tried to distance itself publicly from them in an effort to avoid repeating the domestic political fallout of U.S. involvement in the coup in Chile in 1973. As part of this strategy, Ambassador Hill decided to leave the country before the coup to dispel any notion that he might be pulling the strings behind the scenes. This strategy even convinced some Argentine observers. On February 18, the U.S. Embassy reported that Argentine critics of previous American involvement in internal affairs of other Latin American countries, such as one of the leaders of the UCR and future president Raúl Alfonsín, expressed gratitude for the U.S. refusal to take sides.[47]

Final preparations for the coup took place in the open. On March 22, while Isabel Perón was presiding over a cabinet meeting to discuss ground rules for elections to be held in December, army units were moving into position along the main provincial highways. On the morning of March 23, U.S. Embassy staff noted large troop movements and frequent helicopter flights over the city center of Buenos Aires. During the day, army units occupied television stations, closed down the port, and started to screen passengers at Ezeiza, the international airport of Buenos Aires, for political opponents who might be trying to flee the country.[48] Defying the fact that the military controlled all the strategic points of the country, Isabel Perón held a meeting with her closest advisers in the Casa Rosada, in downtown Buenos Aires, and congressmen met for a last of the so-called multiparty meetings to discuss an institutional solution to the crisis.[49]

The military arrested Isabel Perón on the morning of March 24. By 10:40 A.M. the new military government had been sworn in, the constitution suspended, provincial governors removed, and Congress and the Supreme Court dissolved. Political activities were outlawed, and the rights of trade unions revoked.[50] Even as one of Latin America's bloodiest military dictatorships was about to begin, the U.S. Embassy noted with relief on the evening of March 24, that the "coup [was] accompanied by almost no violence." The embassy thought that the moderate line within the military had prevailed and general reactions

47. Telegram, American Embassy Buenos Aires to Secretary of State, "Government Moves to Silence Critics, Worsens Crisis," February 19, 1976, FOIA Released Documents.

48. Telegram, Buenos Aires to State, "Military Takes Up Positions," March 23, 1976, FOIA Released Documents.

49. Telegram, Buenos Aires to State Department, "Coup in Argentina: SITREP No. 1," March 24, 1976, FOIA Released Documents.

50. Telegram no. 1926, Buenos Aires to State, "Coup in Argentina: SITREP No. 4," March 24, 1976, FOIA Released Documents.

"seem to be one of reserved approval."[51] This judgment was shared by the now censored media. The *Buenos Aires Herald* argued in its editorial that Isabel Perón's government had actually died months ago: "The armed forces only had to organize the funeral."[52] Ricardo Balbín, president of the now-banned opposition UCR, expressed in a conversation with officials at the U.S. Embassy that "there was no question but that the military had no alternative to taking power on March 24" and added that political parties were "almost unanimously disposed to cooperate with the government."[53] Jorge Luis Borges praised the new junta as a "government of gentlemen" who had stepped in to save the country.[54] Even the formerly powerful trade unions seemed to have accepted the military coup as inevitable and might even have preferred to be in the role of opposition to a conservative military government than as partners in a Peronist government that did not share their convictions.[55]

Following the military coup, the de facto government almost immediately achieved what Isabel Perón had attempted in vain: to stabilize the economy and gain the confidence of international investors. Two factors contributed to this success. The military government was able to implement painful economic measures because they violently suppressed dissent. Before the coup, by contrast, organized interest groups had successfully thwarted similar programs by Celestino Rodrigo and Emilio Mondelli. The military government also achieved a closer alignment with the United States. This would serve as a "seal of approval" for international investors and help gain access to substantial loans.

Domestically, the suppression of opposition especially from the highly organized trade unions was the most important element of the stabilization program. Soon after seizing power the military government suspended collective bargaining and the "intervention" of trade unions and prohibited strikes.[56] Weakening the trade union movement was an important part of this economic strategy because it allowed the military government to shift the main burden of adjustment to wage earners, who suffered large losses in real income as nominal

---

51. Telegram, Buenos Aires to State Department, "Coup in Argentina: SITREP No. 8," March 24, 1976, FOIA Released Documents.

52. "Editorial," *Buenos Aires Herald*, March 24, 1976.

53. "Meeting with Representatives of the UCR," December 10, 1976, folder 33: Memoranda of Conversations, December 5–10, 1976, box 3: Argentina: Correspondence U–Argentina: Rogers' Visit, Robert Hill Papers.

54. Borges did not break with the military authorities over their abuses of human rights until 1980. See "Borges Ditches a Regime of 'Gentlemen,'" *Latin America Weekly Report*, May 30, 1980.

55. Drake, *Labor Movements and Dictatorships*, 161.

56. Ibid., 34.

wages were frozen and prices continued to climb.[57] Another important tool to reduce workers' bargaining power was to decrease industrial employment. Executive directors of the IMF understood this policy all too well. Winston Temple-Seminario, Peru's executive director to the IMF, explained during the executive board meeting on the Argentine stand-by arrangement on August 6, 1976, that he "tended to think that additional unemployment would on the whole weaken the position of trade unions and thus facilitate the authorities' intention of reducing real wages on a country-wide basis."[58]

Internationally, the new military government led by General Jorge Rafael Videla sought a close alignment with the United States for ideological as well as pragmatic reasons. The political aims of the government in the international arena were outlined in an internal report titled *Proposición de políticas para el area* (Proposal for the Politics of the Region), which was compiled in May 1976. It described the new Argentine strategy toward the United States, which contrasted sharply with the confrontational attitude of the Peronist government. "The United States is the first power in the Western and Christian world to which we belong by origin, tradition, and cultural and spiritual formation. . . . The recent change in government in our country together with the new beginning in its foreign policy make sure that U.S.-Argentine relations find themselves at a new beginning from which they can progress toward a mutually beneficial association under the sign of maturity and respect."[59]

This pro-American attitude was motivated not only by cultural affinity but also by concrete economic and political interests. The new military authorities believed that in order to reverse the economic tailspin, they needed the support of the United States and the IMF, which would help generate confidence in the new authorities and create a favorable investment climate. Not surprisingly, the first points on the list of actions to be taken to improve U.S.-Argentine relations were economic in nature: the solution of conflicts over expropriations of U.S. companies in Argentina and the reform of the foreign investment law.[60]

Traditionally, scholars have interpreted the economic policies under the military dictatorship of the Proceso de Reorganización Nacional (National

57. Pozzi, "Argentina, 1976–1982."

58. Minutes, Executive Board Meeting, "Argentina—1976 Article VII Consultation and Stand-By Arrangement," August 6, 1976, EBM/76/124, IMF Archives.

59. Memorandum, Dirección General de Política Exterior por Departamento América del Norte, "Proposición de Políticas Para el Área," 24 de mayo 1976, legajo: América de Norte, caja: Archivo Organ. Del Estado Año 1976, Archivos del Ministerio de Relaciones Exteriores y Culto de la República Argentina.

60. Ibid.

Reorganization Process) as "monetarist" or "neoliberal" and stress the importance of the influence of the University of Chicago.[61] However, the new minister of the economy, José Alfredo Martínez de Hoz, was neither an economist
nor the most consistent advocate of neoliberalism. His economic team included
some University of Chicago monetarists, most notably Adolfo Diz, the president of the Central Bank, who was teaching monetary theory at the Centro de
Estudios Monetarios Latinoamericanos in Mexico City when the coup occurred.
However, the overall influence of the Economics Department of the University
of Chicago on the military government was much more limited than in neighboring Chile. Despite generous scholarship support for Argentine economists,
the University of Chicago never established a foothold in Buenos Aires comparable to its presence at the Universidad Católica in Santiago.[62]

Martínez de Hoz and his closest ally, the secretary of planning, Guillermo
Walter Klein, were relatively young and successful lawyers with extensive international experience. Martínez de Hoz had already served as minister of the
economy during the Guido administration in the early 1960s, where he pursued a nationalistic economic policy, introducing among other things the *com-
pra argentina* program, which obliged public agencies to purchase products and
services only from national companies whenever this was possible. This reas-
sured some generals that he was in fact a bona fide nationalist and not an ideologically driven liberal who might undermine the struggle against left-wing
militants with a recessive shock policy.[63] Martínez de Hoz also had known many
of the generals for years through his membership in the informal Grupo Perriaux, a conservative think tank led by Jaime "Jacques" Perriaux, a former secretary of justice under the military government of Juan Carlos Onganía. During
the months preceding the military coup, the Grupo Perriaux became one of the
most important civilian influences on the military commanders.[64]

Martínez de Hoz was deeply influenced by anti-Keynesian, libertarian thinking, an influence he shared with many members of the financial and business
elites in industrial countries. In his first televised address, on April 2, 1976, he
argued that "the state should not operate in spheres of action best undertaken
by private enterprise" and added that the role of the state in society was to be
"subservient to the individual and to intermediate organizations in society."

61. Munck, "'Modern' Military Dictatorship," 58.
62. Biglaiser, "Internationalization of Chicago's Economics," 277.
63. Túrolo, *De Isabel a Videla,* 71.
64. Ibid., 41–42.

He considered the postwar economic model of import-substituting industrialization as state intervention in an economy at its most misguided. He pledged to open Argentina to the world markets, reasoning that in the modern world economy it is "impossible to keep the economy of a country isolated from the rest of the international community."[65] Echoing the main thrust of Friedrich August von Hayek's influential book *The Road to Serfdom*, he held that economic liberalism was a precondition for individual freedom: "Statism and economic totalitarianism are irreconcilable with a political system based on full respect for individual freedom and the rights of man and oriented by the common welfare."[66]

The 1970s saw a hotly contested discussion over whether "liberalization" and opening of the economy could be achieved democratically. After Augusto Pinochet had successfully opened the Chilean economy following the military coup on September 11, 1973, some Chilean economists argued that democracy was a hindrance to economic reform.[67] Mancur Olson's argument that destruction of interest groups through war or dictatorship improved economic dynamism apparently strengthened the case of those calling for what Martínez de Hoz called "vigorous and decisive measures" without interference from elected officials. Friedrich August von Hayek himself gave a further philosophical explanation for why countries could not rely on democratic decision-making to promote progress and economic growth. In his treatise *The Constitution of Liberty*, he argued that "if the majority were asked their opinion of all the changes involved in progress, they would probably want to prevent many of its necessary conditions and consequences and thus ultimately stop progress itself."[68] Von Hayek also explicitly supported the military dictatorships in Chile and Argentina and argued that infringement of civil liberties might be necessary in order to create a liberal state. He stated, "It is possible for a dictator to govern in a liberal way. And it is also possible that a democracy governs with a total lack of liberalism. My personal preference is for a liberal dictator and not for a democratic government lacking in liberalism."[69]

The selection of Martínez de Hoz as minister of the economy was intended

---

65. Minister of the Economy Dr. José Alfredo Martínez de Hoz, "Program for Recovery, Reorganization and Expansion of the Argentine Economy" (speech delivered at the Ministry of the Economy, Buenos Aires, April 2, 1976).

66. "Address by the Minister of Economy Dr. Jose A. Martínez de Hoz at the Buenos Aires Stock Exchange, August 11th, 1978."

67. O'Brien, "Authoritarianism and the New Orthodoxy," 179.

68. Hayek, *Constitution of Liberty*, 50.

69. O'Brien, "Authoritarianism and the New Orthodoxy," 179.

to send a clear signal to international investors that the new political authorities were committed to economic reform, an important condition for attracting desperately needed loans to avert default during the second quarter of the year.[70] Martínez de Hoz's biggest political asset was his impressive international standing and his contacts to banks and businesses abroad. In the 1960s, he had become chairman of the Argentine American Chamber of Commerce. Shortly thereafter, David Rockefeller invited him to join the prestigious International Advisory Committee of The Chase Manhattan Bank, an influential international think tank that met twice a year to discuss international economic and political developments.[71] Following the military coup, Rockefeller helped Martínez de Hoz reach out to business leaders and bankers through a series of small dinners, which he organized for the Argentine minister of the economy.[72] How personal and business interests were intertwined became clear during the first visit of Martínez de Hoz to the United States after assuming office. On Friday, June 18, 1976, Martínez de Hoz addressed the select audience in the River Club in New York City. On the same day José R. Leon, vice president of Chase Manhattan, reported in an internal memorandum to David Rockefeller that the Argentine loan consortium was going ahead as planned and that Argentina would soon receive up to US$950 million in loans to cover its balance of payments deficit.[73] Shortly thereafter, in a second memorandum to David Rockefeller, he reported that a request to return control of the Banco Argentino de Comercio, a Chase Manhattan subsidiary nationalized during the Peronist government, to the U.S. parent company had been granted by Argentine authorities.[74]

Martínez de Hoz proved to be extremely effective at convincing international audiences of his competence and resolve and quickly won over the hearts and minds of his audience in the United States. J. G. Francis, president of the Asiatic Petroleum Corporation, noted admiringly in a letter to David Rockefeller the "classical correctness" of Martínez de Hoz's economic measures. He

70. Schneider, "Material Bases of Technocracy," 78.

71. David Rockefeller to Jose A. Martínez de Hoz, "International Advisory Council," August 6, 1969, David Rockefeller Collection; Jose A. Martínez de Hoz to David Rockefeller, "International Advisory Committee," August 18, 1969, IAC Mtgs—NYC 9/21–23 69, David Rockefeller Collection.

72. Telex, David Rockefeller to Jose Martínez de Hoz, June 3, 1976, DINNER I/H/O Minister of Finance—ARGENTINA JOSE MARTÍNEZ DE HOZ 6/18/76, David Rockefeller Collection.

73. Memorandum, Jose R. Leon to David Rockefeller, "Argentine Loan Consortium," June 18, 1976, DINNER I/H/O Minister of Finance—ARGENTINA JOSE MARTÍNEZ DE HOZ 6/18/76, David Rockefeller Collection.

74. Memorandum, Jose R. Leon to David Rockefeller, "Banco Argentino de Comercio," June 18, 1976, DINNER I/H/O Minister of Finance—ARGENTINA JOSE MARTÍNEZ DE HOZ 6/18/76, David Rockefeller Collection.

bemoaned that "in both the United States and Britain the incipient symptom of a similar situation would tend to be more difficult to deal with on similar lines given the existence in both places of an ineradicable system of political parties and, dare I say it, an almost exaggerated regard for what are known as 'human rights.'"[75]

Ideological affinities also helped the new economic team receive almost immediate support from the IMF.[76] Vito Tanzi, a member of the first IMF mission to visit Buenos Aires after the coup, explained that one of the reasons for the success was that the ideology of the new economic team was "much closer to those of the Fund: trust in the market, not too many controls in the economy." In addition, personal connections appeared to be important. Adolfo Diz, the new president of the Central Bank, had received a Ph.D. from the University of Chicago and previously worked as an adviser to the IMF. "We spoke the same language," Tanzi commented. Martínez de Hoz was initially a much-admired person. "There was a lot of confidence that if anybody could change things, he would be the one."[77]

The Ford administration largely shared this optimistic outlook. Martínez de Hoz visited the United States in June 1976 under the "best circumstances." Secretary of the Treasury William Simon and Chairman of the Federal Reserve Arthur Burns openly supported the Argentine economic program.[78] U.S. government credit agencies such as the Export-Import Bank and the Overseas Private Investment Corporation (OPIC) were eager to extend new loans to Argentina, which they had previously denied to the Peronist administration. In May 1976, B. Thomas Mansbach, director for insurance of OPIC, noted in a letter to Ambassador Hill that the agency had not financed a single project in Argentina since 1970. However, now they were "following with great interest the statements of Argentina's new government concerning the role which they expect foreign private investment to play in the revitalization of the economy."[79] The Export-Import Bank was similarly eager to offer its services to the new economic team.

75. J. G. Francis to David Rockefeller, June 2, 1977, LUNCHEON WITH MIN. OF FINANCE MARTÍNEZ DE HOZ ARGENTINA, 6/2/77, David Rockefeller Collection.

76. Claudio Loser, interview, Washington, D.C., April 7, 2004.

77. Vito Tanzi, interview, Washington, D.C., April 13, 2004.

78. Departamento América del Norte, "Síntesis Informativa No. 3," 17 de Junio, 1976, legajo: América de Norte, caja: Archivo Organ. del Estado Año 1976, Archivos del Ministerio de Relaciones Exteriores y Culto de la República Argentina.

79. B. Thomas Mansbach, Director for Insurance, Latin America, Overseas Private Investment Corporation, to Ambassador Hill, May 17, 1976, folder 12: M, 1976–1977, box 2: Argentina: Correspondence H—Argentina: Correspondence T, Robert Hill Papers.

In a letter to Martínez de Hoz, Stephen M. DuBrul Jr. praised the minister's efforts and promised to reopen the credit lines immediately.[80] Riding on the wave of international support, the immediate external crisis appeared to be solved by mid-July 1976. Foreign reserves rose rapidly because of a financial package of US$1,200 million, which included US$300 million from the IMF successfully negotiated by Martínez de Hoz.[81] An IMF staff report dated July 27, 1976, noted optimistically that "as a result of the improved balance of payments prospects and the large credits being arranged from foreign commercial banks, Argentina's foreign debt problem now appears to be fully manageable."[82]

To stabilize the economy, however, Martínez de Hoz not only needed the confidence and support of international investors and the government of the United States. He also had to convince his fellow Argentines to support his economic project. For this purpose, Martínez de Hoz frequently addressed the nation on radio and television using a technocratic discourse. He stressed that he stood above the "political" debates of the fractured pre-coup polity and spoke out against what he termed "sterile ideological debates, concerning stereotyped isms."[83] Instead, he tried to be the voice of reason, moderation, and inevitability. He called for "the elimination of all false illusions."[84] He rejected the application of ideologically driven "laissez faire" capitalism, explaining that "there is no such thing in any part of the world as free enterprise in the absolute meaning of the word."[85] Giving his economic policies an air of inevitability, he compared his stabilization plan to the action of a responsible driver who tries to stop an out-of-control car.[86]

It is naturally difficult to understand whether the military government achieved its goal of convincing Argentines that their economic strategy was both viable and necessary. Unions and parties were banned, and newspapers sharply censored. The best sources of public opinion are records of secret contacts

---

80. Stephen M. DuBrul Jr., President and Chairman of the Export-Import Bank of the United States, to José A. Martínez de Hoz, July 15, 1976, folder 12: M, 1976–1977, box 2: Argentina: Correspondence H—Argentina: Correspondence T, Robert Hill Papers.

81. "Argentina Gets the IMF Seal of Approval," *Latin America Economic Report*, July 23, 1976, 113.

82. Staff Report for the 1976 Article VIII Consultation, July 27, 1976, SM/76/171, IMF Archives.

83. Martínez de Hoz, "Program for Recovery, Reorganization and Expansion of the Argentine Economy" (cited in full at note 65). Miguel Centeno explains that it is a common feature of technocrats to deny that they follow any particular ideology but instead want to overcome ideological limitations in order to achieve certain goals. See Centeno, "Redefiniendo la tecnocracia," 229.

84. Martínez de Hoz, "Address" (cited in full at note 66).

85. "Address by the Minister of Economy Dr. Jose A. Martínez de Hoz at the International Industrial Conference, San Francisco, Calif., September 1977."

86. "Anuncióse anoche el programa económico," *La Nación*, April 13, 1976.

between the U.S. Embassy and members of the labor unions, the Peronists, the UCR, and the Catholic Church during the period following the coup.[87] These sources indicate that a large part of the population opposed Martínez de Hoz's economic policies. While the papal nuncio defended the military government, noting that Argentina had never been a democracy even before March 24 and that the events should not be judged by European or North American standards, he criticized Martínez de Hoz for placing too heavy of a burden of adjustment on the working class.[88] Ricardo Balbín, leader of the UCR, also sharply criticized Martínez de Hoz's economic measures and described them as deeply unpopular. Enrique Vanoli, political secretary of the UCR, argued, "Martínez de Hoz could not get 2 percent of the vote if he ran in a popular election tomorrow" and expressed puzzlement about the minister's positive reception abroad.[89] Martínez de Hoz seemingly ignored this criticism. For the purpose of economic stabilization, the most important constituency was the holders of financial assets. They were exuberant about the future economic prospects of the country. After the collapse in early 1976, deposits rapidly returned to commercial banks during the second quarter of the year. The exuberance was also reflected in the stock market. The inflation-adjusted value of the stock market index as reported by the daily newspaper *La Nación* rose by a factor of ten between March and September of 1976.[90]

The Argentine experience between 1975 and 1977 showed that gaining the confidence of international investors and faith of the Argentine population at large was a prerequisite to any successful economic program. Neither could be attained without political stability. Following the *Rodrigazo*, the government of Isabel Perón had lost the support and confidence of nearly everybody—including the Peronist trade unions—and was faced with an explicit threat of a military coup. In this context of political disintegration and increasing violence, economic stabilization became impossible. The reluctance of the United States and the IMF

87. "Conversation with Labor Leaders, December 10, 1976" and "Meeting with Representatives of the UCR, Dec. 10, 1976," folder 33: Memorandum of Conversations, December 5–10, 1976, box 3: Argentina: Correspondence U—Argentina: Rogers' Visit, Robert Hill Papers.

88. "Conversation with Papal Nuncio, December 10, 1976," folder 33: Memoranda of Conversations, December 5–10, 1976, box 3: Argentina: Correspondence U—Argentina: Rogers' Visit, Robert Hill Papers.

89. "Meeting with Representatives of the UCR, December 10, 1976," folder 33: Memoranda of Conversations, December 5–10, 1976, box 3: Argentina: Correspondence U—Argentina: Rogers' Visit, Robert Hill Papers.

90. Author's calculations based on various issues of *La Nación*.

to support the struggling Argentine constitutional government reinforced the perception that Isabel Perón's government was finished. Neither the United States nor the IMF directly encouraged the coup plotters but rather assumed a position of neutrality. However, it became obvious that democracy did not represent a value worth defending in and of itself for the U.S. government and the IMF. They sought political and economic stability and would abandon a democratic government if it could not deliver it. Making political stability an implicit condition for economic aid, they sent a clear message to military leaders that they considered the incumbent government incapable of resolving the crisis and made a coup appear inevitable.

The military commanders who assumed office on March 24, 1976 understood this logic all too well. They selected the minister of the economy and tailored the economic policy with the goal in mind of creating political stability and restoring investors' confidence. The full-fledged support the new military government received from the IMF, international financial markets, and the Ford administration vindicated military leaders who had argued for a coup. The initial stabilization was a resounding success for Martínez de Hoz and his economic team. Within weeks, the new authorities reached agreements with banks to roll over existing loans; and by August, with the stand-by agreement with the IMF, the immediate crisis seemed to have passed. The economy recovered from the deep recession in late 1975 and early 1976, and the current account turned positive. Inflation remained high but the threat of hyperinflation, which had existed during the final weeks of the constitutional government, had been averted.

3 THE ORIGINS OF THE FOREIGN DEBT

Compared to the rest of Latin America, Argentina came late to the 1970s debt game. Total foreign debt of all Latin American countries rose almost four-fold from US$44 to US$164 billion between 1973 and 1979, the "golden age" of petrodollar recycling between the first oil shock and the second. During the same period, the Argentine external debt increased from US$6 billion to only US$14 billion. Differences are even more striking when we consider that Argentine net foreign debt actually *fell* during the same period, from US$5 billion to US$4.6 billion. This was mainly due to a large accumulation of foreign reserves by the Central Bank, which reached almost US$10 billion in 1979. The net foreign debt only started to explode in 1980 when the external environment had already become much less favorable to foreign borrowing and the IMF and the U.S. Treasury started to warn of the risks of a financial crisis.

Why did Argentina pursue such a self-defeating strategy? Ever since the outbreak of the international debt crisis in the early 1980s, Argentines have been struggling with the question of whom to blame for the buildup of foreign debt. Martínez de Hoz's policies have come under particularly heavy scrutiny by scholars and journalists and even led to a long and arduous trial.

The trial never reached a final verdict but the judge declared that he had proven "the obvious arbitrariness with which the responsible politicians and economists behaved."[1] Many Argentine analysts believe that this rapid growth of external debt was the result of a deliberate ploy by financial sectors to force Argentina's permanent integration into world capital markets while making a handsome profit in the process.[2] Available evidence, however, suggests that the buildup of foreign debt was not the outgrowth of a well-thought-out strategy and Martínez de Hoz was not a powerful "economy czar." Rather, his economic policies were the outcome of complicated political processes within a deeply divided military government. The compromises that emerged had important inconsistencies. Instead of eliminating inflation, the exchange-rate-based stabilization program led to a dramatic overvaluation of the peso, which led to a growing current account deficit. It also created incentives for banks and companies to assume excessive dollar-denominated debt while expecting that the government would bail them out in case of a crisis.

Scholars often argued that Martínez de Hoz was able to implement, unfettered by public opinion and outside interference, something akin to traditional economic orthodoxy.[3] This view underestimates the deep fragmentation and internal contradictions of government, public enterprises, and bureaucracy in Argentina in the 1970s. The military, which had traditionally been statist, nationalist, and antiliberal, was far from unanimous in its support for the minister of the economy.[4] The Argentine military had been the driving force in the industrialization process during the 1940s and 1950s. As late as the 1970s the Fabricaciones Militares dominated large parts of heavy industry from coal extraction to the production of steel.[5] The Argentine central government was also unable to control the overall budget because provincial and municipal governments as well as public enterprises resisted efforts to restrain spending. More important still, the government could never rely on an efficient and faithful bureaucracy to implement measures adopted at the highest level.[6] The authoritarian nature of the administration also proved to be a severe handicap. The lack of transparency and accountability made it harder to block special interest

---

1. Ballesteros, *Actas*.
2. Schvarzer, *Argentina, 1976–81*.
3. Frenkel and Fanelli, "Argentina y el FMI"; Canitrot, *Orden social y monetarismo;* Müller and Rapetti, "Un quiebre olvidado."
4. Lewis, *Crisis of Argentine Capitalism,* 454.
5. Martin, de Paula, and Gutiérrez, *Los ingenieros militares.*
6. Tanzi, "Rationalizing the Government Budget," 439.

groups and fight corruption. Recent research has shown that Argentina was not an exceptional case of failed market reform in countries where the government refuses to be held accountable for its actions.[7] The lack of accountability and democratic oversight creates an "irresistible temptation to corruption. . . . In the name of freeing market forces by unfree political means, dictators animated less profit seeking than collusive rent seeking. . . . This behavior might explain why, once in power, rulers recoiled from disabling the statist agencies, which they rhetorically condemned as the Trojan horses of populism. They were simply too lucrative."[8]

Miguel Centeno has explained that while politics is the "art of the possible," technocracy is the "science of the optimal."[9] The evidence suggests that Martínez de Hoz was more an astute politician than a pure technocrat. Despite his rhetoric of rationality, consistency, and inevitability, his economic policy was often inconsistent and followed more the political logic of factional struggle within the military authorities than the logic of economic theory. The initial stabilization program of 1976 was an example of this political compromising. Far from being an example of economic orthodoxy, it directly favored the agricultural sector by removing price controls and export taxes while at the same time freezing wages. The result was a large redistribution of income away from traditional Peronist to anti-Peronist sectors. Price stabilization was to be achieved by depressing aggregate demand especially through the lowering of public expenditure.

The military shied away from radical economic measures, fearing social unrest similar to what had followed the *Rodrigazo* a year earlier.[10] The program therefore had to be gradual in nature and avoid high unemployment.[11] Consequently, anti-inflationary measures remained halfhearted and often contradictory. The initial liberalization of prices in 1976 was followed by a series of "price truces" in 1977.[12] After the initial stabilization that brought Argentina back from the brink of hyperinflation, Martínez de Hoz accepted continued high but more stable inflation of 5 to 15 percent per month, hardly an orthodox monetary policy.[13]

Martínez de Hoz's initial economic program was largely uncontested because the military needed him to create confidence in the new authorities in order to

7. Manzetti, "Political Manipulations and Market Reforms Failures."
8. Adelman and Centeno, "Between Liberalism and Neoliberalism," 155.
9. Centeno, "Redefiniendo la tecnocracia," 224.
10. Gerchunoff and Llach, *El ciclo de la ilusión y el desencanto,* 357.
11. Túrolo, *De Isabel a Videla,* 45.
12. Epstein, "Recent Stabilization Programs in Argentina," 997.
13. IPC, nivel general, código 3J001, DataFIEL (accessed May 10, 2005).

regain access to financial markets and resolve the immediate crisis. The successful economic stabilization during the second half of 1976 significantly weakened his bargaining position with the junta, or as Ben Ross Schneider explains it, Martínez de Hoz "succeed[ed] so well in restoring investors' confidence as to make [himself] dispensable."[14] Without the threat of economic collapse hanging over their heads, generals started openly criticizing the minister. In September 1976, the U.S. Embassy reported that the Council of Admirals strongly opposed Martínez de Hoz's economic program.[15] Internal divisions were motivated as much by ideological differences as by personal animosities. Many generals deeply mistrusted Martínez de Hoz, who did not seem to speak their language. Horacio Liendo, minister of labor in the Videla administration, described Martínez de Hoz as a difficult person who did not communicate well with the military. During his long presentations, he would often talk over the heads of the generals and did not allow open discussion of the advantages and disadvantages of the measures he proposed.[16]

The IMF staff on the ground recognized the problems and limitations of the economic policies earlier than the directors in Washington. The briefing for the mission to Argentina in late May 1976 commended Martínez de Hoz and Central Bank president Adolfo Diz because they "espoused an economic philosophy radically different from that of the previous government," but cautioned that the new economic team did not show enough resolve because it was afraid of causing a major recession. It argued: "The Fund staff has considerable doubts that this cautious approach is the best way to proceed and is inclined to believe that a relatively quick adjustment process would have less social and economic costs than a gradual process of scaling down inflation and changing the exchange-rate system over several years."[17]

In 1977 and 1978, once the generals had declared themselves victorious in the war against leftist radicals, they set about trying to win the peace as well, which led to increased internal conflicts within the military junta. The generals lacked the technical knowledge to handle difficult economic questions, which made the gap between the aristocratic civilian minister and the military leaders increasingly unbridgeable. The voices of discontent among the generals grew even louder as Martínez de Hoz's economic measures failed to yield quick results

14. Schneider, "Material Bases of Technocracy," 91.
15. Bureau of Intelligence and Research, Report No. 603, "Argentina: Six Months of Military Government," September 30, 1976, Department of State, Argentina Declassification Project.
16. General Horacio Tomás Liendo, interview, Buenos Aires, May 5, 2004.
17. Briefing for IMF Mission to Argentina, May 20, 1976, IMF Archives.

and the sharp recession in 1978 went hand in hand with continued high inflation.[18] The thrust of the criticism depended on the ideological position and
personal ambition of the person making the criticism. Admiral Emilio Massera,
who imagined himself as president someday, leading some sort of populist coalition, was one of Martínez de Hoz's most outspoken enemies. He scolded Martínez de Hoz for his regressive and antisocial policies: "For every *guerrillero*
that I kill, the minister of the economy is creating five new ones," he explained
publicly.[19] Massera also tried to undermine the power and international standing of de facto president Videla when he told U.S. officials that Videla and his
faction within the army represented a small minority of anti-American, anti-
democratic generals who had secret ties with the Left. He predicted a "redefi-
nition of power" within the following two to three months and suggested that
he might be the next president.[20] Nationalistic officers and those in the military
industrial complex of Fabricaciones Militares were particularly troubled by
Martínez de Hoz's personal relationship with people like David Rockefeller
and accused him of selling Argentina out to the United States and international
financial interests.[21] Over time, the relationship between Martínez de Hoz and
Videla evolved into one of mutual dependence. Martínez de Hoz's standing
depended on the unwavering support of Videla and on the fact that the opposition had no clear alternative to the minister with a comparable international
standing.[22] At the same time, Videla's political future depended on the success
of Martínez de Hoz's economic policies, which increasingly appeared to be the
weak side of his presidency.

It was in this politically difficult environment that Martínez de Hoz took
two of his most controversial and far-reaching measures, the liberalization of
financial markets and the fixing of the exchange rate by way of the *tablita*, a published preannounced devaluation scheme. The financial liberalization started
on June 1, 1977.[23] The main measures included a "decentralization" of deposits—
that is to say, the elimination of a 100 percent reserve requirement—and the
liberalization of interest rates, greatly facilitated entry requirements for new
banks and nonbank financial intermediaries, and the relaxation of restrictions

18. Fontana, "Political Decision Making," 54.

19. "Wir haben Remedur geschaffen," *Der Speigel*, November 7, 1977.

20. Telegram, Buenos Aires to State, "Admiral Massera speaks of divisions in Armed Forces,"
December 9, 1976, Department of State, Argentina Declassification Project.

21. Túrolo, *De Isabel a Videla*, 93.

22. Alejandro Estrada, interview, Buenos Aires, March 1, 2004.

23. De Pablo, *Política económica argentina*, 306.

on transactions in foreign currency.[24] The main goal of these measures was to dismantle the old banking structure where the Central Bank determined who received loans at subsidized rates and to create a competitive banking sector and a higher rate of savings.[25] Financial liberalization was accompanied by universal deposit insurance. This was the most controversial part of the reform. Some members of the economic team correctly predicted that the combination of financial liberalization and universal deposit insurance would create incentives for banks to assume excessive risks while betting on an eventual government bailout—the so-called moral hazard. However, Argentine private banks had sufficient lobbying power to convince Martínez de Hoz that none of them could survive against the competition of public and international banks without such a guarantee.[26]

Insufficient banking supervision aggravated the problem. Banking supervision was weak for personal as well as structural reasons. The president of the Central Bank, Adolfo Diz, had a strong reputation as scholar and specialist in monetary theory but little practical experience managing a financial institution. Many of his colleagues felt that Diz was also somewhat naïve when it came to trusting bankers. Eduardo Zimmermann, the Central Bank director responsible for banking supervision, came from the banking sector and was perceived as representing more the interests of the banks he was supposed to monitor than the country. Banks dragged their feet and actively sought to undermine any effort to bring order in the banking system. When the Argentine Central Bank asked for technical assistance from the United States to improve banking supervision, banks simply refused to cooperate with the advisers, fearing interference with their activities.[27]

The exchange-rate-based anti-inflation program—generally known as the *tablita*—was introduced at the end of 1978 in an even more hostile environment; 1978 had been a recession year, and the country was in the midst of a war scare with neighboring Chile over some small islands in the Beagle Channel in Tierra del Fuego, which strengthened the position of the hard-liners in the military. In early November, war panic spread through Buenos Aires together with rumors that Jorge Rafael Videla had been forced to resign. This led to a wave of deposit withdrawals, a drop in the stock market, and long lines in supermarkets with

---

24. Calvo, "Fractured Liberalism," 519.
25. Martínez de Hoz, *Bases para una Argentina moderna*, 74.
26. Martínez de Hoz, *Quince años después*, 151.
27. Ricardo Arriazu, interview, Buenos Aires, May 19, 2004.

people hoarding essential goods for the eventuality of a war.[28] The threat of hostilities, which reached its climax just before Christmas, augmented the pressure on the economic team to allow for larger spending on imports of military hardware and construction projects in preparation for the war.[29] At the same time, generals grew increasingly restless and frustrated with Martínez de Hoz's failure to bring inflation under control. They wanted to see quick results without a sharp recession, austerity, high interest rates, or high unemployment.[30]

It was during this period of extreme political and military tensions that on December 20, 1978, Martínez de Hoz announced a new economic measure, which promised to eliminate inflation gradually without painful recession. The plan consisted of a series of ever smaller devaluations of the peso against the dollar according to a preannounced schedule and a gradual reduction of tariffs on imports. The program was inspired by the previous Chilean experience where the so-called Chicago Boys had implemented a program based on the monetarist theories of purchasing power parity and the monetary approach to the balance of payments.[31]

Both of these theories worked better on paper than in practice. The theory of purchasing power parity states that if a country is open to international competition, internal inflation cannot exceed world inflation plus the rate of devaluation.[32] This was undoubtedly true in theory but utterly irrelevant in a country whose internal market had been shielded from international competition for nearly half a century. Despite a gradual reduction of tariffs starting in 1976, the "law of one price" did not hold when the *tablita* was introduced in December 1978. The monetary approach to the balance of payments argued that devaluations were not a useful long-term strategy to improve the external balance of payments. For an inflation stabilization program to succeed, the public needed to change the inflationary expectations, which largely determined the money demand. If it failed to do so, a reduction in money creation would lead to capital inflows but not to lower inflation. Commitment to a fixed schedule of devaluation, the theory argued, would change expectations rapidly and without a long and painful recession.[33] While the theory behind the commitment to a fixed schedule of devaluation was sound, the *tablita* never managed

28. Telegram, Buenos Aires to State Department, "The Government Military Situation," November 4, 1978, FOIA Released Documents.

29. Adolfo Diz, interview, Buenos Aires, December 11, 2003.

30. Lewis, *Crisis of Argentine Capitalism,* 456.

31. Valdés, *Pinochet's Economists.*

32. Sourrouille and Lucángeli, *Política económica y procesos de desarrollo,* 79.

33. Machinea, "Use of the Exchange Rate," 91.

to generate enough credibility to make it work. Far from convincing a skeptical population, Martínez de Hoz even failed to gain unanimous support within his own economic team. While the Central Bank under Adolfo Diz and his closest adviser Ricardo Arriazu staunchly defended the preannounced schedule of devaluations, the Department of Commerce under Alejandro Estrada and the Secretary of Finance Juan Alemann doubted the wisdom of the scheme from the very beginning.[34] Alemann later referred to the *tablita* as a "diabolic idea" by Adolfo Diz and his people in the Central Bank.[35]

Martínez de Hoz also failed to administer the prescribed monetarist medicine in a consistent way. Economists long recognized that with predetermined exchange rates, governments need to control the fiscal deficit carefully. Otherwise, domestic inflation will exceed the rate of devaluation and lead to an increasingly overvalued and uncompetitive exchange rate. This overvaluation will gradually erode the competitiveness of domestic companies and lead to a growing current account deficit, which will need to be financed with the help of foreign borrowing. After an initial reduction of the fiscal deficit, fiscal discipline started to slip as early as 1977 when the IMF warned the Argentine authorities that the deficit was "of such a magnitude [that it was] definitely unacceptable."[36] A large part of the deficit was due to operating losses of public enterprises, which amounted to more than 30 percent of public expenditure—almost as much as federal and provincial governments combined.[37]

Reducing public expenditure proved to be an intractable problem. Military leaders regarded public enterprises and whole provinces as personal fiefdoms, and public officials trying to control them received death threats or disappeared. Therefore, public enterprises increased their outlays rather than reducing them during this period. Public investment projects from the Yacyreta hydroelectric dam to an amusement park on the Costanera and the organization of the 1978 Soccer World Cup mysteriously ran far over their initial budgets.[38] Privatizations were unimaginable because of the resistance of large parts of the military, who considered privatizing public companies unpatriotic and potentially dangerous to national security. At the same time, the military and unconstitutional

34. Alejandro Estrada, interview, Buenos Aires, March 1, 2004.

35. Juan Alemann, interview, Buenos Aires, January 12, 2005.

36. Staff Report for the 1977 Article VIII Consultation, IMF Archives.

37. Fundación de Investigaciones Económicas Latinoamericanas (FIEL), *El gastro público en la Argentina, 1960–1988*, 20.

38. This was a charge made by Juan Alemann, in August 1982. See Telegram, Buenos Aires to State Department, "The Scandal Spreads Geometrically," October 20, 1982, State Argentina Declassification Project (1975–84). Also Juan Alemann, interview, Buenos Aires, January 12, 2005.

nature of the regime made foreign investments in public enterprises unthinkable because investors feared that the subsequent constitutional government would repudiate the contracts.[39]

Additional spending for materiel and weapons in preparation for a possible war against Chile only increased the growing deficit. During the period 1974–81, the defense budget more than doubled from less than 2 to almost 4 percent of GDP. In 1977, the military budget amounted to almost a fifth of the central government's spending.[40] After Jimmy Carter cut off military aid to Argentina in early 1977, Germany and France became the largest providers of military equipment. German export statistics show that Argentina received more than one billion dollars worth of German weapons and other military equipment in 1980 and 1981 alone, more than half of all German exports to Argentina during this period.[41] In addition to direct outlays for the purchase of military hardware, the military funneled large parts of Argentina's international reserves into secret bank accounts in Panama, New York, and the Cayman Islands.[42] Marcello Caiola, the head of an IMF mission to Argentina in June 1980, noted that unrecorded military credits might amount to as much as US$1 billion.[43] In late 1982, the Argentine Central Bank reported to the IMF team that this total was probably between US$1 and 2 billion and was unrecoverable.[44] Civilian cabinet members saw military spending as a threat to their economic plan; however, they could do nothing. In identifying and dealing with matters of national security the military was not subject to civilian oversight.[45]

In contrast to the widely accepted notion that Martínez de Hoz's economic policy was characterized by economic austerity, the fastest growing segment of public expenditure was actually social security and welfare spending. During the first two years following the coup, social expenditures had been cut drastically. However, they started rising rapidly again in an obvious effort to buy support from the population. By 1978, they exceeded pre-coup levels, and by

39. José Alfredo Martínez de Hoz, interview, Buenos Aires, August 23, 2003; Lewis, *Crisis of Argentine Capitalism,* 454.

40. It is estimated that Argentina increased military spending from 10 percent of government expenditure in 1975 to almost 19 percent in 1977. Between 1977 and 1980, Argentina imported weapons for an estimated US$1.4 billion. United States Arms Control and Disarmament Agency, *World Military Expenditures and Arms Transfers, 1973–1983.*

41. Rapoport, *Historia,* 808.

42. Christian Brachet, interview, Washington, D.C., April 14, 2004.

43. Memorandum, M. Caiola to the Managing Director, "Mission to Argentina," June 9, 1980, IMF Archives.

44. Christian Brachet, interview, Washington, D.C., April 14, 2004.

45. Juan Alemann, interview, Buenos Aires, January 12, 2005.

1981, spending for social security and welfare had reached a level more than twice that of 1975, the last full year of the "populist" government of Isabel Perón. The main element of these growing outlays for social security was the new pension system, with benefits indexed to inflation. This system became particularly costly in 1980 when contributions to the pension system fell because of the economic slowdown but outlays continued to rise at a rapid pace.[46]

The IMF staff was highly critical of the new strategy of reducing inflation with the help of the *tablita*. The briefing for the IMF mission to Argentina in March 1979 explained that the problems were attributable to a "lack of definition of priorities and to political constraints" and warned of a further appreciation of the currency. This was a serious threat to economic stability because investors could lose confidence in the sustainability of the predetermined exchange rate. The consequence would be massive capital flight and possibly a currency crisis.[47] The following month, Marcello Caiola, who led the IMF mission to Buenos Aires, aired his disappointment with the fiscal, monetary, and income policies. He warned ominously that the "entire program would collapse" if a "convergence between the rates of exchange rate depreciation and inflation should not happen in the next few months."[48]

Martínez de Hoz, however, stood under no obligation to heed warning voices from Washington. While the IMF grew increasingly skeptical of Martínez de Hoz and his economic policies, international investors' enthusiasm for the "Wizard de Hoz" was unabated. Capital inflows into Argentina were so large that Argentina was able to repay all its obligations to the IMF by the end of 1978. The consequence was that the government continued its course of action, and the overvaluation of the peso dramatically worsened, reaching more than 70 percent in early 1981 (see fig. 2). The overvaluation rapidly increased Argentina's purchasing power and created an illusion of prosperity. As the value of their income more than tripled in terms of dollars between 1979 and 1981, middle-class families discovered that vacations in Europe or in Florida were cheaper than in Argentina. Jokes circulated that Argentine tourists to Europe and the United States found prices abroad so attractive that they always said "dame dos" (give me two) when they went shopping. The obvious downside of this development was that domestic products lost the competitive edge against cheap imports, which more than tripled during the brief period from the end of 1978 to early

---

46. Ibid.
47. Briefing to Mission in Argentina, March 7, 1979, IMF Archives.
48. Memorandum, Marcello Caiola to Managing Director, Deputy Managing Director, April 9, 1979, IMF Archives.

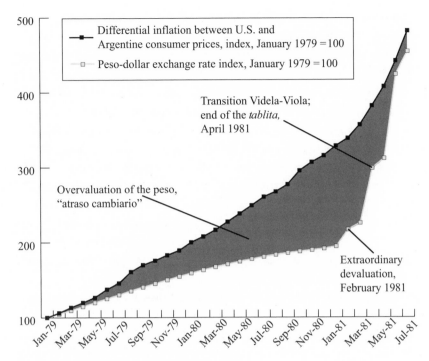

Fig. 2   The overvaluation of the peso, 1979–1981

1981. This contributed to a dramatic deterioration of the current account. While Argentina had enjoyed a healthy surplus of around 3 percent of GDP in 1978, by 1980 it had accumulated a dramatic deficit of more than 6 percent of GDP. The onslaught of imports also accelerated the deindustrialization of the country. While industrial production amounted to almost half of Argentina's national product in the wake of the military coup, by 1981 its share had fallen below 40 percent of GDP.[49]

As long as the Argentine government enjoyed the trust of international financial markets, the ever greater overvaluation of the peso had the additional pernicious effect of encouraging a speculative lending and borrowing boom. Banks and public and private corporations had strong incentives to borrow abroad and invest domestically. As long as the exchange-rate system remained in place, this tactic offered seemingly risk-free profits in a process known as "la bicicleta financiera." The "financial bicycle" evoked the image of a permanent movement in and out of the market taking advantage of short-term opportunities.

49. World Bank, "World Development Indicators."

Banks could reap large profits by borrowing on international markets, lending the funds domestically in pesos, and reconverting the interest and capital payments from the peso debt into dollars at the new exchange rate at the end of the period to cancel the dollar debt. The "profit margin" was the difference between the high lending rate they charged in pesos on the one hand and the low interest rates they paid for the dollar-denominated loans plus the rate of devaluation of the peso on the other. These international lending operations were extremely profitable, with annual profit margins of up to 80 percent. Consequently, bank borrowing abroad surged while the number of commercial banks grew rapidly. Between early June 1977—the moment the financial system was liberalized—and the end of 1980, the number of commercial banks almost doubled from 110 to 207, and the number of financial companies increased from 79 to 135.[50] The foreign borrowing of the ten largest Argentine banks grew more than threefold in these years from just over US$800 million to more than US$2.5 billion.[51]

Large private corporations and public enterprises also had access to international capital markets. They borrowed in dollars but had the largest part of their earnings in pesos. In an environment where domestic inflation exceeded the rate of devaluation, this reduced real borrowing costs because by the time they repaid the debt, the value of the peso relative to the dollar had risen. Between 1977 and early 1981 real borrowing costs were consistently negative for companies with access to international financial markets. Available evidence suggests that large Argentine conglomerates took full advantage of the availability of cheap credit abroad. The two private companies with the largest foreign debt were the gas company Cogasco and the private highway holding company Autopistas Urbanas, which had assumed more than US$2.3 billion in foreign debt by 1983.[52] The steel manufacturer Acindar increased its foreign debt almost four times between 1977 and 1980 from US$80 million to more than US$315 million and reached more than US$800 million by the end of 1983. The paper manufacturing giant Celulosa more than doubled its foreign debt from US$80 million to almost US$200 million between 1977 and 1980 and quadrupled the value again to more than US$800 million in 1983.[53]

Banks engaging in these foreign exchange operations and public and private enterprises contracting debt in dollars should have realized that the peso could

50. Banco Central de la República Argentina, *Memoria anual*, 1980, 111.
51. Schvarzer, *Martínez de Hoz*, 154.
52. Ballesteros, *Actas*, Anexo II.
53. Schvarzer, *Martínez de Hoz*, 153.

not appreciate indefinitely. No matter what happened with the *tablita,* real interest rates would rise in the long term. If the *tablita* were abandoned and the peso devalued, the peso value of the dollar-denominated debt would rise sharply. If the *tablita* were maintained, the country would eventually have to go through years of painful deflation to achieve external balance. This would increase real interest rates and the value of dollar-denominated debt as well. The large profit margins banks enjoyed and the negative real interest rates companies paid on their loans compensated for expected future losses. A prudent banker or executive with foresight would have avoided excessive foreign debt or accumulated reserves anticipating future losses. The fact that most Argentine banks and businesses failed to act prudently reveals that they counted on an eventual government bailout. They made large profits in the short term while anticipating that if a devaluation were to occur, they could either lobby the government to take on the exchange-rate risk or declare outright bankruptcy, leaving the insurer of their deposits, the Central Bank, to cover their losses. Financial liberalization without sufficient supervision, free and universal deposit insurance, and a fixed-exchange-rate regime created the ideal breeding ground where bankruptcy for profit could thrive.[54]

The house of cards started to crumble with a series of external shocks and domestic scandals in late 1979 and early 1980. In early 1979, Mohammad Reza Pahlavi, the shah of Iran, fled to Paris, and Ayatollah Khomeini came to power and declared the foundation of the Islamic Republic of Iran. The turmoil disrupted the important oil sector and sent oil prices soaring.[55] Between March and July of 1979, oil prices rose from US$13 to US$18 per barrel and continued rising to over US$30 in 1980.[56] Therefore, the large current account imbalances, which had been seen after the first oil shock in 1973–74, reemerged. While OPEC countries achieved a surplus of more than US$110 billion in 1980, non-oil developing countries' deficit surpassed US$80 billion.[57] Commercial banks were initially optimistic that the international banking system would be able to handle the recycling of OPEC and other surpluses even more easily than following the first oil shock in 1973 because banks and borrowers had gained a lot of valuable experience with international operations.[58] However, voices warning that

54. Akerlof and Romer, "Looting," 19.

55. Lomax, *Developing Country Debt Crisis,* 41–52.

56. "Precio official del petroleo crudo Arabian light FOB en dolares por barril, código 3E193, DataFIEL (accessed October 6, 2004).

57. Solomon, "Debt of Developing Countries."

58. Mendelsohn and the Group of Thirty, *Outlook for International Bank Lending,* 3.

commercial banks had become overextended in developing countries also grew louder.[59] The Carter administration warned that adjustment to the oil shock would be much harder for developing countries this time. Undersecretary of the Treasury Robert Solomon explained that the "international situation [was] now characterized by greater tension than at any time in recent history," and anticipated that many developing countries would face difficulties in obtaining the necessary external financing."[60]

The most important difference between 1973 and 1979 was the monetary and fiscal policy of the United States, the "elephant in the boat" of the world economy.[61] The negative influence of the United States on developing countries consisted of two, mutually reinforcing parts. The first was the "Volcker Shock." Paul Volcker was sworn in as new chairman of the Board of the Federal Reserve in August 1979 with the mandate to combat the unprecedented rates of inflation. Volcker reasoned that only decisive measures would break inflationary expectations and convinced markets that the Fed would no longer tolerate these high rates of inflation.[62] The decisive measures he enacted consisted of a dramatic tightening of U.S. monetary policy. This resulted in soaring interest rates worldwide. By mid-1981, the U.S. prime rate exceeded 20 percent, and an observer explained that the "real rate of interest was probably higher than any time since the late eighteenth century."[63] Developing countries, which had borrowed heavily under conditions of low or negative real interest rates in the wake of the first oil shock, were hardest hit by this decision. The largest part of the outstanding debt was syndicated loans with banks at flexible interest rates. The sharp rise in interest rates in the United States therefore had a directly negative impact on debtor countries because it increased their costs of debt service.[64]

The effects of the "Volcker shock" were compounded by the economic policy pursued by the incoming Reagan administration. The "collision" between lax fiscal policies driven by Reagan's large tax cuts and tight monetary policies pushed interest rates even higher while the dollar appreciated sharply. Between early 1980 and late 1981, the dollar rose in value against most major currencies (with the notable exception of the Japanese yen) by almost 50 percent. Since

59. Lipson, "International Organization," 614.

60. Senate Foreign Relations Committee—Subcommittee on International Economic Policy, Anthony M. Solomon's statement, February 28, 1980, box 12, Anthony M. Solomon Collection, Jimmy Carter Library.

61. Solomon, "Elephant in the Boat?"

62. Volcker and Gyohten, Changing Fortunes, 166.

63. Solomon, "Elephant in the Boat?" 575.

64. Lipson, "International Organization," 610.

developing countries' foreign debt was almost exclusively denominated in dollars, the revaluation of the U.S. currency also sharply increased the real burden of the foreign debt. Jacques Delors, at the time minister of the economy of the new French socialist government under President François Mitterrand called American interest rates and the appreciation of the dollar a "third oil shock," which could wreak havoc on economies around the world.[65]

In 1980 and 1981, Argentina was extremely vulnerable to these external shocks. Its domestic economic policies were inconsistent, and as a consequence the peso had become increasingly overvalued, the current account had turned sharply negative, and external debt was growing at a rapid pace. Under these circumstances, it was only a question of time until the bubble, driven by ready external financing, would burst and the period of *plata dulce*, sweet money, would come to an end.

Until early 1980, investors and the IMF were optimistic about the sustainability of Argentine external debt. While the IMF had warned the Argentine authorities of the threat posed by external indebtedness and criticized the profligate borrowing of public sector enterprises, it had also acknowledged that "Argentina's external debt [was] not particularly high when compared with most other developing countries."[66] By late 1979, public external debt had reached just under US$10 billion—twice as much as four years earlier. However, at the same time international reserves had increased even more rapidly. In late 1979, they amounted to more than half the total foreign debt and exceeded the entire public debt. Investors and the IMF were also comforted by the fact that the largest part of the public debt had not been incurred by the central government or the Central Bank but by public enterprises. According to the testimony of Martínez de Hoz during the trial against him, public enterprises used external financing to invest heavily in long overdue infrastructure projects amounting to more than US$50 billion during the four years between 1976 and 1980, a fifth of which represented imported capital goods.[67]

This was not the only reason for the surge in the foreign debt of public enterprises. They also incurred large operating losses during the period 1976–81. They were squeezed between institutional inertia, which made it impossible to

65. Quoted in "Franco-American Blinkers," *New York Times*, June 26, 1981.

66. Memorandum, Marcello Caiola to Managing Director, Deputy Managing Director, April 9, 1979, IMF Archives.

67. "Observaciones al informe presentado por los peritos ad-hoc el 10 de abril de 1991." Document presented by José A. Martínez de Hoz during the trial "Olmos, Alejandro S/dcia." Courtesy of José A. Martínez de Hoz.

reduce costs, and the government's insistence that prices could not be adjusted to reflect these costs in order to avoid fueling inflation.[68] At the same time, the government had decided that starting in 1977 public enterprises could no longer draw on the central government's budget to finance their operating losses but had to resort to capital markets. The intention of this measure was to reduce monetary emission and to expose public enterprises to market scrutiny.[69] However, market scrutiny remained elusive because international banks were awash with liquidity and all too willing to lend large amounts of capital to public enterprises whose debt was explicitly or implicitly guaranteed by the government. As an unintended side effect, the government lost even more control over public enterprises, which could now bypass the Ministry of the Economy and access financial markets directly.

Only when confidence in the sustainability of the fixed-exchange-rate system started to disappear in early 1980, did the true dimension of the debt problem become apparent. The first blow was the banking crisis, which started in April 1980 when the Central Bank had to intervene in three of the largest private banks in Argentina, which had incurred great losses in excessively risky or even illegal operations. The Banco de Intercambio Regional (BIR), the Banco Oddone, and the Banco de los Andes were guilty of the three most infamous examples of graft and fraudulent bankruptcy during the period. While some smaller banks and finance companies had been liquidated before, the consequences of collapse of these three large banks were much more dramatic. They set the stage for a one of the largest bank runs in Argentine history.[70]

The BIR had grown from a small bank in the province of Corrientes to the largest private bank in Argentina within only a few years by offering the highest interest rates to depositors, up to 9 percentage points above what the other banks were paying. Observers remember that customers were so eager to deposit their money that the bank often had to keep its doors open until late at night

68. Documentos de la sentencia sobre la deuda externa "Olmos, Alejandro S/dcia"- Expte N. 7.723/98" (from now on abbreviated as DSDD). GUILLERMO WALTER KLEIN, secretario de programación y coordinación económica (Fs. 2741, 5296/302), defends this decision, while JUAN BUSTOS FERNANDEZ, presidente de Y.P.F. S.E. (fs. 2216/17, 2632 y 3169), criticizes it heavily. Bustos Fernández states that until 1978 the regulated prices for oil and derivatives still covered the variable costs of production. In 1980 they amounted only to 50 percent of costs. In his opinion, YPF would not have needed to incur debt if they had been allowed to set prices according to world market conditions.

69. JOSE ALFREDO ANTONIO MARTÍNEZ DE HOZ, ministro de economía de la nación (Fs. 2684, 3673/85, 3795/96 y 5304/17), DSDD.

70. Fernández, "La crisis financiera argentina," 11–12.

"hand[ing] out coffee and biscuits to people queuing to put their money in."[71] At the same time, the bank would lend funds to second- and third-rate customers, charging them a high-risk premium in return. By the time the BIR was closed down by the Argentine Central Bank in late March 1981, less than half of its loan portfolio was performing normally. The flamboyant chairman, José Rafael Trozzo, was a prominent member of the conservative Opus Dei and used his apparent success in banking to gain access to powerful circles in Argentina and abroad. His closest associates were Robert Hill, former U.S. ambassador in Argentina; Sir David Nicolson, conservative member of the European Parliament; and Olivier Giscard d'Estaing, brother of the French president and founder of the Centre Européen de Coopération Internationale (CECI). In Argentina, Trozzo enjoyed unparalleled access to top-ranking military leaders, especially Admiral Emilio Massera, who presumably wanted Trozzo to succeed Martínez de Hoz as minister of the economy.[72] The end of the BIR could have been part of a gangster movie. With the help of his political connections, Trozzo managed to resist inspections of an increasingly suspicious Central Bank for several months. When the Central Bank finally sent four inspectors to audit the bank, all four resigned simultaneously and started working for the bank they were supposed to be auditing.[73] When the inspections finally started with a new team of inspectors, the BIR headquarters in Buenos Aires burned down under mysterious circumstances, killing three employees and destroying much of their records.[74]

The banking crisis of March and April 1980 was a serious blow to Martínez de Hoz's economic plan and undermined confidence in the minister. The Central Bank fulfilled its obligations under the deposit insurance scheme at a staggering cost. During the month of April alone, the Central Bank had to issue rediscounts for more than US$2 billion, the equivalent of 27 percent of the Argentine monetary base.[75] Yet while this episode undermined the confidence in Martínez de Hoz and his economic policies, reserves recovered by midyear when the worst part of the crisis seemed to be over.

The second and ultimately fatal blow to confidence in the program was political. The year 1981 was a critical year for Argentina; it marked the end of Videla's five-year term as de facto president. The armed forces lacked strong leadership

71. "The Amazing Career of José Rafael Trozzo," *Euromoney,* June 1980, 15.
72. Ibid., 20.
73. Martínez de Hoz, *Quince años después,* 166.
74. "The Amazing Career of José Rafael Trozzo," *Euromoney,* June 1980, 20.
75. Calvo, "Fractured Liberalism," 519.

and were deeply divided in their approach to economic policymaking. The institutional fragmentation of the military government was enshrined in the statute of the *Proceso,* which established that the de facto president was subordinate to, and served at the pleasure of, the commanders of the three branches of the armed services.[76] In order to avoid strong "personalization" of military rule— something Argentine conservatives had been afraid of throughout the twentieth century—the presidential term was limited to five years. In 1978, the military junta decided that they would need to select a new de facto president by September–October 1980 to assume power at the end of March 1981.

This transition of power proved to be much more contentious and costly than the military had foreseen when it had established these rules. This was partially a problem of timing. By 1980, the threat represented by "subversion," which had initially united the military and given it a common purpose, had largely disappeared. At the same time, the economic project associated with the name of José Martínez de Hoz was widely perceived as a failure. The wave of bank runs in early 1980 and growing protest by important industrial and agricultural interest groups nurtured the perception among important civilian and military circles that a radical change was necessary. In October 1980, some five hundred representatives of the business sector came together in the interior city of Rosario and openly criticized the economic policy of Martínez de Hoz. In the final declaration, they called for the adoption of an emergency economic program to stop the crisis. They proposed a wholesale reversal of everything Martínez de Hoz stood for and called for a bailout of financially strapped companies and protection of domestic industry against foreign competition.[77]

Roberto Viola, retired commander-in-chief of the army, classmate, and long-time friend of Jorge Rafael Videla, was the natural choice for his succession. He enjoyed the trust of Videla but shared the concerns of the critics of the regime. Viola favored a radical departure from the economic policies pursued by Martínez de Hoz, an open dialogue with trade unions, and a relatively rapid political opening of the country.[78] With this agenda, Viola faced strong opposition from two different sectors of the military during the nomination process, economic liberals who had supported Martínez de Hoz's economic measures and saw Viola as a threat to their economic project and political hard-liners who wanted to delay political liberalization as long as possible. The navy insisted

76. Argentina, Junta militar, *Documentos básicos,* 17.
77. "Críticas al plan económico en la reunión de Rosario," *La Nación,* October 19, 1980.
78. Fontana, "Political Decision Making," 120.

that the military *Proceso* first needed to be deepened before a political opening could start at the earliest between 1984 and 1987. Viola, by contrast, hoped to be the last de facto president and tried to achieve a faster transition to democracy.[79] Personal animosities and rival ambitions added to the explosive situation. The navy commander Admiral Armando Lambruschini tried to stop Viola's nomination by offering the navy's support to General Leopoldo Galtieri, the army commander, under the condition that he help fulfill one of the navy's long-standing ambitions: the occupation of the Malvinas.[80] In September 1980, Galtieri turned down Lambruschini's offer because Viola's support within the army still appeared to be strong. However, just over a year later, in December 1981, Galtieri would take the navy at its word and oust Viola from the presidency, promising to take action against the British islands in the South Atlantic. Despite the internal opposition, the military junta announced the election of Roberto Viola to succeed Videla on October 3, 1980. However, Viola emerged weakened from the very beginning. While the navy finally decided not to openly vote against him, the deep divisions within the junta became a matter of public record because of the unusual delay of the announcement.

With the appointment of Viola as next de facto president in early October began the six-month transition period, which heightened insecurity with respect to future economic policies. Viola's entourage repeatedly made public statements indicating that they believed the Argentine economy to be in crisis and Martínez de Hoz to blame for the problems.[81] Viola himself, by contrast, did not appear in public and refused to nominate a successor for Martínez de Hoz. His spokesman during the period of transition, Alfredo Olivera, explained that Viola—being aware of his political weakness and vulnerability—was convinced that he needed to act with the utmost prudence during this difficult period. Viola felt that any thoughtless statement could further destabilize the situation and make it even more difficult for him to build a new power base once he assumed the presidency.[82] However, absent any clear statements about future economic policies, the "silence of Viola" contributed to a growing sense of political and economic unease. Rumors about an impending devaluation eroded the remaining trust in Martínez de Hoz's economic management. By October 1980, only 5 percent of a sample of bankers polled by a newspaper reportedly

79. Túrolo, *De Isabel a Videla*, 275.
80. Fontana, "Political Decision Making," 123.
81. Túrolo, *De Isabel a Videla*, 284.
82. Alfredo Olivera, interview, Buenos Aires, January 11, 2005.

believed that the government would stand by its predetermined exchange-rate schedule until the following March.[83]

The loss of confidence in the future of the *tablita* led to rampant capital flight; more than US$10 billion left the country between early 1980 and March 1981. This represented more than 60 percent of the increase of foreign debt during the same period and equaled 80 percent of the total private foreign debt at the end of the March 1981.[84] Faced with a loss of confidence and massive capital flight, the government's best response would have been to abandon the policy of fixed exchange rate and financial opening by either imposing exchange controls or abandoning the *tablita* and devaluing the peso. However, since the minister of the economy had staked his personal reputation on the continuity of his policy of economic opening and the maintenance of the *tablita*, such a move would have entailed a large political cost for Martínez de Hoz. Richard Cooper warned in an article published in 1971 that the political consequences of devaluation created a "sharp conflict between the personal interest of those in authority and the interest of the country, a conflict that has to be resolved by those same persons, and which often may be resolved at the expense of the country."[85] The final year of the tenure of Martínez de Hoz in the Ministry of the Economy displayed this precise pattern. Afraid of the political fallout of a devaluation, the outgoing government defended the fix with increasingly desperate measures in an apparent case of what behavioral scientists call "escalation of commitment."[86] They hoped their determined defense of the peso could stop the run on the currency by convincing investors that the Argentine government would stand by their promise to maintain the fixed exchange rate.[87]

With the economic program starting to fall apart, Martínez de Hoz and his economic team tried to put up a brave face in order to convince international investors that the situation was under control. An article on the Argentine minister of the economy by the financial magazine *Euromoney* in January 1981 quoted Martínez de Hoz as saying that the "country [had] achieved by hard work and discipline a stability that won't be affected whether or not he retires in March."[88] Francisco Soldati, Argentina's chief debt negotiator in the Central Bank, boasted

83. Gerchunoff and Llach, *El ciclo de la ilusión y el desencanto*, 367.

84. Schvarzer, *Implantación de un modelo económico*, 56.

85. Cooper, "Currency Devaluation in Developing Countries," 30.

86. Whyte, Saks, and Hook, "When Success Breeds Failure," 416.

87. Manuel Solanet, interview, Buenos Aires, January 10, 2005.

88. "Martínez de Hoz Insists That, If He Goes, the Policies Will Stay," *Euromoney*, January 1981, 2.

that his job was considerably easier than a year earlier because foreign banks knew that Argentina was healthy.[89] *Euromoney* concluded that Martínez de Hoz had salvaged the economy "from the ineptitude, bungling and greed of the previous 30 years." The biggest challenge was now to "get used to success."[90]

While the international press was still celebrating Martínez de Hoz as "Wizard de Hoz" in early 1981, the government was resorting to increasingly desperate measures. Central government debt rose by more than US$1.2 billion in just three months, while public enterprises, pressured by the Central Bank, started to assume additional foreign debt in dollars in order to have dollars on hand in case they were needed.[91] These public companies often had very little real demand for capital themselves, rather they were *fronting* for the Central Bank, which was growing increasingly desperate to attract funds to shore up its dwindling international reserves.[92] The state-owned petroleum company, Yacimientos Petrolíferos Fiscales (YPF), borrowed almost US$600 million in three months, apparently under orders from the Central Bank. It remains unclear who exactly gave these orders, since Adolfo Diz, president of the Central Bank, denied having ordered state-owned companies to assume additional debt to prop up international reserves but acknowledged that these orders had come to his attention during his time in office.[93] The otherwise orthodox president of the Central Bank even gave up sound monetary policy during the run-up to the transition. During late 1980 and early 1981, the fiscal deficit was almost entirely financed by the printing press. This abrupt change in monetary policy was caused by the fear that if the Treasury had relied on domestic or international capital markets to finance the deficit, it would have driven up interest rates to unsustainable levels. However, inflationary financing predictably caused rising inflation and further capital outflows.[94]

With only a few months left until the transition of power, the team of Martínez de Hoz was seen as a lame duck, and had to negotiate its strategic decisions with the yet to be formally nominated incoming team.[95] In early 1981,

89. "Francisco Soldati: Banks Are Aware That Argentina Is Healthy," *Euromoney,* January 1981, 33–36.

90. "Trying to Get Used to Success," *Euromoney,* January 1981, 9–14.

91. JOSÉ LUIS MACHINEA, gerente de finanzas públicas del B.C.R.A. (Fs. 5059/70), DSDD.

92. Mario Teijeiro, interview, Buenos Aires, December 15, 2003.

93. FRANCISCO PÍO NORBERTO SOLDATI, director del B.C.R.A. (Fs. 4610/15), ADOLFO DIZ, presidente del B.C.R.A. (Fs. 5071/79), DSDD.

94. Telegram, Buenos Aires to State Department, "The Economic Legacy of Martinez de Hoz," February 6, 1981.

95. Adolfo Diz, interview, Buenos Aires, March 12, 2004.

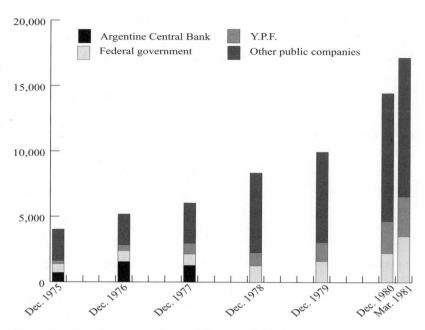

Fig. 3   Growth and structure of the public external debt between December 31, 1975, and March 31, 1981 in millions of U.S. dollars

Martínez de Hoz applied intense pressure on Viola and his economic advisers to commit to a common strategy on exchange-rate policy. He hoped this would help improve the credibility of the *tablita* and stop capital flight. A meeting in early February between the outgoing minister of the economy and Lorenzo Sigaut, the chief economic adviser of the incoming president, Lorenzo Sigaut, concluded with a lukewarm agreement to devalue the peso by 10 percent with a promise to continue with the *tablita* until August. However, neither Martínez de Hoz nor Sigaut publicly endorsed this move, and withdrawals of dollars continued in anticipation of a sharp devaluation with the change in government. The loss of public confidence was such that Martínez de Hoz's spokesman had to officially deny rumors that the minister had resigned the day after the meeting.[96]

Each side believed the other was betraying the common cause. Lorenzo Sigaut and his advisers perceived Martínez de Hoz as unwilling to assume the political cost of his misguided policies and believed that he had tried to sabotage the transition to show that he was irreplaceable.[97] The economic team of Martínez

96. "Martínez de Hoz no renunció," *La Nación*, February 4, 1981.
97. Lorenzo Sigaut, interview, Buenos Aires, December 23, 2004.

de Hoz felt betrayed by Viola and his men, who publicly remained silent about their plans for the time after the transition of power but privately made it clear that they wanted to break with the past and undo many policies Martínez de Hoz had established since the coup.[98] The transition of power in the Ministry of the Economy in late March 1981 took place in a setting of mutual distrust and was a grotesque demonstration of how differently the outgoing and incoming economic teams judged the economic situation. Martínez de Hoz declared victory in his struggle against inflation and explained in his last public address that a new equilibrium of prices and exchange rate could be reached within a matter of months if sensible economic policies were pursued.[99] Meanwhile, Lorenzo Sigaut was getting ready to declare an economic emergency.[100]

The foreign debt problem in Argentina originated in the combination of an incomplete financial liberalization and a mismanaged exchange-rate-based stabilization program in a deeply antiliberal political environment. A large part of the military junta was not only antiliberal in their economic thinking—they favored state intervention and control over free markets—they were also antiliberal in their political thinking, which undermined efforts to establish an open and flexible economy. The de facto government rejected basic principles of accountability, and military leaders often behaved as if the provinces and public enterprises under their control were personal fiefdoms rather than public patrimony. The combination of press censorship and open death threats for dissidents also made it impossible to denounce corruption.

Under these circumstances, financial liberalization combined with deposit insurance and a virtually fixed exchange rate was an open invitation for abuse and personal enrichment. The years 1979 and 1980 saw a speculative boom fueled by foreign and domestic lending at negative real interest rates. The preannounced exchange rate of the *tablita* eliminated the exchange-rate risk, and the combination of deposit insurance and lax supervision by the Central Bank eliminated the last incentives to responsible behavior on the part of commercial banks. The large spread between domestic peso interest rates and dollar interest rates in international financial markets also created strong incentives

98. Martínez de Hoz, *Quince años después*, 216.

99. "Palabras pronunciadas por el Sr. Ministro de Economía, Dr. José A. Martínez de Hoz, en el mensaje dirigido al país al finalizar su gestión de cinco años al frente de la cartera a su cargo, marzo 12 de 1981," *Boletín Semanal de Ministerio de Economía*, March 23, 1981.

100. "Mensaje del ministro de economía, Hacienda y finanzas, Dr. Lorenzo Sigaut, 1 de abril de 1981," *Boletín del Ministerio de Economía*, 1981, 856.

for companies to assume debt in dollars. Public enterprises joined in the borrowing frenzy because the government tried to eliminate the vast fiscal outlays to them by forcing them to finance deficits on capital markets.

The system was dynamically unstable. Since inflation always remained above the rate of devaluation, the peso became increasingly overvalued. Trade liberalization added to the pressure on domestic companies and led to a trade deficit in 1979–80. The easiest solution would have been an unscheduled and substantial devaluation of the peso. However, the large dollar-denominated debt made this a dangerous and unattractive proposition because such a devaluation would have caused a wave of bankruptcies in the private sector and made servicing the public debt more costly. Consequently, the economic authorities started defending the *tablita* in an increasingly desperate way while confidence in their success slipped even more as the incoming administration under General Roberto Viola wavered on their support for the exchange-rate-based stabilization program. During the crisis of 1981, the system displayed its worst flaws: it inspired economic actors to speculate not only against the maintenance of the exchange-rate system but also on an eventual bailout by the government. Fortunes were made during a span of only a few months at the expense of the Argentine state and future taxpayers.

4 THE SELF-DESTRUCTION OF THE MILITARY DICTATORSHIP

We will finally have a government of gentlemen.
—JORGE LUÍS BORGES (1976)

The military should accept the responsibility for the economic disaster, for the ethical disaster, for the War of the Malvinas, the defeat, they are implicated in horrible things . . . the disappearances. . . . They are crazy people without scruples.
—JORGE LUÍS BORGES (1982)

Even in their worst nightmares, the generals who overthrew Isabel Perón in March 1976 could not have imagined the ignominious retreat to the barracks they would be making seven years later. The armed forces had played a significant role in modern Argentine politics since General José Félix Uriburu ousted Hipólito Yrigoyen in 1930 in the midst of the Great Depression.[1] During economic and political crises, civilians had called upon the military to save the *patria*, and the generals enjoyed widespread support at the beginning of their rule in 1976.[2] The years between 1980 and 1982 profoundly changed the face of Argentine politics. Economic disintegration and the military humiliation in the South Atlantic War discredited the armed forces as an institution to such an extent that in July 1982, the novelist Ernesto Sabato complained, "Our military men are not even fit to wage war."[3]

---

1. Goldwert, *Democracy, Militarism and Nationalism in Argentina*; Goldwert, "Rise of Modern Militarism in Argentina"; Potash, *Army and Politics in Argentina*; Potash, "Changing Role of the Military in Argentina."
2. Rouquié, "El poder militar en la Argentina de hoy."
3. "Argentines Are Seeking Ways to Overcome Series of Losses," *New York Times*, July 12, 1982.

The breakdown of the military dictatorship can be attributed to a variety of factors, among them the strengthening of civil society in defiance of violent political repression.[4] However, the deep divisions between various factions within the military government were perhaps the single most important reason for the economic and political implosion during the period 1981–82. These divisions manifested themselves in the mismanaged transition between the outgoing Videla and the incoming Viola administrations, and in the "palace coup" against Viola in December 1981. The main consequence was a complete lack of continuity in policymaking as the country started to slip into chaos. Between March 1981 and August 1982, Argentina had no fewer than five de facto presidents and six ministers of the economy. The political and economic instability also opened the door to military hard-liners who wanted to realize their long-held dream, to retake the disputed Falkland/Malvinas Islands from the United Kingdom, if necessary by force. The defeat in the South Atlantic exposed the complete failure of the military's ambitious project to reorganize state, society, and economy and paved the way for a return to democracy.

The transition of government from President Jorge Rafael Videla to Roberto Viola in late March 1981 occurred at a time when Argentina was once more teetering on the brink of economic crisis. Martínez de Hoz's economic policy had created a dangerous time bomb consisting of an overvalued peso and a large and growing current account deficit. A recession in industry, construction, and commerce; faltering confidence in the financial system; continued capital flight; and the unsustainably high public sector deficit further contributed to a worsening of the situation. Argentina had faced similar current account crises in the past; governments devalued the currency and tightened the belt on domestic consumption in order to reduce imports, bolster exports, and jump-start domestic industry.[5] What made the situation in early 1981 unprecedented was the high foreign debt. A sharp devaluation, instead of ameliorating the crisis, now threatened to bankrupt many large corporations and wipe out the entire domestic financial system.[6] International observers were keenly aware of this dilemma. The U.S. Embassy and the IMF internally expressed their concern that the incoming Argentine government might be overwhelmed by the challenges it would face.[7] Important economists, such as MIT's Rudiger Dornbusch, shared

---

4. Feitlowitz, *Lexicon of Terror.*
5. Díaz Alejandro, "Stop-Go Cycles."
6. Calvo and Reinhart, "Fear of Floating."
7. Telegram, Buenos Aires to State Department, "The Economic Legacy of Martinez de Hoz,"

the gloomy outlook, explaining that the new economic team had inherited only problems.[8]

The new government had to devise an economic policy that would simultaneously overcome the recession and balance the external accounts while avoiding a massive default on the foreign debt. Balancing these three conflicting demands would have been a challenging task even under favorable external circumstances. Unfortunately, 1981 was a particularly difficult year in the international financial markets. Real interest rates were at all-time highs, and most industrial countries were in deep recession. The IMF's "World Economic Outlook" for 1981 described the situation as "grim" especially for non-oil developing countries. It warned that some countries might be unable to borrow all the capital they needed on international markets, which might precipitate widespread crises.[9] The new minister of the economy's political weakness and lack of experience further complicated the situation. De facto president Roberto Viola had deliberately weakened the position of the minister of the economy in his cabinet because he wanted to avoid the emergence of a politically powerful minister comparable to Martínez de Hoz who might challenge his authority.[10] He divided the Ministry of the Economy into five ministries without a clear leadership or unequivocal direction. Lorenzo Sigaut was little more than a *primus inter pares* in a team where each minister represented an interest group and tried to implement policies favorable to his constituency. Eduardo Oxenford, the new minister of industry, had been president of the Alpargatas textile company and the state interventor of the Unión Industrial Argentina (UIA) and had attacked Martínez de Hoz repeatedly for hurting the interests of domestic industry. Jorge Aguado, minister of agriculture, had previously been the president of the Argentine Rural Confederation. General Diego Urricariet, minister of public works and services, had previously been at the helm of the powerful military-industrial Fabricaciones Militares and frequently clashed with Martínez de Hoz over the role of public enterprises in the Argentine economy.[11] The result was an economic policy worked out by trial and error that had no clear direction and which ultimately proved to be disastrous.

February 6, 1981; Argentina—Staff Report for the 1981 Article IV Consultation, December 2, 1981, SM/81/233, 3, IMF Archives.

8. Dornbusch, "Argentina Since Martinez De Hoz," 13.

9. International Monetary Fund, "World Economic Outlook," 56.

10. Smith, *Authoritarianism*, 243.

11. George L. Reeves, president, Chase Bank Buenos Aires to James W. Bergford, executive vice president, Chase Manhattan Bank, New York, "Re: President Designates Roberto E. Viola's Cabinet," David Rockefeller Collection.

Lorenzo Sigaut initially failed to recognize his political weakness and the scale of the debt problem. The latter was partly due to a lack of information on the actual size of the foreign debt.[12] He hoped that a relatively small devaluation could balance the external account and restore competitiveness. The first of a series of packages that he announced on April 1 was a one-time 30 percent devaluation of the peso against the dollar, after which he pledged to continue with a scheme of a predetermined devaluation.[13] He promised that businesses would benefit from a special rediscount facility of the Central Bank, which would help consolidate the internal debt of industry and agriculture. At the same time, he tried to consolidate the public finances by levying new export taxes, raising public tariffs, and freezing the salaries of public employees. The initial results of his program were positive. Capital flows reversed immediately, and by the end of April reserves had risen by more than US$1.5 billion. Only in May did it become obvious that the initial devaluation had not been large enough to balance the external account, and the fiscal measures fell far short of their goal. While the fiscal deficit surged, reserves started to fall again rapidly.[14]

June 1981 became the defining month for Sigaut's term in office. Public confidence in his policies collapsed as the lines in front of the exchange houses in the banking district of Buenos Aires, the "Microcentro," grew longer and the peso reached new lows against the dollar. By the end of the month, Sigaut had become a laughingstock not only in financial circles but also in large parts of the population. The crisis started in late May when the minister of trade, Carlos Garcia Martínez, made off-the-record remarks that the country was teetering on the brink of economic collapse. The run on the peso that followed had such proportions that after spending US$600 million in an effort to shore up the currency, the Central Bank closed foreign exchange markets on June 2 and the peso was again sharply devalued.[15] A confident Sigaut boasted in a press conference that from now on "nobody in their right state of mind could again claim that the peso was overvalued. With today's measures it is undervalued."[16] Even within his economic team, not everybody agreed. Julio Gómez and Martin

---

12. Lorenzo Sigaut, interview, Buenos Aires, December 23, 2004.

13. Cellini and Pombo, "Los cinco meses del Dr. Sigaut," 22.

14. Argentina—Staff Report for the 1981 Article IV Consultation, December 2, 1981, SM/81/233, 4, IMF Archives.

15. "Argentina: Pesocide," *Economist*, June 6, 1981.

16. "Devaluase el peso en un 30 por ciento: La nueva paridad rige desde hoy y no está acompañada de medidas compensatorias. Ajuste del 6% en junio y seguro cambiario. Renuncias," *La Nación*, June 2, 1981.

Lagos, president and vice president of the Central Bank, resigned in protest. They argued that only a free float of the peso could help solve the crisis of confidence in economic policymaking in Argentina.[17] Sigaut was convinced that he knew better and wanted to keep intervening in the foreign exchange market and continue with the system of incremental monthly devaluations. On Friday, June 20, 1981, he stated in an interview on a morning radio show, "This time, those who bet on foreign currency are really going to lose." The response of the markets was immediate and unmistakable. The selling of the peso was so strong that Sigaut was forced not only to devalue the peso by another 30 percent the following Monday but also to impose a system of multiple exchange rates and exchange restrictions.[18] On the black market, the dollar rose even more, reaching almost nine thousand pesos to the dollar, more than three times as much as on April 1.

The June meltdown added a new political and financial dimension to the crisis. With inflation rising sharply and unemployment at record heights, the military junta started to face increasing public opposition. In June, Viola confronted a large-scale strike of autoworkers, which ended with the arrest of more than a thousand workers.[19] For a de facto president who wanted to prepare the country for transition to democracy, this event undermined his claim to legitimacy. The second major devaluation of the peso also directly threatened to bankrupt companies and banks, which had assumed a large dollar-denominated debt during the heyday of the *tablita*. To save the heavily indebted private sector, the government resorted to emergency measures that would ultimately amount to a complete bailout for private borrowers with dollar-denominated debt. While debtors rejoiced, these measures had costly long-term implications for Argentina.

With the devaluation of June 2, Sigaut made the vague promise to compensate companies with liabilities in dollars for the losses they incurred from the devaluation.[20] The Central Bank later specified that under certain circumstances, companies that managed to extend their external liabilities by at least 540 days would benefit from this guarantee.[21] With further devaluations over the course

17. "Financial Panic and Political Rumors Shake Buenos Aires," *Latin American Weekly Report*, June 5, 1981.

18. Kannenguiser, *La maldita herencia*, 32.

19. "Argentine Regime Severely Strained by Economic Woes," *New York Times*, July 5, 1981.

20. "Devaluase el peso en un 30 por ciento: La nueva paridad rige desde hoy y no está acompañada de medidas compensatorias. Ajuste del 6% en junio y seguro cambiario. Renuncias," *La Nación*, June 2, 1981.

21. Argentina—Staff Report for the 1981 Article IV Consultation, December 2, 1981, SM/81/233, 4, IMF Archives.

of the next year and a half, the predictable consequence was a large-scale nationalization of foreign debt. Individuals who managed to get their dollar assets out of the country benefited particularly from these measures because they saw their liabilities reduced to a small fraction of their previous value while their assets remained untouched. Available evidence suggests that some entrepreneurs even created fictitious "paper loans" worth up to US$5 billion to take full advantage of this opportunity.[22]

The second half of 1981 echoed the final months of Isabel Perón's government. Inflation exceeded an annualized rate of 120 percent in July and continued at high levels afterward. Compared to the previous year, GDP fell by more than 10 percent while real wages continued to shrink and the budget deficit ballooned to almost 10 percent of GDP. The economic meltdown coincided with what appeared to be an orchestrated attempt to undermine Viola's political base.[23] During the nomination process for his successor, it had become clear that Roberto Viola did not enjoy the full support of all three branches of the armed forces. With the economy faltering during the southern winter of 1981, frictions within the military grew dangerously. Leopoldo Galtieri, the new commander-in-chief of the army, and Cristino Nicolaides, commander of the Third Army, started to challenge Viola publicly on his efforts toward political opening. While Viola was suggesting that political parties participate in the selection of the next chief executive, Galtieri publicly emphasized that the president was subordinate to the military junta and had to follow their orders. He also directly rejected any political opening and warned Viola not to "revive dead myths, worn-out ideas, and degrading populism."[24] The disaffection of the armed forces with the economic team of Lorenzo Sigaut also became increasingly vocal and direct during the second half of 1981. In the winter (July–September 1981) issue, the *Revista Militar* featured cartoons addressing the effects of the economic crisis on the morale of the troops. One of them showed two officers explaining to their subordinates that they could no longer afford ammunition and so needed to kill their enemies with "indifference" (see fig. 4).

In September 1981, Eduardo Girling, chief of the Argentine Naval Intelligence, confided to a member of the U.S. delegation that he was "particularly worried about the current economic situation and its ultimate political impact." He explained that he feared the army would topple Viola if the situation did not

22. Smith, *Authoritarianism*, 243.
23. "Financial Panic and Political Rumours Shake Buenos Aires," *Latin American Weekly Report*, June 5, 1981.
24. Fontana, "Political Decision Making," 129.

Fig. 4 "And because we ran out of ammunition, we are going to kill the enemy with indifference." Cartoon from *Revista Militar,* July–September 1981

improve and added that the army seemed to be united behind Leopoldo Galtieri, who "is the man . . . to do something if anything is done."[25]

Not unlike the situation in late 1975, the political crisis exacerbated the economic crisis in a vicious circle. Sigaut's economic policy was tightly interwoven with Roberto Viola's political fortunes. Sigaut's failure to control the faltering economy and to inspire confidence weakened Viola's position, and Viola's political weakness rendered Sigaut increasingly unable to implement his proposed measures. In early November, with a new run on the dollar fueled by rumors of a regime change, Sigaut for the first time publicly admitted that Argentina had "tremendous problems with its external debt" and added that the total external debt had reached some US$29 billion and that private debt needed to be refinanced in order to help them "digest the immense financial burden."[26] This statement led to yet another run on the peso, which drove the exchange

25. Pol Files, Townsend Friedman, "Conversation with Admiral Girling," September 17, 1981, State Argentina Declassification Project (1975–84).

26. "A la deuda externa se refirió Sigaut," *La Nación,* November 5, 1981.

rate temporarily as high as 14,500 pesos to the dollar. The image of Sigaut being chased by the markets became the symbol of the perceived inability of the Viola administration to control events. In late October and early November 1981, rumors that the government was about to be overthrown were circulating so widely in Buenos Aires that even the conservative—and heavily censored— newspaper *La Nación* responded to them.[27]

The power vacuum was soon filled "Argentine style." On November 11, 1981, Argentines woke up to a strangely familiar situation: a weak and unpopular president was suddenly declared "sick" and given a period of "repose" to regain his strength.[28] General Horacio Liendo, Viola's minister of the interior, became interim president on November 20.[29] Liendo moved fast to enact sweeping changes in the economic order, which suggests that he knew that Viola would not return to power. Since Viola refused to give Liendo permission to reshuffle the cabinet, the revamping of the economy occurred from behind the scenes.[30] The government unveiled a new economic plan on November 30, 1981, that differed sharply from previous policies. The author of the plan was a young Harvard-trained economist named Domingo Cavallo. He had come to Buenos Aires as Liendo's protégée, who had gotten to know him from his work at the Fundación Mediterránea, an economic think tank in Córdoba.[31] Cavallo's exact political function initially remained a mystery. He gave an interview claiming to be Lorenzo Sigaut's spokesman.[32] However, the very next day he had to retract that statement while at the same time denying that there were any disagreements within the government.[33] Behind the scenes, Cavallo's comments had outraged Liendo, who felt that Cavallo had sidestepped the institutional hierarchy.[34] In fact, Cavallo was only an undersecretary in the ministry of interior but his close contact with the interim president gave him important political leeway to implement his ideas.

27. "La vieja técnica del rumor," *La Nación,* November 1, 1981.

28. "Viola guardará un período de reposo: Permanece desde ayer en la quinta presidencial y no retornaría a su despacho hasta la semana próxima," *La Nación,* November 11, 1981.

29. "Decídese hoy sobre el ejercicio del P.E.: Liendo lo informó tras reunirse con Viola. Habrá nuevo parte médico. La *Junta* Militar resolverá de acuerdo con lo que fija el estatuto," *La Nación,* November 20, 1981.

30. "Argentine Army Debates Next Step as Liendo Becomes Interim President," *Latin America Weekly Report,* November 27, 1981.

31. Thompson, *"Think Tanks" en la Argentina.*

32. "Exclusivo: El gobierno explica su plan," *Ámbito Financiero,* December 1, 1981.

33. "Cavallo: Las explicaciones que di, de ninguna manera han sido desautorizadas," *Ámbito Financiero,* December 3, 1981.

34. General Horacio Tomás Liendo, interview, Buenos Aires, May 5, 2004.

Cavallo was driven by the conviction that the main problem of the Argentine economy was the high debt burden of individuals and companies, which made further investment impossible. He blamed Martínez de Hoz's economic policies for unfairly favoring the so-called *patria financiera,* the financial and banking interests in the city of Buenos Aires, at the expense of supposedly honest businesses who found it impossible to pay the high interest rates. The young economist had the ambitious goal of redefining the rules of the game of the Argentine economy in order to break inflationary inertia and put Argentina on a sustainable path to growth. He was convinced that a radical financial reform, which would restore incentives to invest and produce in industry, agriculture, and services, was necessary.[35]

The Cavallo Plan consisted of fixing interest rates below the rate of inflation. Cavallo hoped this would help to reduce the real value of domestic public and private debt quickly, a process Cavallo euphemistically called "licuación," and tried to convince politicians and the population at large that everybody would benefit from it. To alleviate the burden on debtors who had assumed liabilities in dollars, he enacted new exchange guarantees.

Even though the Cavallo Plan represented a radical departure from Sigaut's muddling through, the economic consequences were initially limited. The political fallout, by contrast, was as swift as it was dramatic. Only days after the new measures were announced, former minister of the economy José Martínez de Hoz took the unusual step of publicly denouncing his successors' economic policies. Martínez de Hoz commented that Argentina was returning to the economic mismanagement of 1975 and called for a new minister of the economy "whose name alone would inspire enough confidence to reestablish economic stability."[36] Lorenzo Sigaut and Horacio Liendo reacted to these critical comments with outrage. They publicly accused Martínez de Hoz of being responsible for the economic problems and attacked him for trying to "impose elitist criteria" as if the country could be governed against the true national interests and shaped to his own personal image.[37] Only two days after the publication of Martínez de Hoz's comments and the day after the reaction of Liendo and Sigaut had been printed in major newspapers in Argentina, the military junta made it clear whom they supported. A palace coup ousted Roberto Viola and replaced him with a military hard-liner, Leopoldo Galtieri. Galtieri immediately fired

---

35. Domingo Cavallo, interview, Cambridge, Mass., April 8, 2004.
36. "Críticas declaraciones del ex ministro Martínez de Hoz," *La Nación,* December 8, 1981.
37. "Liendo y Sigaut refutan al doctor Martínez de Hoz," *La Nación,* December 9, 1981.

Lorenzo Sigaut and Domingo Cavallo and called on Roberto Alemann, a close friend of Martínez de Hoz, to take the helm of the Ministry of the Economy. The coalition behind the palace coup consisted of three sectors with potentially contradictory interests, namely political hard-liners, economic liberals, and military hawks. Political hard-liners supported Galtieri because they believed him to be a bulwark against democratic opening. Economic liberals had two goals. On the one hand, they hoped that Galtieri would undo the economic measures applied by Sigaut and Cavallo and return the country to the economic model championed by Martínez de Hoz. On the other hand, they wanted to deepen their alignment with the West and especially with the United States, with whom Galtieri had built up strong ties. Finally, hawks in the navy supported the palace coup on the condition that Galtieri would assume an aggressive policy against Britain in the South Atlantic.[38] As would soon become obvious, the military adventure in the South Atlantic trumped all other concerns and directly contradicted efforts to reestablish economic stability or to strengthen political ties with the West. The war isolated the country politically and economically. Economic liberalization would be impossible to achieve during wartime, and a militarily aggressive country would not be able to gain international investors' confidence. Galtieri's failed Malvinas gamble would also ultimately speed the transition to democracy, not delay it.

Political events in Washington initially seemed to support Galtieri. Ronald Reagan's victory over the incumbent Jimmy Carter led to a radical shift in U.S. policy toward Argentina. Reagan had consistently criticized Carter's focus on human rights and accused him of making "a mess of our relations with the planet's seventh largest country, Argentina, a nation with which we should be close friends" while at the same time praising the Argentine military junta for eliminating the "terrorist threat."[39] Before the coup, Galtieri was widely perceived as "Washington's man" in Buenos Aires. Galtieri traveled to Washington in early November 1981 to attend the annual meeting of army leaders of the Americas where he met with his U.S. counterparts. Secretary of Defense Caspar Weinberger and National Security Adviser Richard Allen reportedly described him as a "magnificent person" and an "impressive general."[40] U.S and Argentine military interests also seemed closely aligned in the area of hemispheric

38. Argentina, Comisión Rattenbach, *Informe Rattenbach*, 40; also see the interview with Nicanor Costa Méndez published in Mack, *Der Falkland (Malvinas)-Konflikt*, 212.

39. Vacs, "Delicate Balance," 33.

40. "Viola's Health Wanes and Galtieri Gets the US Seal of Approval," *Latin American Weekly Report*, November 13, 1981.

security, with Argentina's military actively supporting the anticommunist strategy in Central America.[41]

President Reagan's new diplomatic team also included some of Argentina's most vocal defenders against human rights activists. The new U.S. ambassador in Buenos Aires, Harry Shlaudeman, had been an assistant secretary in the State Department during the Ford administration and had encouraged the Argentine government "to get the terrorist problem over as soon as possible" during late 1976.[42] Jeane Kirkpatrick, new U.S. ambassador at the United Nations, had previously explained that the Argentine dictatorship was only "moderately repressive" and deserved U.S. military, economic, and political support.[43] Kirkpatrick's support for the Argentine dictatorship even continued during the military conflict with the United Kingdom. This would lead to a sharp conflict with Secretary of State Alexander Haig, whom she accused of being a "Brit in American clothes . . . insensitive to [Latin] cultures." She warned that U.S. policy would irreparably damage "the solid working relationship of trust nurtured through so many administrations."[44]

The human rights certification, which the State Department had to send to Congress every year, reflected the Reagan administration's effort to build stronger ties with Argentina and to downplay human rights abuses. It noted, "Since 1979 terrorism has been under control and human rights conditions have improved significantly." It explained that during 1981 only "one possible case" of disappearance had been reported, political freedom was expanded, and there was no evidence for the use of torture during interrogations.[45] In early March 1982, Esteban Takacs, Argentine ambassador in Washington, declared triumphantly, "Relations with the United States could not be any better."[46]

Argentina desperately needed better relations with the United States in order to restore investors' confidence, which would allow them to roll over some US\$7.2 billion of external debt falling due in 1982 and contract US\$3.5 billion in fresh loans to cover the current account deficit.[47] Roberto Alemann appeared to be

41. Feldman, "The United States Role in the Malvinas Crisis."

42. Telegram, American Embassy Buenos Aires to Secretary of State, "Foreign Minister Guzzetti Euphoric over Visit to United States," October 19, 1976, State Argentina Declassification Project (1975–84).

43. Kirkpatrick, "Dictatorships and Double Standards."

44. Quoted in "Reagan's Aides at War," *Newsweek* (U.S. edition), June 7, 1982.

45. Telegram, Buenos Aires to State Department, "Argentine Certification," February 2, 1982, State Argentina Declassification Project (1975–84).

46. "Relaciones con los EE.UU.," *La Nación*, March 2, 1982.

47. Kannenguiser, *La maldita herencia*, 36.

the ideal candidate for this task. A conservative economist of Swiss-German descent, Alemann was a bona fide economic liberal with close ties to former minister of the economy Martínez de Hoz. He enjoyed excellent international contacts through his work as ambassador to the United States starting in 1962 and long-standing contacts with the international banking community through his advisory function for the Union Bank of Switzerland (UBS).

Alemann's economic policy meant a complete reversal of every important economic measure taken since June and especially of the Cavallo Plan. The first economic measures aimed at reassuring investors by lifting exchange restrictions, unifying the exchange rate and allowing the peso to float, and liberating interest rates.[48] Alemann promised to bring inflation under control with the help of a stringent austerity program at the heart of which stood the three "Ds," namely disinflation, deregulation, and privatization of public enterprises (*desestatización*).[49] The burden of the anti-inflation program fell heavily on wage earners, whose salaries were frozen and who therefore experienced a rapid decline in purchasing power.[50]

The local financial press greeted the measures euphorically. *Ámbito Financiero* praised Roberto Alemann for his "revolutionary intent to achieve economic growth in freedom and serious monetary policy."[51] The international financial community was also impressed with the new minister. Christian Brachet, head of the IMF mission in early 1982, remembered, "Roberto [Alemann] and we were completely on the same wavelength. To a certain degree, he was even more orthodox than we were."[52] In the April 1982 issue, published just days before the outbreak of hostilities, *Euromoney* Magazine lauded Alemann for "trying to break Argentina of its bad habits" and underlined his sincerity and perseverance with the words, "What he says goes."[53]

Subsequent events would quickly reveal the political limitations Alemann faced in his effort to revamp the economy. In sharp contrast to the situation in 1976, when the military coup was widely supported by the Argentine public,

48. Supplement to the Staff Report for the 1981 Article IV Consultations, February 25, 1982, SM/81/233, Supplement 1, IMF Archives.

49. Solanet, *Notas sobre la guerra de Malvinas*, 8.

50. Jorge Schvarzer, "De la recesión con inflación a la inflación con recesión," *El Economista, Guía de Consulta*, December 1982.

51. "Roberto Alemann significa el revolucionario intento de expandir el país en libertad y con seriedad monetaria," *Ámbito Financiero*, December 21, 1981.

52. Christian Brachet, interview, Washington, D.C., April 14, 2004.

53. Alan Robinson, "Roberto Alemann Treats Inflation as a Personal Enemy," *Euromoney*, April 1982, 17–25.

tired of Peronist mismanagement, this time the military was widely blamed by the public for their mismanagement and the economic meltdown. The population's patience with the military government's economic experiments was running out. The briefing papers for Undersecretary Enders's visit to Argentina in March 1982 noted that "the deep recession and the draconian economic measures, after six years of military rule, are raising social tensions, give strong encouragement to the civilian opposition, now more vocal than ever, and leave the regime isolated." At the same time, it warned that "if the present conservative government should fail with its economic program, this would mean the end of liberal market economics in Argentina and the country would turn back towards a more dirigist course."[54]

Even more damaging for Alemann's economic program was the fact that Galtieri's political and military ambitions left little room for an orthodox economic policy of domestic liberalization and simultaneous opening of the economy to world markets. Galtieri publicly endorsed Alemann and his stringent economic measures. This included an important reduction in the defense budget and the privatization of key public enterprises. In his inaugural speech, Galtieri stated confidently that he would not accept any excuses for not privatizing.[55] However, this rhetoric had little to do with the reality of the dictatorship, where large parts of the military continued to oppose the idea of privatizing the public enterprises it controlled directly. Preparations for a military operation in the South Atlantic also ruled out any reduction in the military budget. Galtieri's support for Alemann's economic policies was therefore halfhearted at best. Galtieri did not subscribe to the long-term vision of Argentina with a small and efficient state fully integrated in the Western World. Instead, he used Alemann's status among economic liberals to win support for his presidential ambitions.

Available evidence suggests that the invasion of the Falkland/Malvinas Islands was part of the pact between the navy commander Admiral Jorge Anaya and the army commander Leopoldo Galtieri. In exchange for Anaya's support in the palace coup against Roberto Viola, Galtieri pledged to implement the plan, which Anaya had developed for Admiral Massera as early as 1977.[56] The official report

54. Telegram, Buenos Aires to State Department, "Travel of Assistant Secretary Enders; Overview of Argentina," March 3, 1982, State Argentina Declassification Project (1975–84).

55. "No acepto excusas para no privatizar, afirmo Galtieri," *Ámbito Financiero,* December 24, 1981.

56. See, e.g., Corradi, *Fitful Republic,* 138, and Cardoso, Kirschbaum, and Van der Kooy, *Falklands—the Secret Plot.*

of the Argentine armed forces investigating their strategic and tactical failures during the military campaign—the Rattenbach Report—confirmed that Leopoldo Galtieri and Jorge Anaya already had a clear plan for a military occupation of the islands in the South Atlantic when Galtieri assumed the presidency in mid-December 1981.[57] At the same time, Galtieri briefed his minister of foreign affairs, Nicanor Costa Méndez, that retaking the islands had highest priority.[58]

Galtieri underestimated the economic and political costs of the military adventure. This can partly be explained with a deeply flawed perception of a possible British response to the invasion. Galtieri believed that an invasion without bloodshed on the British side could serve as a strong bargaining chip for a subsequent diplomatic solution favorable to Argentina.[59] His close and cordial relations with the Reagan administration also created the dangerous illusion that the United States would remain neutral in a conflict with the United Kingdom or even lean on the government in London to reach a diplomatic compromise and avoid a military showdown.[60]

The military junta apparently never consulted with the economic team prior to the landing on the islands. Robert Alemann and his right-hand man Manuel Solanet claim to have been unaware of the strategic planning for the invasion.[61] These explanations are unconvincing. The buildup of military tensions between Argentina and the Britain following a series of incidents on the South Georgia islands in March 1982 could hardly have escaped Alemann's attention. He also must have been aware of the navy's long-standing desire to resolve the conflict over the island group by force if necessary. Alemann could have warned Galtieri how dangerous the military adventure would be for the Argentine economy even if a full-scale military showdown was avoided. British banks had underwritten the second-largest part of Argentine debt, a total of US$4.5 billion, with Lloyds Bank being the single largest creditor.[62]

The Argentine invasion started in the early morning of April 2, 1982, only hours after the United Kingdom had informed an urgently convoked session of the U.N. Security Council that Argentine invasion forces were heading toward

57. Argentina, Comisión Rattenbach, *Informe Rattenbach*, 40.

58. Interview with Nicanor Costa Méndez, published in Mack, *Der Falkland (Malvinas)-Konflikt*, 212.

59. Manuel Solanet, secretary of finance, interview, Buenos Aires, January 10, 2005.

60. Feldman, "The United States Role in the Malvinas Crisis," 5–7.

61. Alemann, *La política económica*; Roberto Alemann, interview, Buenos Aires, June 20, 2003; Manuel Solanet, interview, Buenos Aires, January 10, 2005.

62. "Relevamiento de la deuda externa Argentina," Comunicado No. 4645 del BCRA del 7–11–84, DSDD.

the Falkland Islands.[63] By the following day, it became clear that Galtieri's gamble had not paid off. The British government would not accept the invasion as a fait accompli. The House of Commons virtually unanimously called for military action to retake the islands, and Margaret Thatcher announced that the British Aircraft Carrier *Invincible* would set sail on April 5 to lead a task force of between thirty-five and forty ships to the South Atlantic.[64]

With the outbreak of hostilities, Alemann's liberal economic program came to an abrupt end. While large crowds gathered on the Plaza de Mayo to cheer Galtieri, an immediate run on the banks and the national currency showed that confidence in the success of the operation was actually very low. Argentine banks lost more than 4 percent of their deposits during the first days of April. By April 3, the government saw itself obliged to enact exchange restrictions to stop the outflow of dollars.[65] Foreign exchange was only available with explicit permission from the Central Bank. This was intended to help stem the tide of capital flight and maintain adequate exchange reserves for the purchase of armaments. Alemann believed that maintaining large enough foreign reserves would help generate confidence in Argentina's ability to pay its debt, making it easier to roll over the outstanding loans during the conflict.[66] The peso, whose value had been determined freely by market forces during the first three months of 1982, was devalued sharply and subsequently fixed in value through the direct intervention of the Central Bank. Capital controls immediately led to the development of a large black market premium reflecting investors' fears about the future of Alemann's economic program. In mid-April, the CIA started to worry about the broader risk the armed confrontation posed for the Argentine economy, which could be "severe" especially if the war were prolonged.[67]

Foreign obligations were paid with the help of newly issued dollar-denominated bonds, called BONEX.[68] This had severe undesired consequences: private obligations were paid with government bonds at a favorable exchange

63. Department of State—Operations Center—Falkland Working Group, Situation Report No. 1, "Falklands Situation as of 0600 EST, April 2, 1982, Falklands/Malvinas (intelligence and press items) (2), Fontaine, Roger: Files Box 90134, Ronald Reagan Presidential Library.

64. Department of State—Operations Center—Falkland Working Group, Situation Report No. 5, "Falklands Situation as of 1700 EST, April 3, 1982, Falklands/Malvinas (intelligence and press items) (2), Fontaine, Roger: Files Box 90134, Ronald Reagan Presidential Library.

65. "Medio Año de Política Económica: 22 de diciembre de 1981 a 30 de junio de 1982," *Boletín Semanal del Ministerio de Economía*, July 5, 1982.

66. Alemann, *La política económica*, 12.

67. Central Intelligence Agency Documents, "Falkland Islands Dispute: Economic Impact," April 15, 1982, Declassified Documents of the National Security Council, 6.

68. Alemann, *La política económica*, 14.

rate. This allowed for subsidized service payments for private debtors and directly increased public debt. Additionally, it allowed for large speculative profits for those with access to domestic and foreign BONEX markets. The war economy also derailed Alemann's monetary orthodoxy. During April alone, the money supply increased by more than 50 percent, so that the total money supply more than tripled between the end of December and late April. An Argentine analyst noted that printing of money was the only strategic industry that worked at full capacity during these critical months.[69]

Actual hostilities ended on June 14, with a decisive British victory at Port Stanley. The blood toll was considerable with more than 650 Argentine and 255 British soldiers and sailors killed and almost two thousand wounded. By contrast, direct material costs of the war were relatively limited for Argentina. The British naval blockade, which became operational two weeks after the invasion with the arrival of two nuclear-powered submarines, was so effective that Argentina was unable to send supplies to the islands by ship. After the sinking of the cruiser *General Belgrano* on May 4, 1982, the navy was too afraid to let military vessels (including the aircraft carrier *25 de Mayo*) confront the British fleet. Consequently, the Argentine forces had little heavy equipment and not a single tank at their disposal during the battle for control of the two main islands.[70] The most costly losses for the Argentine armed forces were fighter aircrafts and helicopters shot down. Manuel Solanet, secretary of finance during the conflict, estimated the material losses amounted to roughly US$900 million.[71]

The direct cost of military equipment was only a small part of the damage done to the Argentine economy. The effect of a widely honored trade ban and financial sanctions imposed by United Kingdom were much costlier and longer lasting. Trade with Britain, New Zealand, and Canada came to a complete halt. The European Community halfheartedly followed suit, enacting a ban on new trade with Argentina but exempting goods under prior existing contracts. Since the trade embargo of the EEC only came into force on April 16, many Argentine exporters used the transition period to shore up contracts, which would remain exempted from the embargo. Consequently, the effects of the embargo were felt with considerable delay. While exports to the EEC fell by only 18 percent compared to the previous year in April, they had fallen by two-thirds in June and by more than 80 percent in September. The impact of the sanctions

69. Schvarzer, "De la recesión" (see note 50).
70. Manuel Solanet, interview, Buenos Aires, January 10, 2005.
71. Solanet, *Notas sobre la guerra de Malvinas*, 97.

was cushioned by the refusal of Japan, Spain, and Latin American countries to participate in the embargo and the fact that the United States merely suspended import-export credits. Still, the overall effect of the embargo on Argentine exports was sizable. Exports fell by 20 and 40 percent compared to the previous year in May and June respectively, and the negative effect lasted for the remainder of the year. Imports were also sharply lower. However, the fall in imports started before the outbreak of hostilities. This suggests that the main reason was not the embargo but rather the fallout of economic crisis, shortage of foreign exchange, and a new system of import controls under which each importer needed to prove the urgent necessity of the goods being imported.[72]

The financial sanction imposed by the United Kingdom had limited immediate effects but would sharply disrupt Argentina's ability to access international capital markets for years to come, pushing the country into de facto default during the military conflict. Since the Argentine authorities anticipated the freezing of Argentine financial assets in the United Kingdom in case of hostilities, they started withdrawing international reserves that had been deposited with the Bank of England and with commercial banks in the United Kingdom on March 20.[73] The Central Bank also secretly informed large state-owned banks, such as the Banco Nación and Banco de la Provincia de Buenos Aires to transfer their funds to offshore accounts ahead of the imposition of British sanctions. Only US$1.45 billion were ultimately frozen during the hostilities. They largely belonged to private citizens who were caught off guard by the invasion. The only exception was US$70 million, which the army's weapons purchase commission had forgotten to withdraw from British banks before the outbreak of hostilities.[74]

Argentina retaliated against the British financial sanctions by freezing British assets in Argentina and restricting payments to British banks.[75] While this move satisfied the nationalistic impulse, it actually hurt Argentine interests and complicated Alemann's debt negotiation strategy. Argentina needed bank cooperation to roll over existing loans, which were falling due during the first half of the year under extremely unfavorable external circumstances. The country also

---

72. Secretary of Finance Manuel Solanet, "La Economía Argentina Frente al Conflicto Bélico" (speech delivered at the stock exchange, Córdoba, May 28, 1982); reproduced in *Boletín Semanal del Ministerio de Economía*, June 7, 1982.

73. Solanet, *Notas sobre la guerra de Malvinas*, 20.

74. Kannenguiser, *La maldita herencia*, 38.

75. Central Intelligence Agency Documents, "Falkland Islands Dispute: Economic Impact," April 15, 1982, 5, Declassified Documents of the National Security Council.

needed a continued inflow of foreign capital to finance the large current account deficit. During the year 1982, the Argentine government had anticipated borrowing US$3.5 billion to finance the current account deficit and needed to roll over more than US$7 billion of foreign debt, which was falling due during the remainder of the year.[76] These plans were now at serious risk. The war undermined bankers' confidence in the reliability of the Argentine authorities. At the same time, financial sanctions between Argentina and the United Kingdom, which hosted two of Argentina's largest creditor banks, started to have an effect on commercial transactions. By excluding British banks from service payments on foreign debt, Argentina risked being declared in default on a large part of its foreign obligations. Most foreign liabilities were bank loans made by banking syndicates, not individual banks. The loan contracts contained "sharing clauses," which implied that banks had to share the payments with each other in case a part of the payment was not made. The nonpayment of a part of the outstanding payment could lead to a formal default on the entire loan, a so-called cross default. To avoid this scenario, the Argentine authorities decided to pay the share due the British banks into escrow accounts that would be accessible as soon as the sanctions were lifted.[77]

Despite the difficult circumstances, Alemann made every effort to maintain a working relationship with the country's creditors. He flew to the interim committee meeting of the IMF in Helsinki in mid-May to plead his case before the international financial community and later continued to Zurich and New York to reassure international banks. He received assurances that existing debt would continue to be rolled over. A leading banker explained that "there [was] no other way" than to go along with the Argentine proposal at this point.[78] The U.S. Cabinet Council of Economic Affairs was also deeply concerned about the financial future of Argentina and expected that the country would urgently need an IMF intervention by the time the armed conflict came to an end in order to stabilize the situation. They were particularly worried about the potential fallout for U.S. banks should Argentina and Mexico declare a cessation of payments on their external obligations simultaneously, a possibility they would not rule out, given the precarious state of Mexico's finances.[79] By the end of the war, Argentina had accumulated more than US$2 billion in external arrears and

76. Alemann, *La política económica,* 15.

77. "Argentines See Jump in Inflation," *New York Times,* May 12, 1982.

78. "Argentina Is Assured on Short-Term Debts," *New York Times,* May 18, 1982.

79. Minutes, Cabinet Council on Economic Affairs, May 20, 1982, case file 068967, FG010-02, WHORM Subject File, Ronald Reagan Presidential Library.

enjoyed no international support, which would have helped them normalize the situation quickly.[80]

During the months following the end of hostilities, the Argentine military confronted the economic and political fallout from economic chaos and military defeat. Argentina seemed to fall into collective depression. During the official mass for the ruling junta, the priest said in his homily that "fear, skepticism, distrust and partisanship abound in difficult times."[81] In a similar vein, the novelist Ernesto Sabato explained in an interview with *Gente*, a general interest weekly: "I think this is the last chance for the nation. We can get out of the swamp or remain in total frustration—forever."[82] When Northern Argentina suffered from major flooding in mid-1982, a bitter joke circulated. "It's not that the waters are rising. The country is sinking."[83]

The armed forces were now so divided that election of a new de facto president caused the rupture of the military junta. The air force argued that a civilian instead of another general should head the next government, while the army insisted that it had always been their prerogative to field the president. The navy insisted that Nicanor Costa Méndez remain minister of foreign affairs, which Reynaldo Bignone, the presidential candidate for the army, refused to accept. Since it was impossible to reach the unanimity of the junta required by statues of the *Proceso* over these disagreements, the army took direct responsibility for the leadership of the country, and the navy and the air force withdrew from the junta in protest.[84]

Reynaldo Bignone found himself in an extremely precarious political situation. The military burdened him with unrealistic expectations concerning negotiations with Britain over the future of the islands in the South Atlantic. Business groups expected rapid stimulation of the economy and a significant alleviation of the debt burden. And trade unions were pushing for higher real wages.[85] The U.S. Embassy noted that Bignone's strategy was "to identify himself with the transition to democracy, thereby gaining the tacit support of the parties, labor and the church, and disarming—so far—the opposition whose criticism could be construed as an attempt to interrupt the process of return

---

80. Boughton, *Silent Revolution*, 329.
81. "Argentines Are Seeking Ways to Overcome Series of Losses," *New York Times*, July 12, 1982.
82. "A New Wave of Movie Makers Cry for Argentina," *New York Times*, October 19, 1983.
83. "Argentina After the Falklands," *New York Times*, December 26, 1982.
84. Bignone, *El último de facto II*, 122.
85. "Argentina: Union Wage Demands Add to the Pressure," *Latin American Weekly Report*, August 20, 1982.

to civilian rule."[86] One would normally not expect such a weak and divided government to be able to enact far-reaching economic reforms. Indeed, in his inaugural speech Bignone pledged that he would not offer great changes during the period of transition to democracy.[87] During the first two months of his administration, however, the very fragmentation of the government made it possible for individual actors—especially the president of the Central Bank, Domingo Cavallo—to take far-reaching measures that would have been impossible to implement in the absence of political chaos and without the declaration of yet another economic emergency.

The nomination process of the minister of the economy and the president of the Central Bank reflected the conflictual nature of policymaking. Reynaldo Bignone later explained that he would have preferred to keep Roberto Alemann as minister of the economy and continue economic policies similar to those applied before the outbreak of the war. However, this was a politically impossible choice. The *multipartidaria*, the organization of democratic parties whose support Bignone needed for a seamless transition to democracy, was highly critical of Alemann's performance because they associated him with the military government's economic liberalism, which they held responsible for the economic crisis. The new commander-in-chief of the army, General Cristino Nicolaides, pushed Bignone to nominate Domingo Cavallo minister of the economy. Nicolaides had met Cavallo in 1981 when he was the commander of the Third Army Corps in Córdoba. The young and ambitious economist soon became his protégée.[88] Bignone, however, did not trust Cavallo enough to make him minister of the economy, arguing that he was too young and lacked experience. Instead, he chose José Maria Dagnino Pastore. Dagnino Pastore was an experienced economist who had been minister of the economy during the military government of Juan Carlos Onganía in 1969–70. Cavallo had to be content with the presumably less important position of president of the Central Bank.[89] However, as would soon become obvious, Cavallo once again sidestepped his nominal superior in an effort to implement the far-reaching economic reforms he had planned.

In his first televised address, the new minister of the economy laid out the ambitious program, which included stimulating the economy, creating new

86. Telegram, Buenos Aires to State Department, "President Bignones Performance and Prospects," September 16, 1982, State Argentina Declassification Project (1975–84).

87. "Argentine Leader Sworn in, Vows No 'Great Changes,'" *Washington Post*, July 2, 1982.

88. N'Haux, *Menem-Cavallo*, 208.

89. Bignone, *El último de facto II*, 126.

employment, and radically redesigning the financial system. Dagnino Pastore explained: "The Argentine economy is in a state of destruction without precedents, which can really be qualified as a national emergency. The decision is equally clear: we have to act with urgency."[90] He directly blamed the opening of financial markets for the deterioration of the situation, calling the open financial system the "crux of the nation's experiment in a free market economy." Only a fundamental restructuring of the economy could alleviate this "explosive situation."[91] Fearing that heavily indebted private companies and banks would collapse and cause a depression and hyperinflation, Dagnino Pastore and Cavallo initiated a dramatic rescue operation.[92] Cavallo proposed a controlled process of inflating away domestic debt, his famous "licuación," with artificially low interest rates and a brief inflationary shock ("golpe inflacionario"), which would reduce the real value of domestic debt.[93] This program strongly resembled his previous efforts in the Ministry of the Interior during late November / early December 1981. He promised to help every sector of society, while nobody except for "speculators" would have to pay for it. In a nationally televised speech on July 14, 1982, Cavallo explained that families with mortgages or personal loans needed urgent help because the principal of their debt had risen rapidly through indexation and interest payments and had reached astronomical levels. Businesses with debt in pesos would equally enjoy a massive reduction of their debt burden. External debt would benefit from generous exchange guarantees.[94]

The *Review of the River Plate*, a biweekly financial magazine, reacted to the announcement with outrage, calling Cavallo the "new führer of the economy, now enthroned in one of the greatest temples of Argentine dirigisme, the Central Bank."[95] The financial daily *Ámbito Financiero* shared the frustration and explained that this new economic program meant a return to the times of dirigisme and economic authoritarianism but conceded that this step was perhaps inevitable to avoid a full-scale collapse of the industrial base.[96] Cavallo, moreover, not only angered the financial sector with his policies but also alienated his colleagues at the Central Bank with his management practices and

90. "El Programa Económico: Mensaje del ministro de Economía, Doctor José Maria Dagnino Pastore"; reprinted in *Boletín Semanal del Ministerio de Economía*, July 12, 1982.

91. "Argentina Readies Curbs on Economy," *New York Times*, July 6, 1982.

92. Horacio Tomás Liendo (h), interview, Buenos Aires, December 4, 2003.

93. Domingo Cavallo, "Brodersohn miente" (press conference, Córdoba, August 5, 1987).

94. "Alcances y mecanismos de la reforma financiera," *Boletín Semanal del Ministerio de Economía*, July 19, 1982.

95. "The Dagnino Plan," *Review of the River Plate*, July 14, 1982.

96. "Giro de 180 Grados en la estrategia económica," *Ámbito Financiero*, July 6, 1982.

leadership style. Colleagues in the Central Bank complained that Cavallo had fixed ideas on how to solve given problems and would not listen to any advice from Central Bank staff.[97] He also developed a furious work style in an effort to implement his economic projects as quickly as possible. The flood of directives—more than 170 in fifty days—overwhelmed the Central Banks staff and the financial institutions that had to implement them. Christian Brachet, who led the first IMF mission to Argentina after the end of hostilities, explained that Cavallo destroyed the morale of the Central Bank staff. "When we came back with the new economic team in October/November 1982, the staff was all devastated and in a state of shock."[98]

The *licuación* of domestic debt implied a large-scale redistribution of wealth from savers to debtors. Within two months, the real value of domestic debt—both private and public fell by around 20 percent. Cavallo even boasted that the real value of Argentine internal debt had fallen by more than a third during his tenure.[99] The reaction of the stock market was immediate. Between early July and mid-August the stock market index more than doubled even when taking the high rate of inflation into consideration.[100] "The debtors celebrated the Cavallo program with a "Santo Cavallo day," an economist working in the Central Bank during this period, recounted.[101] Despite Cavallo's promises that "authentic savers" would not be the victims of his scheme, the real value of savings in the banking system fell sharply. The inflation-adjusted value of saving accounts and time deposits fell by almost 40 percent during the brief period between July and September.[102]

The even more lasting legacy was the nationalization of private foreign debt. Private foreign debt had frequently benefited from exchange guarantees, most recently during Cavallo's brief tenure at the Ministry of the Interior in November 1981 and previously by Lorenzo Sigaut in June 1981. However, the guarantees of July 1982 offered even more favorable conditions than previous ones. Cavallo gave companies who had borrowed abroad the option to pay the Central Bank in pesos. The Central Bank would then take over the foreign debt in dollars. The exchange guarantee was indexed with the rate of inflation, and

97. Ernesto Gaba, interview, Buenos Aires, January 13, 2004.

98. Christian Brachet, interview, Washington, D.C., April 14, 2004.

99. Cavallo, "Brodersohn miente" (see note 93). Cavallo's calculations are based on the dollar value of peso-denominated debt, which fell much more sharply because of the devaluation of the peso.

100. Author's calculations based on published records from the newspaper *La Nación*.

101. Ernesto Gaba, interview, Buenos Aires, January 13, 2004.

102. Author's calculations are based on data from DataFIEL.

Cavallo insisted that this assured that companies would not unload their foreign debt at the taxpayers' expense.[103] In fact, the opposite was true. The exchange guarantee used the inflation rate of two months prior to the current one as its basis. During these two months, however, inflation spiked. Consequently, debtors could lighten the burden of their debt by almost half in these two months alone. When inflation started to fall during the last quarter of the year, however, this system threatened to raise the real value of debt.[104] Companies with large foreign debt vigorously lobbied the Central Bank to implement changes in the guarantee in order to avoid this scenario. One of the vice presidents of the Argentine Central Bank, Rodolfo C. Clutterbuck, took a leadership role in this process. He ordered the Central Bank staff to prepare for a change in the basis of the exchange guarantee from past inflation to the tightly controlled interest rate, which was considerably below the rate of inflation. His intentions were not entirely altruistic; Clutterbuck had previously been a director of the textile company Alpargatas, one of the most heavily indebted Argentine companies.[105] Over the previous years, Alpargatas had accumulated some US$220 million in foreign debt and desperately needed debt relief. Cavallo remembered that he resisted the implementation of these changes because he felt that the state should not assume the private foreign debt in its entirety. The Central Bank therefore implemented this change in policy only after Cavallo had been forced to resign its presidency on August 24.[106] The consequences of these two exchange guarantee schemes were dramatic. The Central Bank assumed the debt in dollars and only received strongly depreciated pesos—worth as little as a third of the dollar amount of the debt—from the private debtors in return at the end of 1983. While in late 1980 the private sector had been responsible for almost half of the US$26 billion in foreign debt, by the end of 1982 public and publicly guaranteed debt made up almost 90 percent of a total of US$44 billion, adding almost US$24 billion to the public foreign debt.[107]

The furious activity in the Ministry of the Economy and the Central Bank could not obscure the deep divisions between the heads of the two institutions. While Dagnino Pastore favored a strategy of gradual stabilization, Cavallo tried

103. Domingo Cavallo, interview, Cambridge, Mass., April 8, 2004.

104. Author's calculations based on inflation, controlled interest rate, and financial and commercial exchange rate data published in Banco Central de la República Argentina, *Memoria Annual*, 1984.

105. José Agustin Uriarte, interview, Buenos Aires, June 23, 2004.

106. Domingo Cavallo, interview, Cambridge, Mass., April 8, 2004.

107. Arriazu, Leone, and Lopez Murphy, *Políticas macroeconómicas y endeudamiento privado*, 216.

to impose a radical reform of financial markets from the Central Bank. Another conflict arose out of different opinions on negotiations with the United Kingdom.[108] The military was adamantly opposed to direct negotiations between Argentina and the United Kingdom with respect to the lifting of financial sanctions. Consequently, it would not even allow the minister of the economy to talk to the British on the telephone. This led to the bizarre result that Argentine and British negotiators had to meet in Montevideo, the capital of neighboring Uruguay, for secret conversations. Domingo Cavallo, apparently under the influence of commander-in-chief of the army Nicolaides, tried to undermine Dagnino Pastore's efforts to remove mutual financial sanctions.[109] The most important problem between the two, however, was Cavallo's ambition to become minister of the economy himself.[110] A combination of these conflicts finally led to Dagnino Pastore's and Cavallo's resignation of during the last week of August 1982. The resignation of the economic team came only days after a statement by a finance minister some five thousand miles to the north of Buenos Aires had rattled financial markets. On Friday, August 20, 1982, the minister of finance of Mexico, Jesús Silva Herzog, informed bankers in New York that his country would be unable to repay the loan coming due the following Monday. The meltdown in Mexico would soon transform a localized debt crisis into an international one.

Argentina had already entered into the logic of the debt crisis with the series of devaluations that followed the transition of power from Jorge Rafael Videla to Roberto Viola in April 1981. What turned an unfavorable balance of payments into an unmanageable debt? The crisis occurred at the moment the second oil shock and sharply higher interests rates caused by the radical anti-inflationary measures adopted by the new chairman of the Federal Reserve known as the "Volcker shock" had rendered world financial markets extremely fragile. The Argentine government's initial reaction to the crisis was inept and demonstrated little understanding of its nature and extent. Instead of applying a consistent policy and reassuring markets and the population that the government was bringing the situation under control, the new minister of the economy vacillated in his policy. His clumsy public statements further undermined the confidence,

108. "Argentina: Wehbe Confident of Gaining Breathing Space," *Latin American Weekly Report*, September 10, 1982.

109. Interview on May 31, 2004, in Buenos Aires, with a high official in the Ministry of the Economy during this period who prefers to remain anonymous.

110. Bignone, *El último de facto II*, 131.

turning him into a laughingstock toward the end of the year. The growing political crisis aggravated the economic crisis. By the second half of 1980, but especially after the inauguration of the new de facto president Roberto Viola, political differences within the armed forces burst into the open, not only over economic policies of the new administration, but over the entire political project of the *Proceso*. This combination of looming economic crisis and a power struggle within the armed forces set the stage for one of the most dramatic and chaotic episodes in Argentine history. Within the span of little over a year, four different presidents governed Argentina, and economic policy experienced five fundamental changes of direction, each of them justified by the supposed necessities of an economic emergency. The fact that each of the main actors in the economic scene—Lorenzo Sigaut, Roberto Alemann, and Domingo Cavallo— had a genuine sense of mission further compounded the chaos. They not only wanted to alleviate the crisis and stabilize the economy but also sought to replace the economic model in effect when they took office with one of their own because they believed it to be fundamentally flawed. Lorenzo Sigaut and Domingo Cavallo were driven by the belief that the economic policies of José Martínez de Hoz had unfairly favored financial interests, the *patria financiera,* and had opened the economy to the detriment of domestic business and agricultural interests. This needed to be undone if Argentine was to return to long-term growth. Roberto Alemann hoped to achieve the opposite—a genuine insertion of Argentina into the world economy and rationalization of the public sector through large-scale privatization of state-run companies, which were dominated by the armed forces. Each of the successive ministers of the economy ignored the political weakness and fragmentation of the government they belonged to. While none of them could muster enough support to implement a consistent new economic structure, each of them successfully disrupted the previous government's economic measures. It was much easier to play the spoiler than to take a constructive role in rebuilding the country.

5 THE INTERNATIONAL DEBT CRISIS AND THE RETURN TO DEMOCRACY

International financial markets initially shrugged off the military conflict in the South Atlantic and Argentina's de facto cessation of payments in early April as isolated events. Lending to Latin American countries continued almost unabated through the summer of 1982. This deceptive sense of tranquility gave way to panic, however, when Jesús Silva Herzog, minister of finance of Mexico, informed bankers in New York on August 20, 1982, that his country would be unable to repay the loan coming due the following Monday.[1] Bankers, who for years considered Latin America a region of boundless economic potential, suddenly realized that they had dangerously overextended themselves and were now effectively trapped in the logic of the debt crisis. If they stopped lending new money to heavily indebted countries, those countries would be unable to service the old loans. A default of some major borrowers threatened the very survival of some of the largest commercial banks. If they continued lending money to heavily indebted countries, they would further increase their banks' exposure to countries of doubtful solvency, an action they could not to justify to stockholders and

1. Boughton, *Silent Revolution*, 268.

bank regulators.[2] Faced with the patent inability of the banking sector to resolve the crisis on its own, the IMF and the Federal Reserve Bank decided to
intervene by coordinating continued bank lending while trying to convince
governments in heavily indebted countries to tighten their belts. Both institutions were more concerned with the stability and survival of the world financial
system than with the effects of the looming debt crisis on the heavily indebted
countries themselves.

The main problem facing Argentina during the period of transition to democratic rule at the end of 1983 was not the external debt crisis but rather the
question of how to come to terms with the legacy of the military dictatorship.
The outgoing military government under Reynaldo Bignone had to deal not
only with economic meltdown but also with growing disintegration of the military in the face of military defeat and the consequences of human rights abuses
during the height of the so-called Dirty War against left-wing insurgents, which
the armed forces had waged throughout the 1970s. After a few weeks of frantic
activity following the Argentine surrender at Port Stanley on June 14, 1982,
Argentina became politically paralyzed at the very moment the international
financial crisis, which was spreading from Mexico, required decisive action.
Military leaders were so deeply divided and preoccupied with covering up crimes
and failures during the previous six years that they were unable to reach agreement on almost any important political project. The transitional nature of the
Bignone administration added to its weakness. Since its only legitimacy originated in a promise to return the country to democracy, every political decision
with long-term implications required at least tacit approval of the *multipartidaria*, a council of traditional political parties, which was loath to be associated
with any adjustment program. Weak, internally divided, and without legitimacy,
the outgoing military administration lacked the political power to implement
harsh economic reforms, distribute the costs of war and foreign debt, and impose sacrifices on any sector of society. In this political paralysis, the Bignone
administration resorted to postponing important decisions in an effort to "pass
the buck" to the next government.[3]

The outbreak of the international debt crisis should not have come as a complete surprise to anyone who followed the financial markets. The easy phase of
petrodollar recycling had ended in 1979 when two new shocks hit the financial

---

2. Lipson, "Bankers' Dilemmas."
3. Della Paolera, Irigoin, and Bózzoli, "Passing the Buck."

markets. The "Volcker shock" was caused by the decision of the Federal Reserve of the United States, under the leadership of the new chairman Paul Volcker, to fight persistent inflation with tight monetary policy. The consequence was a sharp increase in real interest rates in the United States and on international financial markets. Given that most developing countries had contracted bank loans at flexible interest rates, this increase immediately translated into sharply higher interest payments on foreign debt. Second, the overthrow of Mohammad Reza Pahlavi, the shah of Iran, led to sharply higher oil prices and triggered the second oil shock. Both developments led to a sharp worldwide recession and large current account imbalances between oil-exporting and oil-importing countries.[4]

The crisis first manifested itself in Eastern Europe in early 1981 when Poland suspended payments on the principal of its foreign debt of US$27 billion accumulated over the previous decade.[5] Poland was soon followed by Hungary and Yugoslavia, which were equally unable to roll over their bank loans.[6] Argentina started to suffer under the weight of foreign debt at the same time as Poland when the incoming Viola administration was forced to abandon the quasi-fixed exchange-rate regime following a sharp loss of reserves. In early 1982, the U.S. financial press was still downplaying the danger that the high debt burden of developing countries posed to the international banking system. While the business magazine *Forbes* worried about the financial health of the U.S. banking sector, it was primarily concerned about "small- and middle-market commercial and industrial loans . . . real estate . . . and single family homes with excesses of pyramiding mortgages."[7] In mid-April, the same magazine argued there was no need to worry about the banking industry at all because banks had adequate reserves for possible debt write-offs.[8]

Mexico and Argentina's financial woes were well known, but most analysts believed that those countries would adopt sustainable long-term strategies and their loans would be rolled over. Following a large devaluation of the Mexican peso in January 1982, *Barron's* reported that currency specialists shared the broad sentiment that "Mexican authorities would go to great lengths to avoid outright devaluation." They estimated that "by the end of 1982, the peso would be down another 12 percent or so."[9] This forecast proved to be spectacularly wrong.

4. Solomon, "Debt of Developing Countries."
5. James, *International Monetary Cooperation Since Bretton Woods*, 361.
6. Boughton, *Silent Revolution*, 269.
7. Allan Sloan, "Industry Report: Banks," *Forbes*, January 4, 1982, 74.
8. Ben Weberman, "Will the Bad Apples Spoil the Entire Barrel," *Forbes*, April 12, 1982.
9. Richard A. Donnell, "Corner the World . . . Wither the Peso," *Barron's*, January 11, 1982.

In fact, the peso would fall from 26.3 to the dollar to 160, less than one-sixth of its previous value. In late February 1982, after more devaluations of the peso, a Merrill Lynch analyst was still bullish on Mexico and recommended Mexican stocks as a "good long-term buy on a 12-months view."[10] In April 1982, *Euromoney* sounded a more cautious note, arguing that "the Carnival is over in Latin America" and reported, "Bankers are imposing stiffer terms even on the most stable countries of Latin America." However, they argued that Latin American countries had proven themselves able to adjust to international disturbances remarkably well and expressed confidence that they would be able to bounce back rapidly.[11] Only with the end of hostilities in the South Atlantic did observers start to worry about the sustainability of loans to developing countries. In June 1982, *Forbes* predicted, "Long after the guns are silenced, the Falkland Islands war may be remembered as the beginning of the end of the wildest international credit binge the world has seen." It continued to warn that American and international banks would soon need to accept that they "are sitting on billions of dollars' worth of paper that isn't worth anything like the face value."[12]

Mexico in the summer of 1982 had much in common with the Argentina of early 1981. Mexico had pursued a fixed-exchange-rate system, not unlike the Argentine *tablita*, and President Lopez Portillo had pledged his political prestige on its maintenance, promising to "defend the peso like a dog."[13] The fixed exchange rate was intended to reduce the stubbornly high rates of inflation but ultimately led to a significant overvaluation of the Mexican peso. Over the previous years, the Mexican economy had grown at a rapid pace of almost 8 percent per year because the price of oil, Mexico's most important export, was high throughout the period, and because Mexico had had easy access to foreign loans for domestic investment and consumption. During these boom years, Mexico built up more than US$86 billion in foreign debt, almost twice as much as Argentina had. By February 1982, the Mexican authorities were forced to break their pledge with a 30 percent devaluation in the face of a rapid outflow of international reserves. However, the Mexican government still enjoyed access to international financial markets after it concluded a US$2.5 billion "jumbo loan" with a broad syndicate of banks led by Bank of America in June 1982.[14]

10. "The International Trader," *Barron's*, February 22, 1982.

11. Charles Grant, "The Carnival Is Over, But There's Always Next Year," Latin American Survey, *Euromoney*, April 1982.

12. Norman Gall and Isabel de Souza, "Enough," *Forbes*, June 21, 1982.

13. "Lopez Portillo Plays for High Economic Stakes," *Financial Times* (London), February 23, 1982.

14. James, *International Monetary Cooperation Since Bretton Woods*, 363.

Not unlike Argentina in 1981, transition of power between two governments accelerated the economic meltdown. The Institutional Revolutionary Party (P.R.I.) had ruled Mexico since 1929. The outcome of the elections, which were held on July 4, 1982, was therefore a foregone conclusion with Miguel De la Madrid Hurtado, the P.R.I. candidate, winning with almost 75 percent of the votes cast.[15] The long transition period between the election and the inauguration of the new president on December 1, however, created uncertainty concerning long-term economic policies. This manifested itself in rising capital flight during the remainder of July. The Mexican Crisis exploded during the first two weeks of August. On August 5, Mexico established a dual exchange-rate system with a tightly controlled "preferential" market and a freely floating "general" market.[16] This amounted to a large devaluation of the peso and was intended to stop the rapid outflow of foreign exchange from the already depleted coffers of the Central Bank and thus to protect Mexico's relations with the international banking system. Still, many observers underestimated the severity of the crisis. On August 10, the U.S. Embassy in Mexico City expressed relief that the Mexican authorities had decided to "maintain international credit standing rather than opt for a 'siege economy' that would include a formal debt rescheduling." The memorandum continued to argue, "The Mexican crisis is far from over, but there is a very slight possibility that the most recent measures could constitute the peak of the crisis."[17] However, on the following day, Wednesday August 11, the Mexican minister of finance, Jesús Silva Herzog, learned that commercial banks were refusing to roll over principal payments on loans falling due the following Monday. Over the weekend, Silva Herzog flew to Washington to plead for emergency aid from the IMF and the U.S. Treasury. While the IMF agreed to open negotiations, it was unable to release funds without a formal agreement and approval from the Board of Directors. Short-term emergency aid would need to come from the U.S. government, which agreed to prepay US$1 billion in oil shipments at a preferential price, extend loans under the auspices of the Commodity Credit Corporation, and grant a currency swap line under the Exchange Stabilization Fund.[18] These short-term loans helped avoid an immediate default after the bank holiday was over, but they did not

15. "Mexican Is Elected by a Wide Margin," *New York Times,* July 6, 1982.

16. Telegram, Mexico to State Department, "GOM establishes dual parity system: Bank of Mexico withdraws from foreign exchange market again," August 6, 1982, FOIA Released Documents.

17. Telegram, Mexico to State Department, "Reasons for and Implications of Dual Exchange Rate System," August 10, 1982, FOIA Released Documents.

18. Boughton, *Silent Revolution,* 293.

solve the underlying problem that billions of dollars of loans were falling due during the remainder of the year while international banks were unwilling to lend additional funds to the country in crisis.

While the origins and the nature of the Mexican crisis were not radically different from similar crises in Eastern Europe and Argentina, the political and economic consequences were much more far-reaching. One reason was that this crisis could not be explained by some unique and special circumstances such as the political crisis surrounding the declaration of the martial law by General Wojciech Jaruzelski in 1981 in the case of Poland or the South Atlantic War in early 1982 in the case of Argentina. Instead, it raised the question of sustainability of the large foreign debt that many developing countries had accumulated during the preceding decade. More immediately, with a total foreign debt of US$86 billion, Mexico had far larger external liabilities than the other countries that had experienced similar crises during the previous year.

This translated into dangerously high exposure for many U.S., European, and Japanese banks.[19] With most developing countries having trouble servicing their debt, commercial bank claims on countries in financial distress reached almost US$350 billion in late 1982. The three largest Latin American debtor countries (Brazil, Mexico, and Argentina) alone accounted for no less than US$145 billion in syndicated bank loans.[20] The exposure of U.S. banks to Latin American loans was particularly large. Mexican debt accounted for roughly 44 percent of the capital of the nine largest U.S. banks.[21] Furthermore, in mid-1982 these same banks had loans outstanding to Argentina, Brazil, and Mexico worth 112.5 percent of their capital.[22] Citicorp alone had lent almost US$9 billion to the big three Latin America debtor countries by 1982, 160 percent of its primary capital and more than 100 percent of total capital funds (see Table 1).[23]

Given this dire scenario, it was not surprising that during the fall of 1982 politicians and bankers in industrial countries were intensely concerned that a default of one or more large developing countries could trigger an uncontrollable

19. Kraft, *Mexican Rescue,* 9.

20. Acting Secretary to Members of the Executive Board, "Payment Difficulties Involving Debt to Commercial Banks," March 9, 1983, SM/83/47, IMF Archives.

21. Kraft, *Mexican Rescue,* 9.

22. Senate Committee on Banking, Housing, and Urban Affairs, *Proposals for Legislation to Increase the Resources of the International Monetary Fund: Hearing Before the Subcommittee on International Finance and Monetary Policy,* Paul Volcker's statement, 98th Cong., 1st sess., February 17, 1983.

23. For Citicorp's exposure, see "Citibank's Pervasive Influence on International Lending," *Business Week,* May 16, 1983. For the bank's capital, see Citicorp, "Citicorp reports," 3.

Table 1.   Major U.S. Lenders to Latin America: Outstanding Loans as of December 31, 1983 (in millions of U.S. dollars)

	Mexico	Brazil	Argentina	Venezuela	Percent of total assets
Manufacturers					
Hanover	$1,915	$2,130	$1,321	$1,084	10.0%
Citicorp	$2,900	$4,700	$1,090	$1,500	7.6%
Chase Manhattan	$1,553	$2,560	$775	$1,226	7.5%
Chemical N.Y.	$1,414	$1,276	$370	$776	7.5%
J. P. Morgan	$1,174	$1,785	$741	$464	7.2%
Bankers Trust N.Y.	$1,286	$743	$230	$436	6.7%
BankAmerica	$2,741	$2,484	$300	$1614	5.9%
Wells Fargo	$655	$568	$100	$279	5.9%
Continental Illinois	$699	$476	$383	$436	4.7%
First Chicago	$870	$689	NA	NA	4.3%

Source: "A War of Nerves over Latin Debt," Business Week, June 18, 1984.

meltdown of world financial markets. Johannes Witteveen, former managing director of the IMF, publicly warned, "A crisis in confidence in the international banking system could turn this prolonged recession into a real depression."[24] The Federal Reserve under the leadership of Paul Volcker was also intensely concerned about the health of the banking system. In a meeting of the Federal Open Market Committee, he stated: "This is not a time . . . for business as usual, certainly, in the international area. I don't think it's time for business as usual in the domestic area either. Extraordinary things may have to be done. We haven't had a parallel to this situation historically except to the extent 1929 was a parallel."[25]

The Reagan administration did not share this sense of urgency. After the initial intervention on behalf of Mexico, the U.S. government refused to assume a leadership role in the collective effort to solve the unfolding crisis. Secretary of the Treasury Donald Regan was "asleep on the switch" and failed to realize the seriousness of the crisis.[26] In early September 1982, he explained in a presentation before the Cabinet Council of Economic Affairs that the Mexican crisis was merely a liquidity crisis. He argued that the short-term loans extended by the United States in late August had "served to stabilize the situation for the

24. "Less Risk, More Worry for the Banks," New York Times, October 10, 1982.
25. Board of Governors of the Federal Reserve System, Federal Open Market Committee Transcripts, Meeting of October 5, 1982.
26. Kraft, Mexican Rescue.

very short-run." The long-term solution required a reduction of the fiscal deficit and an improvement of the balance of trade.[27]

The Reagan administration also faced domestic opposition to assuming a more active role in solving the unfolding debt crisis. A large part of the Republican Party opposed any intervention on behalf of overextended financial institutions and heavily indebted countries on ideological grounds. They had traditionally been hostile to the IMF and strongly opposed emergency loans to heavily indebted countries, which they perceived as a "bailout" of big banks and corrupt governments. When the Reagan administration asked Congress to approve an increase of the IMF quota to allow the multinational institution to cope with the fallout of the debt crisis in mid-1983, many conservatives were outraged. On July 30, 1983, a *Washington Times* editorial argued: "The US$8.4 billion IMF-bank bailout bill the Reagan administration got conned into supporting is expected to sail through the House this week. Better it should sail out of the window."[28] A conservative lobbying group, the Conservative Caucus, even started an advertising campaign against the IMF programs explaining, "America's Big Banks got themselves—and us—into a lot of trouble—and now they want US TAXPAYERS to bail them out." A political cartoon titled "The Great Bank Robbery" depicted Secretary of the Treasury Donald Regan and Chase Manhattan's David Rockefeller running out of a bank with guns in their hands to rob a helpless taxpayer.[29]

From the very beginning, debt negotiations across Latin America were marked by conflicts over two interrelated questions. What was the nature of the crisis, and who was to blame for it? Solutions to the crisis depended on the answers to these questions. The question of the nature of the debt crisis was often framed in terms of liquidity versus solvency. These terms have their origin in corporate finance. Insolvency occurs when the value of a company's liabilities exceed its assets. Illiquidity, by contrast, occurs when a company has insufficient liquid funds to cover its payments as they come due. The former case normally leads to the company's liquidation, whereas additional lending and debt restructuring under the supervision of a bankruptcy court is the best solution in the latter case. For sovereign lenders the difference between a liquidity crisis

27. Minutes, Cabinet Council on Economic Affairs, September 9, 1982, case file 077455, FG010-02, WHORM Subject File, Ronald Reagan Presidential Library.

28. "The Bailout No One Needs," *Washington Times,* July 30, 1983.

29. Advertisment by the Conservative Caucus published in various American newspapers. Source: Memorandum, Richard A. Viguerie to Conservative Leaders, "The Big Bank Bailout," August 15, 1983, OA11152 IMF Funding [International Monetary Fund], Jacobi, Mary Jo: Files, White House Staff and Office Files, Ronald Reagan Presidential Library.

and a solvency crisis is much harder to define. Technically, countries cannot become insolvent, because their assets will always exceed their liabilities. This is probably what Walter Wriston, the CEO of Citibank, had in mind when he boldly stated in an op-ed piece in the New York Times in September 1982 that "countries don't go bankrupt."[30] However, the solvency criterion used in corporate finance is entirely meaningless in the case of a sovereign borrower because—short of military intervention—real assets such as national territory cannot be seized and turned into cash. The ability of a country to service foreign debt is therefore not determined by its physical assets but rather by the willingness and ability of the government to sacrifice the welfare of its citizens.[31] The Federal Reserve Bank recognized this risk early on. Paul Volcker explained in October 1982, "It gets into political questions as well as economic questions at some point. The country may say 'Is it worthwhile to meet them [the debt payments] whether they can or cannot theoretically?'"[32] A government can decide that in the face of insurmountable debt, austerity measures offer too few short-term political benefits to risk alienating important constituencies. Governments can therefore find it advantageous to delay economic adjustment even at the risk of making the crisis more severe in the long term.

The question of who was to blame for the foreign debt proved to be even more contentious. It was played out on two levels, namely between debtor and creditor countries and within the debtor countries between the sectors that had supposedly benefited from the buildup of foreign debt and those which had to bear the burden of adjustment. Critics of debtor countries pointed out that governments had "squandered their resources during the "fat years" when credit was easily accessible. The crisis was therefore a just punishment for previous irresponsibility.[33] Critics of the international financial system sharply disagreed, pointing out that most of Latin America had not acted irresponsibly before the outbreak of the crisis. They wondered "how well the exemplary mass punishment [fits] the alleged individual crime" and argued that the main reason for the crisis had been a series of unexpected events such as the second oil shock and the "Volcker Shock."[34] Others squarely blamed banks for the crisis because they had known of the economic problems and the corruption of the countries they were lending to. Their lending was driven by their "greed and stupidity."[35]

30. Walter Wriston, "Banking Against Disaster," New York Times, September 14, 1982.
31. Lomax, Developing Country Debt Crisis, 62.
32. Federal Open Market Committee Transcripts, Meeting of October 5, 1982.
33. Schuker, American "Reparations" to Germany, 135.
34. Díaz Alejandro, "Latin American Debt," 335.
35. Lissakers, Banks, Borrowers, and the Establishment, 10.

These theoretical discussions had very concrete repercussions during the debt renegotiations that took place over the course of the subsequent decade. If creditor banks deserved some of the blame for the debt crisis because they had lent without a prudent assessment of the risk involved, they also deserved to shoulder some of the burden of adjustment in the form of involuntary additional lending or partial write-offs of outstanding loans. If the responsibility for the debt crisis was squarely the debtor countries', by contrast, they should be expected to bear the full burden of the debt and adopt all necessary measures to repay the debt to the last cent. Debtor countries adopted the former position, bankers, the latter. Indeed, the banks steadfastly refused to admit any fault on their part and called on debtor countries to live up to their contractual obligations.[36]

Perhaps even more politically explosive was the conflict within debtor countries over whom or which sector within society to blame for the crisis. The years of easy availability of foreign capital had created unprecedented opportunities to make money with clever stock and bond market investment. In many countries, the traditional elites looked down upon these "new rich" of the *patria financiera,* while those who had failed to profit from these opportunities themselves regarded them with envy and suspicion. Worse, when the crisis broke out in 1981–82, most countries perceived that they had no choice but to bail out private investors who had assumed large liabilities in foreign currency in order to avoid a collapse of the financial system. While the external debt was thus nationalized, private assets transferred abroad during the same time—according to some estimates amounting to between 50 and 80 percent of the total external debt—remained untouched.[37] This created the impression that thieves with white gloves had looted the national treasure and that therefore a large part of the debt was fraudulent.[38] Furthermore, since capital was more mobile than labor and countries desperately needed to attract new capital, the brunt of the burden of adjustment fell on labor in the form of lower real salaries and on small savers who had been unable to get their money out of the country before the collapse. This perceived injustice would make it much harder for governments to win the political support for tough adjustment measures and created the temptation to gain broad support by defying the creditor banks or the IMF.

36. John Reed, interview, New York, July 23, 2004; Juan V. Sourrouille, interview, Buenos Aires, June 9, 2004.

37. Telegram, Buenos Aires to State Department, "Stemming Capital Flight: A Key to Argentina's Economic Future," December 18, 1987; Basualdo and Kulfas, "Fuga de capitales"; Padilla del Bosque, *Estimación de la fuga de capitales.*

38. Beveraggi Allende, *El vaciamiento económico de Argentina.*

The sense of injustice was reinforced by the fact that the IMF and the U.S. government initially focused all their attention on avoiding the default of large debtor countries and protecting commercial banks. Anthony Solomon, chairman of the Federal Reserve Bank of New York, favored extending new loans to countries as a cheap way to avoid a direct bailout. He stated, "If everything goes to hell, then the amounts of both public assistance and losses to the banking system are going to be huge. I can't conceive that the United States would not step in ultimately and do what was necessary to restore order in Mexico to tame the chaotic situation."[39] Behind closed doors, members of the board of governors of the Federal Reserve Bank made it clear that their prime concern was to save the U.S. banking system. If this involved helping heavily indebted countries, this was a welcome side effect. Because such a large share of the debt was owed by only three Latin American countries—Mexico, Brazil, and Argentina—they received particular attention. Paul Volcker explained in a meeting of the Federal Open Market Committee in December 1982: "If we get Mexico, Brazil, and Argentina settled . . . I would think the rest of these [debtor countries] can go and hang there, to put it bluntly. I don't think it presents a threat to the world banking system if we have these big countries stabilized, and that had been the [focus of the] whole effort."[40] Henry Kissinger was even more outspoken about the fact that the main purpose of any measure needed to be to protect the banking system. In January 1983, he called for a collective effort to "save the world economy." He argued, "The first step must be to change the bargaining framework; the debtors should be deprived—to the extent possible—of the weapon of default. The industrial democracies urgently require a safety net permitting some emergency governmental assistance to threatened financial institutions. This would reduce both the sense of panic and the debtor's capacity for blackmail."[41]

The effects of adjustment in heavily indebted countries were only taken into consideration to the extent that a radical and immediate adjustment was deemed impossible to implement and might push countries into openly defaulting on their external obligations. IMF economists used projections of economic growth and balance of payments after all the politically possible austerity measures had been taken into account in order to compute the "borrowing requirements" of a country that needed to be financed. The IMF argued that a joint effort of private banks and multilateral financial institutions was necessary because neither

39. Federal Open Market Committee Transcripts, Meeting of December 20–21, 1982.
40. Ibid.
41. Henry A. Kissinger, "Saving the World Economy," *Newsweek,* January 24, 1983.

of the two could bear the burden alone. The managing director, Jacques de Larosière, also recognized a shared responsibility of private creditors and debtor countries and tried to "bail in" the banks by obliging them to extend new loans to the struggling economies.[42] Since new loans were generally larger than the principal payments but smaller than the entire debt service payments, the countries suffered from capital outflows while the total debt kept rising. Additional lending came attached to adjustment programs, which were—at least on paper—stringent and painful. The combination of rising debt, IMF-prescribed austerity, and net-capital outflows raised sharp criticism within developing countries as well as from scholars in the North. They argued that the actions amounted to little more than "muddling through" without resolving the underlying problem while at the same time effecting massive resource transfers from poor to rich countries at the cost of deep recession in the former.[43]

Earlier than most, the IMF started to recognize the limitations of the "muddling through" strategy. By the spring of 1983, the IMF took a more pessimistic view of the long-term prospects of the affected countries and hinted that some countries might suffer from a solvency crisis. In an internal document titled "Fund Policies and External Debt Service Problems," the IMF staff warned that domestic adjustment, important as it might be to lessen the "crisis of confidence," might not be enough to solve the crisis. It recognized that "for a number of countries, the debt service problems they face are of such a magnitude that efforts to reduce sufficiently their external current account imbalances by domestic adjustment measures alone may prove to be extremely difficult." It explained that these countries critically depended on an improvement in the international environment, including lower interest rates and increased demand for their exports in industrial countries. "In addition, and aside from the granting of debt relief which has become necessary in many instances, the availability of balance of payments assistance from official sources and multilateral institutions will play a crucial role."[44] The CIA shared the IMF's pessimism. In early 1983, the agency warned ominously that the IMF-led measures to resolve the debt crisis might be insufficient and economic recovery might not be rapid enough to avoid social and political instability in developing countries.[45] The case of Argentina would soon prove how correct the CIA's assessment had been.

42. Jacques de Larosière, interview, Princeton, April 20, 2004.

43. Dornbusch, "World Debt Problem," 138; Lissakers, Banks, Borrowers, and the Establishment, 10.

44. "Fund Policies and External Debt Servicing Problems," March 8, 1983, SM/83/45, 5, IMF Archives.

45. Memorandum, Norman A. Bailey to William B. Clark, "CIA Report on the IMF and the International Debt Crisis," May 5, 1983, International Monetary Fund, Vol. 1 [of 2], Executive Secretariat:

Paradoxically, Argentina was originally not a victim of the wider debt crisis but actually benefited from the diversion of attention away from its disastrous economic policies and military aggression. In April 1982, financial sanctions and the cessation of payments on external obligations during the South Atlantic War had turned Argentina into a pariah on world financial markets. Banks were hesitant to refinance the foreign debt of an unstable, bankrupt, aggressive country. An isolated default by Argentina would have hurt banks but would not have endangered the survival of some of the largest players in the world financial system.

The unfolding financial crisis, which came to a fore in August 1982, suddenly changed this perception. With Mexico, Brazil, and most of the rest of Latin America in crisis, the default of any major Latin American country on its foreign obligations now posed a vital threat. In the eyes of the international financial community, the outbreak of the international debt crisis thus transformed Argentina from a pariah into just another Latin American country affected by the crisis. The sense of urgency was such that even the United Kingdom under Prime Minister Margaret Thatcher became convinced that it was in her best interest to help the erstwhile enemy.[46] The Argentine government also benefited politically from the fallout from the Mexican crisis. A general international debt crisis now created the impression that the country had fallen into an "a trap set for them by the international financial system"[47] rather than one of its own making.

When the Mexican crisis brought the debt problem to international attention during the fall of 1982, Argentina was already economically and politically exhausted from more than a year of permanent debt crisis. The sharp devaluations following the abandoning of the *tablita* in April 1981 had required a massive bailout of private foreign debtors and an involuntary rescheduling of a large part of the foreign debt. The South Atlantic War had further contributed to the political and financial breakdown and isolation of the country. While trade and financial sanctions did not have an immediate impact on the ability or willingness of the Argentine authorities to fight the war, they severely added to the political and economic problems of the new military government under de facto president Reynaldo Bignone. In mid-August, Argentina faced the prospect of an

NSC Records, Subject File C–K, Box 3 of 5, White House Staff and Office Files, Ronald Reagan Presidential Library.

46. British involvement in the international "lifeboat" operation for Argentina shortly after the end of hostilities infuriated many British MPs. "Anger at Loans," *Financial Times*, January 28, 1983.

47. Hirschman, "Political Economy of Latin American Development," 16.

imminent default on almost US$40 billion in foreign debt. The financial sanctions during the war contributed to a shortening of maturities. Some US$12 billion were falling due before the end of the year. In addition, the suspension of payments led to a massive buildup of overdue interest and principal payments, which amounted to more than US$2.5 billion in arrears by the end of 1982.

Argentina would have needed an IMF program even in the absence of the Mexican crisis. By May 1982, the U.S. Cabinet Council of Economic Affairs noted that Argentina would urgently need an IMF intervention by the time the war ended in order to stabilize its economy.[48] During the two months following the end of hostilities, Argentina did nothing to restore confidence and economic order. By August, the rate of inflation was at the highest level since the military coup had overthrown Isabel Perón in March 1976, and the economy was shrinking at an annualized rate of more than 10 percent.[49] The economic crisis was compounded by a political and military crisis. During the initial months of his tenure, Reynaldo Bignone had only a tenuous hold on power and lacked political authority because he could not count on the support of the navy and the air force after they had walked out of the junta in protest over his appointment. This open split within the military complicated economic policymaking because the economic team under the leadership of the minister of the economy Jorge Wehbe and the president of the Central Bank Julio González del Solar had to clear all their undertakings not only with President Bignone and the army but afterward separately with the air force and the navy as well.[50] The only unifying factor was the fear that a return to democracy would lead to the prosecution of those who had participated in the "Dirty War." This created a political atmosphere that valued secrecy over accountability and the covering up of past mistakes over the solution of present problems. Only with the retirement of the chiefs of the air force and the navy, General Basilio Lami Dozo and Admiral Anaya, on September 10, 1982, did all three branches of the armed forces reestablish the junta. This significantly strengthened the hand of Bignone during the pending negotiations with Argentina's creditors.[51]

It was under these grim circumstances that Jorge Wehbe traveled to Toronto for the World Bank/IMF Annual Meeting in early September 1982. During the meeting, Wehbe formally asked the IMF for help, and de Larosière agreed to

48. Minutes, Cabinet Council on Economic Affairs, May 20, 1982, case file 068967, FG010-02, WHORM Subject File, Ronald Reagan Presidential Library.

49. GDP at 1970 prices. Source: DataFIEL, código 5C002 (accessed March 31, 2005).

50. Christian Brachet, interview, Washington, D.C., April 14, 2004.

51. Fontana, "Political Decision Making," 172.

send a mission to Buenos Aires immediately to start the annual Article IV consultation and begin negotiations on a stand-by arrangement of some US$1.41 billion.[52] In addition to the stand-by arrangement, Argentina applied for a drawing under the Compensatory Financing Facility of US$489 million.[53] The negotiations that ensued were extraordinarily difficult. The South Atlantic War had left in its wake not only material losses but also deep mutual mistrust between Argentina and many of the key members of the IMF's Board of Executive Directors. Without the looming international crisis, which made it imperative for industrial countries to avoid the open default of such a large debtor country, their resistance to accommodating Argentina would have been much more difficult to break.

The financial sanctions imposed during the war were the most contentious issue. Key commanders of the armed forces opposed the lifting of sanctions against the United Kingdom. In early September, an internal navy memorandum criticizing the Bignone administration for its "vacillating foreign policy," that is to say, its conciliatory attitude toward the United Kingdom, was leaked to the press.[54] The minister of foreign affairs also wanted sanctions to remain in place, hoping to be able to lift them himself in exchange for British concessions on the question of the islands' sovereignty.[55] Under intense pressure from the IMF and the U.S. Treasury, Argentine authorities finally agreed to a compromise. While financial sanctions would formally remain in effect, Argentina would disburse some US$270 million in principal and interest to U.K. banks, compensating them for the amount they would have received over the previous six months and promise to keep future payments current. This cleared the way for negotiations with creditor banks. Argentina needed to clear its arrears before the IMF would finalize any agreement, and this it could not do unless the creditor banks agreed to roll over existing loans and extend new credits.[56]

The British government was equally hesitant to help Argentina recover its financial stability. In negotiations with the IMF, the United Kingdom urged caution when extending fresh loans to the military government, fearing the proceeds

---

52. Boughton, *Silent Revolution*, 332.

53. Staff Report for the 1982 Article IV Consultation and Request for Stand-by Arrangement, January 10, 1983, EBS/83/8, IMF Archives.

54. Telegram, Buenos Aires to State Department, "President Bignones Performance and Prospects," September 16, 1982, State Argentina Declassification Project (1975–84), 6.

55. Telegram, Buenos Aires to State Department, "Current Argentine Government: Weakness, Fragmentation, Instability," September 9, 1982, State Argentina Declassification Project (1975–84).

56. "Argentina/U.K. Financial Sanctions," Draft, September 13, 1982, folder 1: Falkland Islands, Subject Files, 1981–1985, box 144, Donald T. Regan Papers.

could be used to purchase new military equipment.[57] When de Larosière tried to assemble a loan package to Argentina comparable to the one offered to Mexico, British creditor banks openly resisted, citing the discriminatory practices of Argentina against them.[58] The intention of the British government was to lift financial sanctions against Argentina only as part of a comprehensive agreement between the two countries, which would have included an official cessation of hostilities and normalization of trade.[59] However, in the face of growing fears of an Argentine default on its external obligations, the United Kingdom agreed to lift financial sanctions in mid-September even without a full normalization of economic and political ties between the two countries. Later in the year, the British government also supported the IMF program to help Argentina—over the objections of many Conservatives in Parliament, who complained publicly that Argentina was spending large amounts of money to restock and modernize its armed forces while at the same time pleading for financial aid from the international community. The criticism was at least partially justified. In 1983, Argentina imported military equipment worth almost US$1 billion— compared to an average of only US$500 million per year during the previous five years—and signed large new orders to replace materiel lost during the war.[60] The *Financial Times* columnist Samuel Brittan argued, "If you must fight, don't lend," and blamed the Bank of England for convincing the government that "British banks must take part in credits to Argentina to prevent the 'collapse of any bank or banks' involved in lending to Latin America." Brittan continued, "The implication is the semi-Marxist one that the capitalist system is so precarious that we cannot pick or choose to whom we make loans."[61]

The second major concern was whether Argentina would qualify for drawing upon the Compensatory Financing Facility. These loans were normally restricted to cases where unforeseen external shocks had brought about an external payments crisis.[62] The problem with the Argentine case was that the fall of exports had not been caused by an external event but rather by a war that Argentina itself had started. The executive directors, hard-pressed not to let Argentina fall at a time of a looming worldwide financial crisis, decided to consider the war as outside the control of the economic authorities. They argued

57. Mario Teijeiro, interview, Buenos Aires, December 15, 2003.

58. Jacques de Larosière, interview, Princeton, April 20, 2004.

59. "'Complications' in Buenos Aires Delay British Lifting Fiscal Curbs," *Washington Post*, September 14, 1982.

60. López, "Gasto militar en la Argentina," 325.

61. Samuel Brittan, "When You Must Fight, Don't Lend," *Financial Times*, February 3, 1983.

62. Stiles, *Negotiating Debt*, 173.

that Roberto Alemann, the minister of the economy during the Galtieri government, had been unaware of the decision to go to war, and that his economic policy had been going in the right direction before the outbreak of hostilities. Argentina was therefore eligible to draw upon Compensatory Financing funds.[63]

A third problem was that the statutes of the IMF barred the institution from lending to countries that had accumulated unpaid principal or interest on their foreign debt—"lending into arrears." A deal with the IMF therefore hinged on a simultaneous agreement with the creditor banks. This gave the creditor banks disproportionate bargaining power because they could veto any IMF agreement simply by refusing to roll over existing loans and extend new loans to cover the accrued interest.[64] The agreement between Argentina and the creditor banks became the main obstacle to the successful conclusion of the negotiations. By the end of October, an agreement in principle was reached that allowed for a short-term loan of US$500 million from the Bank for International Settlements.[65] In mid-November, de Larosière made a dramatic appeal to private banks to procure more funding to allow Argentina to clear its arrears in order to qualify for the stand-by agreement.[66] John Reed, CEO of Citibank, one of the largest creditor banks to Latin American countries, remembered, "We all went along with the IMF in part because we were scared."[67] By December 10, an agreement was reached with the advisory committee of the creditor banks, which opened the door for a deal with the IMF, which was signed on December 31, 1982.[68]

The agreement between Argentina and its creditors would only offer a brief respite for the weak Argentine government, which enjoyed little domestic support and even less legitimacy. Since the early 1980s, scholars have been discussing whether democracies or dictatorships are better able to cope with economic crises.[69] They argued that transition democracies enjoyed greater legitimacy and the goodwill of the population, which would make it easier to implement painful economic measures. However, they were more susceptible to pressures from social actors and found it harder to say "no" to any important constituent.[70] Dictatorships, by contrast, are supposed to benefit from "bureaucratic

63. Boughton, *Silent Revolution*, 335.
64. Mario Teijeiro, interview, Buenos Aires, December 15, 2003.
65. "Argentina Gets Loan," *New York Times*, February 28, 1983.
66. Jacques de Larosière, interview, Princeton, April 20, 2004.
67. John Reed, interview, New York, July 23, 2004.
68. Boughton, *Silent Revolution*, 334.
69. Centeno, "Between Rocky Democracies and Hard Markets."
70. Malloy, "Politics of Transition"; Skidmore, "Politics of Economic Stabilization."

insulation," the ability to disregard the opposition from excluded social groups, which creates the opportunity to impose unpopular measures.[71]

The final sixteen months of the Argentine *Proceso*—between August 1982 and December 1983—show that a weak, internally divided dictatorship, paralyzed by the desire not to alienate democratic parties and the public ahead of the transition of power, combines the worst elements of both forms of government. It was unable to impose unpopular measures by fiat because it could not reach consensus within the governing military on what to do and lacked the power and the will to repress dissenting opinions in civil society. At the same time, the *Proceso* was unable to create popular trust and legitimacy or generate a wide consensus on what sacrifices might be needed for the common good because the military was widely seen as the main cause of the high foreign debt and economic malaise.

Immediately following the defeat in the South Atlantic War, the Argentine military government realized that it needed to move toward democratization; however, it harbored hopes that it could control the process. The military junta wanted to promote a conservative party and shelter itself from prosecution for human rights abuses, following the example of Spain, where the transition to democracy had taken place on Franco's terms. However, an authoritarian regime that has achieved little of importance before the transition to democracy begins is generally incapable of controlling the transition itself.[72] The Argentine military government of the *Proceso* had nothing to show for its six years in power. After economic crisis and military humiliation, even Argentines who had supported the military coup in 1976 were turning their backs on the de facto government. When the international debt crisis began in August 1982, the prestige of the Argentine military authorities was at an all-time low. It was therefore surprising that the Bignone administration was able to implement sweeping changes in the economic structure of the country during the two months in office under the leadership of José Maria Dagnino Pastore in the Ministry of the Economy and Domingo Cavallo in the Central Bank. As the U.S. ambassador in Buenos Aires, Harry Shlaudeman, noted in September 1982, the problem with the Argentine government was not that there was no government. "When the entire structure of the financial system can be changed overnight by fiat there is too much government. There is, however, no strong overall leader in a government made

---

71. Geddes, "Politics of Economic Liberalization," 197; Kaufman, "Democratic and Authoritarian Responses to the Debt Issue," 482.
72. Viola and Mainwaring, "Transitions to Democracy," 195.

up of many overlapping empires and authority and clean policy lines are often absent."

After the cabinet reshuffling in mid-August 1982, which coincided with the beginning of the debt crisis in Mexico, the government became increasingly paralyzed. One of the most obvious signs of faltering control was the growing fiscal deficit, which rose sharply from just under 10 percent of GDP in 1981 to more than 35 percent the subsequent year, only to stay above 25 percent in 1983. The reasons for this dramatic shortfall were rising expenditures and falling tax revenues. The military expenditure remained an important part of the ballooning budget deficit; both the army and the air force started pressuring the Bignone administration to increase the purchase of weapons massively beyond the mere replacement of lost equipment during the military confrontation.[73] Tax receipts fell sharply because of rising tax evasion. The IMF estimated that as much as half of the value-added tax remained unpaid and blamed that shortfall on a "basic weakness in the tax auditing machinery." In addition, with high rates of inflation many people simply delayed tax payments, preferring to pay relatively small late fees.[74]

By far the largest part of this deficit, however, was not of a budgetary but of a "quasi-fiscal" nature, mostly the losses suffered by the Central Bank. There were two main reasons for Central Bank losses to rise sharply in the wake of the war: exchange guarantees and the modification of the so-called *cuenta regulación*. Minister of the Economy Jorge Wehbe and president of the Central Bank Julio González del Solar decided that the Central Bank would no longer charge interests on loans to the government. At the same time, it continued to pay close to market interest on the reserves, which commercial banks had to deposit with the Central Bank. With monthly rates of inflation of more than 15 percent, interest-free loans to the government represented a huge subsidy to the government but enormous losses for the Central Bank.[75] Christian Brachet, who headed various IMF missions to Argentina between 1982 and 1983, called this decision "completely criminal" and remembered that it changed the working practice of the IMF. From then on the quasi-fiscal deficit of a country became an additional key variable the IMF would use to judge a country's compliance with a Fund agreement.[76]

73. Telegram 820909, AMEMBASSY BUENOS AIRES to SECSTATE, "Current Argentine Government: Weakness, Fragmentation, Instability," September 9, 1982.

74. Staff Report for the 1982 Article IV Consultation and Request for Stand-by Arrangement, January 10, 1983, EBS/83/8, IMF Archives.

75. José Agustín Uriarte, interview, Buenos Aires, June 23, 2004.

76. Christian Brachet, interview, Washington, D.C., April 14, 2004.

The second half of 1982 also saw an acceleration of the nationalization of private external debt. In addition to the exchange guarantees installed by Domingo Cavallo and then modified to make them even more attractive for debtors by his successor González del Solar, and which in this period amounted to more than US$4 billion, the Argentine Central Bank also resorted to offering bonds, so-called BONEX, to private companies to pay their arrears to commercial banks. During the third quarter of 1982 alone, roughly US$1 billion in BONEX and an additional US$800 million in exchange-rate swaps were sold, which represented an exchange rate guarantee to its buyers.[77] The rescheduling of foreign debt with the help of exchange guarantees during 1981 had the unintended—but entirely predictable—consequence that a large amount of guaranteed foreign debt fell due at the same time in late 1982 and early 1983. The IMF estimated that almost US$1.5 billion matured during the last five weeks of 1982 and more than US$1.7 billion during the first quarter of 1983. This created the risk of a financial meltdown, which an IMF official reportedly called "Argentina's end-of-year financial Hiroshima." The Argentine Central Bank did not have the foreign exchange to fulfill its obligations under the exchange guarantee. The economic authorities were afraid that letting the private sector roll over these loans by repaying them at the guaranteed rate and renewing them at the current exchange rate would be extremely inflationary. After all, the guarantees had been contracted at an exchange rate of between four and seven thousand pesos per U.S. dollar but at the end of 1982 the peso stood at nearly fifty thousand per U.S. dollar.[78]

As the end of military rule approached, the political horizon narrowed significantly, and the focus of the government's attention shifted from stabilizing the economy to protecting the interests of the armed forces. The most divisive question was how to deal with the legacy of the "Dirty War." In late February and early March of 1983, the military announced that it was preparing a document on the "struggle against terrorism" and affirmed that it intended "to lower the curtain and never speak of the matter" again. At the same time, the junta was drafting the so-called Law of National Pacification, which granted amnesty to those members of the armed forces guilty of human rights abuses.[79] As the political authority of Reynaldo Bignone progressively disintegrated, it became obvious that he would not even be able to protect members of the armed forces

77. Argentina—Staff Report for the 1982 Article IV Consultations and Request for Stand-By Arrangement, January 10, 1983, IMF Archives.

78. "Averting a Financial Hiroshima," *Latin American Weekly Report*, November 26, 1982.

79. Fontana, "Political Decision Making," 177.

from prosecution after the return to democracy.[80] The military government, which had been feared for years for "disappearing" opponents, had not only lost control of the streets, where strikes and demonstrations grew ever more numerous, but also of the courts of justice, where judges started to assert their independence.

A series of armed robberies in Córdoba in broad daylight symbolized the powerlessness of the government to control the streets. The police stood by without interfering because of a "lock-in" strike for higher salaries. The under-secretary of the economy, Victor Poggi, noted, "The state can do nothing any-more but pay salaries." In fact, even the ability to pay salaries was seriously threatened. As the elections neared, the Bignone administration's political and economic room to maneuver grew ever narrower. With the military govern-ment's legislative body, the Comisión de Asesoramiento Legislativo—CAL, delaying changes in the tax code and amid rising uncertainty regarding the eco-nomic policy of the next constitutional government, tax collection fell sharply.[81] Paying the outlays with the help of the printing press was equally uncertain because the workers at the mint went on strike in September. At the same time, the government lost control over the judicial system. This became particularly obvious on October 4, when the president of the Central Bank, Julio González del Solar, was arrested at the airport on his return from Washington on the order of Oscar Pinto Kramer, a judge from Rio Gallegos. The judge charged González del Solar with treason for conceding foreign jurisdiction over the foreign debt of a state-owned company, Aerolíneas Argentinas.[82]

In October 1983, as elections approached, Argentina was again facing imme-diate default on its external obligations. The outgoing military government decided that it would be unable to reach an agreement with creditors before the elections but hoped to reach a deal before the transfer of power. The U.S. Embassy noted on October 19, 1983: "The Central Bank probably recognizes that the 1983–84 IMF program is finished, but it wishes to reserve at least a pub-lic façade that relations with the IMF are good to avoid another possible finan-cial crisis before the elections."[83] The main problem was that the presidential candidates of both opposition parties avoided comment on the debt issue. This caution was partially fueled by the widespread belief that an elected government

---

80. Viola and Mainwaring, "Transitions to Democracy," 192.

81. Telegram, Buenos Aires to State Department, "Economic Notes: Number 22," October 5, 1983.

82. Kannenguiser, La maldita herencia, 47.

83. Telegram, Buenos Aires to State Department, "Status of Refinancing Program," October 19, 1983.

would be able to negotiate substantially better terms with creditors than the military government could. Both the Peronists and the Radicals agreed in principle that the debt needed to be honored, but they added the caveat that the legality of the debt had to be investigated first.

The Peronists under their presidential candidate Ítalo Luder were significantly more supportive of the military administration than the UCR.[84] Secret negotiations between the military and the Peronists, especially the trade unions CGT-RA and the Group of 62, were meant to prepare for a smooth transition. The trade unions and the military government agreed on the fundamental principle that the transition should take place without major disruptions, and the unions therefore pledged to "refrain from any major strikes or provocative acts that could endanger the democratization process." The army hoped that after the expected victory of Peronism, the new constitutional government would protect the military from prosecution for human rights abuses and wrongdoing during the South Atlantic conflict.[85] Union leader Jorge Triaca confirmed that secret negotiations between the military government and Peronism actually took place. He described this as something completely natural because everybody expected the PJ to win the elections, and both the incoming and the outgoing administration had an interest in a transition without major problems.[86]

Raúl Alfonsín, the presidential candidate of the UCR, took a much more antagonistic approach toward the Bignone administration. He denounced the secret contacts between the Peronist unions and the military and advocated prosecuting human rights violators. On the economic front, he rejected the agreements between the Argentine government and its creditors, calling the interest rates "usurious." Alfonsín also tried to distance himself from the negotiations with the IMF and other creditors and announced publicly that he would not participate in any negotiations with creditors prior to the transition. Privately, however, Alfonsín could not ignore the severity of the financial crisis and secretly sent his economic adviser Bernardo Grinspun to Washington to meet with the IMF in September 1983.[87]

The results of the presidential elections held on October 30, 1983, surprised observers. Winning a clear majority of 52 percent of the popular vote against a

84. Telegram, Buenos Aires to State Department, "Can Argentine Default Be Avoided over the Next 6–12 Months?" October 11, 1983.

85. Telegram, Buenos Aires to State Department, "Interior Minister Denies Labor-Military Pact," April 14, 1983, State Argentina Declassification Project (1975–84).

86. Jorge Triaca, interview, Buenos Aires, February 25, 2004.

87. Telegram, Buenos Aires to State Department, "Can Argentine Default Be Avoided over the Next 6–12 Months?" October 11, 1983.

mere 40 percent for Ítalo Luder, Raúl Alfonsín, the charismatic candidate of the UCR, managed what had previously been considered impossible: victory over the Peronists in a free election. However, Alfonsín's triumph was not complete. While the Radical Party won the majority in Congress, the humiliated Peronists won the Senate. In the face of his lack of authority, outgoing President Bignone agreed to bring forward the transition of government from late January 1984 to December 10, 1983.

The Argentine debt crisis had already begun with the transition between the Videla and Viola administrations, more than a year before the meltdown in Mexico in August 1982. It turned into a de facto cessation of payments during the South Atlantic War between April and June 1982. By the time hostilities ended, successive military governments had not only ruined Argentine finances but also destroyed domestic and international trust in its ability to resolve the crisis on its own. The internationalization of the debt crisis with the announcement by the Mexican authorities that they would be unable to continue servicing their debt helped Argentina in the short term. Creditor banks and industrial countries' governments wanted to avoid the default of a large debtor country at any cost and were therefore willing to overlook Argentina's reckless economic policies and military aggression in an effort to reach a rescheduling agreement.

Despite the international goodwill and the Bignone administration's publicly stated intent to solve the most pressing economic problems in order to hand over a stable country to a democratic successor government, the last eighteen months of the *Proceso* saw a considerable worsening of the Argentine economic and political crisis. Weak and internally divided, the military authorities were unable to design and implement a consistent response to the economic meltdown. The looming transition to democracy further complicated economic policymaking, since long-term planning would have required at least the tacit support of the civilian opposition. Under these circumstances, the relative lenience of international creditors proved to be more of a curse than a blessing. It helped the outgoing military government postpone painful measures. Despite Argentina's loss of access to international financial markets, the foreign debt continued to expand at a rapid pace because of involuntary lending by creditor banks and loans from multilateral financial institutions such as the IMF. At the same time, the negotiations between the military government and the international creditors delegitimized the process of debt renegotiation in the eyes of many Argentines, who believed that the military was selling out the country to international financial institutions.

The new constitutional government, which assumed office in December 1983, would have to cope with the wide gap between popular expectations of a much easier solution under democratic rule and the dire reality of the debt crisis. While civilians had promised to undo the economic legacy of the military dictatorship, increase real wages, and resist austerity and IMF-imposed economic programs, they had to learn the hard lesson that with the high external debt burden there was no going back to the populist postwar economic model.

6 CAN DEMOCRACY FEED A NATION?

With democracy you can eat; with democracy you can educate;
with democracy you can cure.
—RAÚL ALFONSÍN

With the transition to democracy in December 1983, the dynamics of economic policymaking changed dramatically. After seven years of political repression and more than three years of economic chaos, Argentines once again
started to look toward the future with optimism.[1] Many believed that the
charismatic new president, Raúl Alfonsín, would be able to live up to his campaign promise to restore the integrity of the constitutional order, strengthen
democracy, restore social justice, and return the country to a path of economic growth. This political and economic idealism created the context for
an intense clash of the Argentine government with the domestic opposition
on the one hand and international banks and the IMF on the other. However, high expectations were soon disappointed, for the first year of democracy was one of almost permanent economic and political crisis.

Alfonsín's initial attempt to lay a basis for economic growth with social
justice unraveled so quickly because the newly elected government could not
escape the political logic of transition to democracy. Following the disastrous
failure of the *Proceso*, it was natural for the new democratic government to

1. Smith, *Authoritarianism*, 272.

reject everything the military had stood for. Large parts of Argentine society, blaming economic liberalism for the economic crisis, agreed with Alfonsín's effort to undo the military legacy by returning to the developmentalist economic model of the 1960s. However, this model was inappropriate to the domestic and international situation. The most important difference was the existence of the large foreign debt the military dictatorship had left behind.[2] The foreign debt reduced Alfonsín's room for maneuver because the government had to spend a large and growing share of its budget on debt service payments. It also reduced the autonomy to implement economic policies the government saw fit because they became the subject of permanent scrutiny from international financial markets and the IMF. The fact that the debt had been accumulated by an unconstitutional government also posed a political problem. To accept the burden of servicing it was perceived as an implicit endorsement of the economic policies of the military government. Alfonsín consequently felt compelled to oppose economic austerity, resist IMF conditions, and call for a massive debt reduction.[3] After more than a year of constant confrontation and without any substantial advances to show for it, Alfonsín was forced to radically change course in early 1985, adopting a less idealistic and more conciliatory approach proposed by a group of technocrats surrounding the secretary of planning, Juan Vital Sourrouille.

The economic policies pursued during seven years of repressive dictatorship had severely impoverished the country. The per capita GDP had fallen by almost 10 percent between 1980 and 1983 and was 4 percent lower than a decade earlier.[4] Industrial production had fallen even more dramatically—by over 20 percent—between 1975 and 1982, and industrial employment had shrunk by over 40 percent.[5] The economic crisis, which started in 1980, had also drastically increased the number of people living below the statistical poverty line to more than half the Argentine population in 1982 as compared to only 31.3 percent two years earlier.[6] At the same time, the legacy of the military dictatorship limited the range of available economic policy options. The large fiscal deficit together with uncontrollable inflation significantly constrained fiscal and monetary policies,

2. Schvarzer, *Un modelo sin retorno.*
3. Stiles, "Argentina's Bargaining with the IMF."
4. Based on data provided by Della Paolera and Taylor in *A New Economic History of Argentina.*
5. In terms of value added in constant 1970 pesos. World Bank, *Argentina: Economic Memorandum,* 2:381.
6. Instituto Nacional de Estadística y Censos de la República, *La pobreza urbana en la Argentina.*

while the high external debt made it impossible to finance a recovery with the help of additional loans or to jump-start the economy with a devaluation of the peso.

The difficulties inherited from the outgoing military government were compounded by the weakness of the incoming Alfonsín administration. Alfonsín's Radical Party lacked political experience because it had been out of power for eighteen years.[7] Alfonsín himself had never held elected office, and Bernardo Grinspun, Alfonsín's first minister of the economy, did not understand the changes that had taken place in the Argentine and world economies that had occurred during the previous two decades.[8] Grinspun had risen to power thanks to his unflagging loyalty to the party and his close personal ties with Alfonsín.[9] Some observers and even close allies considered Grinspun entirely incompetent to run the Ministry of the Economy at such a critical juncture. Some even suggested that he was mentally imbalanced.[10] The absence of a well-staffed and disciplined bureaucratic apparatus to deal with complicated economic policy made the situation even more precarious. Argentina was not unique in this regard. The new authorities of countries in transition often want to start with a clean slate of bureaucrats but find it impossible to recruit well-qualified but untarnished civil servants to replace those who had worked in key positions during the previous administration. In the case of Argentina, the problem was further aggravated by civil servants' low salaries. According to a World Bank study, civil servants' real salaries fell by almost 30 percent between 1980 and 1983 and amounted to only half the level of a decade earlier.[11] The U.S. Embassy observed that when Alfonsín assumed office on December 10, "work had not even started on the budget for the year beginning January 1" because so few qualified bureaucrats had been left in this section of the Ministry of the Economy.[12]

Alfonsín also lacked full political backing from his own party, the Unión Cívica Radical (UCR), which was deeply divided over the future direction of the economy. The sector of the UCR most closely aligned with the president, "Renovación y Cambio" (Renewal and Change), endorsed a leftist ideology and admired European social democracy. The youth movement of the "Junta

7. Gerchunoff and Llach, *El ciclo de la ilusión y el desencanto,* 394.

8. Huneeus, "Technocrats and Politicians," 191.

9. Grinspun, "Intenciones de política económica," 24.

10. Rodolfo Pousa, interview, Buenos Aires, May 26, 2004; Mario Teijeiro, interview, Buenos Aires, December 15, 2003.

11. World Bank, *Argentina: Economic Memorandum,* 2:62.

12. Telegram, Buenos Aires to State Department, "The Difficulties in the Argentine Economic Situation," September 15, 1984, 5.

Coordinadora Nacional de la Juventud Radical," which stood even further to the left, also supported him. The main internal opposition was the "national" or center-right wing of the party. Its most prominent representatives were the governor of Córdoba, Eduardo Angeloz, the UCR presidential candidate in 1989, and senator and future president Fernando De la Rúa.[13] While there was substantial disagreement between the two traditional wings of the Radical Party, they agreed that the state should play a major role in the economy and rejected the economic policies of the military government as "neoliberal."[14·]

Alfonsín's surprising electoral triumph over the Peronist candidate Ítalo Luder also represented a clear victory for the left wing of the UCR, which reflected itself in Alfonsín's economic program. The economic plan on which Alfonsín had campaigned, "Bases para la Acción Económica del Gobierno Democrático," openly defied the orthodox economic thinking of the IMF and Martínez de Hoz, whose monetarism or neoliberalism it held responsible for the economic meltdown. It rejected the notion that overcoming the crisis required a period of austerity, stating that the democratic government would "not tie its hands because of arguments invoking false theoretical or 'realistic' principles in its struggle to improve the most difficult social situations."[15] Instead, it looked for inspiration in Keynesian theory and aimed at rapidly alleviating poverty and social injustice through public works projects, a sharp increase in real wages, and reduction of the real interest rate.[16]

The notion that external constraints could be ignored was sharply contested even within the government. The young and mostly foreign-educated technocrats around the planning secretary Juan Vital Sourrouille believed that restoring stability had to be the government's first priority. They reasoned that social programs would be impossible to implement in any meaningful way under a permanent economic emergency and near hyperinflationary conditions.[17] Adolfo Canitrot, a colleague of Sourrouille, remembered that the left wing of the UCR frequently clashed with these technocrats during the first year of the Alfonsín presidency. Consequently, Grinspun tried to exclude the economic team around Sourrouille as much as possible from important decisions.[18] The conflict became deeply divisive partly because Sourrouille and his followers were not affiliated

13. Huser, *Argentine Civil-Military Relations from Alfonsín to Menem,* 48.

14. Huneeus, "Technocrats and Politicians," 185.

15. *Bases para la acción económica del gobierno democrático;* reprinted in Grinspun, *La evolución de la economía Argentina.*

16. Ibid.

17. Daniel Heymann, interview, Buenos Aires, May 27, 2004.

18. Adolfo Canitrot, interview, Buenos Aires, May 24, 2004.

with the ruling party. This aroused suspicion of disloyalty among the party hierarchy, the *historicos*. Jaime Baintrub, director of the Central Bank during the first two years of the Alfonsín administration and closely associated with the left wing of the Radical Party, complained that Sourrouille was betraying what was at the heart of Radicalism.[19]

The implementation of a Keynesian economic program faced the insurmountable obstacle that public expenditure and the deficit were already at all-time highs before Alfonsín assumed office. During the constant economic crisis of 1981–82, public expenditure had grown from half of Argentine GDP to around 80 percent of it. The combined fiscal and quasi-fiscal deficit reached a staggering 40 percent of GDP during the same period, indicating that the Argentine government was able to pay only half of its outlays out of current income. The high foreign debt burden was responsible for a large part of the expenditure. Interest payments were substantial and amounted to between 6 and 8 percent of GDP in 1983 and 1984. More important were the consequences of exchange guarantees on private foreign debt during the previous two years. They were partially responsible for the large losses of the Central Bank, the so-called quasi-fiscal deficit, which amounted to more than a third of the public sector deficit in 1983 and more than half of it in 1984.[20]

Since the country had lost access to voluntary lending from international financial markets, the government could not borrow abroad to finance the budget deficit. The only available options were involuntary external financing, domestic borrowing, and the printing press. The first of these options was only available in the context of an agreement with creditor banks and the IMF, which was difficult to reach and contradicted the government's ideological position. Domestic financing through borrowing or through money creation had severe drawbacks as well because it directly fueled the spiraling inflation, which had already reached 400 percent annually when Alfonsín assumed office in December 1983. Argentina had reached a critical threshold of inflationary financing. As the population grew hesitant to hold pesos, the Central Bank had to print pesos at an ever higher rate in order to reap the necessary benefits from the "inflation tax." Between 1983 and 1984, inflation almost doubled from 350 to 650 percent, while the "inflation tax" remained constant at about 5 percent of GDP.[21] This was clearly not a sustainable strategy.

19. Jaime Baintrub, interview, Buenos Aires, July 2, 2003.
20. Fundación de Investigaciones Económicas Latinoamericanas and Consejo Empresario Argentino, *El Gasto público en la Argentina.*
21. Kiguel and Neumeyer, "Inflation and Seigniorage in Argentina," 37.

In early 1984, the Alfonsín administration faced an impossible situation. Spending cuts were extremely unpopular because they smacked of "neoliberal orthodoxy" and were widely opposed as recessionary and socially unjust. At the same time, the Argentine population grew increasingly weary of high and rising rates of inflation.[22] The government therefore pledged to make fighting inflation one of its main political objectives. Bernardo Grinspun promised to reduce inflation and the fiscal deficit without a recession. This program ran counter to what most economists and the IMF considered sound policy. He wanted to raise real wages, but denied that this would be inflationary because companies had spare capacity and increasing demand would lower the per-unit costs. He argued that artificially low interest rates would compensate companies for higher wage costs and induce them to invest more in capital equipment, while strict price controls would stop speculation and cost-driven inflation.[23]

Most Argentine economists were appalled by Grinspun's plan. Even Raúl Prebisch, the octogenarian economist from the heterodox CEPAL in Santiago de Chile, opposed the proposed measures. In March and April 1984, he explained that Grinspun had lost control over the situation and sharply criticized the government for lacking a clear strategy for dealing with the national crisis.[24] At the same time, he warned that the government's policies were based on "dangerous illusions" and stressed that tough measures needed to be taken to stop inflation and consolidate the economy with or without the support of the IMF.[25]

The domestic economic crisis was compounded by a growing external crisis caused by the almost US$45 billion in foreign debt the military government had accumulated over the previous seven years. The short maturities added to the immediacy of the crisis. Within the span of a year, Argentina would need to refinance more than a third of its total foreign debt, as US$12 billion of public debt and over US$5 billion in private loans were either due by the end of 1983 or would fall due during 1984.[26] From the first day in office, the threat of a default loomed large over the Alfonsín administration. Negotiations between the outgoing military government and Argentina's creditors broke down in the

22. Carlos Moyano Llerena, "La batalla contra la inflación," *La Nación,* December 8, 1983; "Grinspun anticipó que en los próximos días se adoptarán medidas muy duras" and "Inflación y mensaje del Presidente," *La Nación,* December 29, 1983; *Bases para la acción económica del gobierno democrático,* reprinted in Grinspun, *La evolución de la economía Argentina,* 17.

23. Sheahan, *Patterns of Development in Latin America,* 104.

24. "La Nación con el Dr. Raúl Prebisch," *La Nación,* April 15, 1984.

25. Raúl Prebisch, "Hacia el consenso en la recuperación," *La Nación,* May 13, 1984.

26. Banco Central de la República Argentina, Comunicado No 4645, "Relevamiento de la deuda externa Argentina," 7 de setiembre de 1984, DSDD.

run-up to the election and the transition to democracy. The U.S. Embassy in Buenos Aires warned in early October 1983, "given Argentina's poor reputation, British concerns, and the already overdue first payment on the bridge loan," there is a serious risk of Argentina defaulting on its foreign debt over the following six to twelve months.[27]

For the incoming Alfonsín administration, foreign debt represented not only an economic but also an immensely important political problem because it was a legacy of the hated military dictatorship. This created a shared conviction that the foreign debt was of questionable legitimacy. During the presidential campaign and the first months in office, Alfonsín and Grinspun reiterated that they would only honor "legitimate debt."[28] Based on information available at the time, they estimated that a large part of the debt was of doubtful legality and legitimacy and hoped that careful scrutiny could help identify these fraudulent loan contracts and thus reduce the amount of foreign debt.[29] The legitimacy of the debt became subject to a drawn-out investigation, which reached its conclusions in early September 1984. The results disappointed those who had hoped that it would reduce the debt burden. Only a few claims were deemed unfounded, the most famous example was a loan for the purchase of military helicopters from the United Kingdom, whose delivery had been canceled due to the outbreak of hostilities while the corresponding loan remained on the books.[30] Largely, however, the inquiry concluded that foreign obligations had been contracted under the legal norms in force at the time of signature and were thus legally binding.[31]

The domestic political repercussions of the discussion about the legitimacy of foreign debt, however, did not come to a close with this report. Popular perceptions that the debt was illegitimate significantly reduced the willingness to assume the financial and political costs of it and created a political climate in which servicing the debt was perceived as endorsing the economic policies of the military government. The widely held belief that the economic policies of the dictatorship had been "neoliberal" and "imposed by the IMF" delegitimized the process of economic liberalization in the eyes of a large segment of the Argentine

27. Telegram, Buenos Aires to State Department, "Can Argentine Default Be Avoided over the Next 6–12 Months?" October 11, 1983.
28. Telegram, Buenos Aires to State Department, "Summary of the Statement of the Government's Economic Program," February 3, 1984.
29. Banco Central de la República Argentina, Comunicado No 4645, "Relevamiento de la deuda externa Argentina," 7 de setiembre de 1984, DSDD.
30. Juan V. Sourrouille, interview, Buenos Aires, June 9, 2004.
31. Schvarzer, Implantacion de un modelo economico, 89.

population and set the scene for a public showdown between the Alfonsín administration and its international creditors, including the IMF. Alfonsín and Grinspun publicly attacked the IMF for always prescribing the same "medicine of recession and misery" in order to solve the economic crisis.[32] Instead, the newly elected government wanted "our country to grow, to increase wages, and to fight inflation."[33]

The widely held belief that Argentina was in a strong bargaining position vis-à-vis its creditors contributed to the confrontational policy. Argentina depended less on imports than most countries affected by the debt crisis. It was virtually self-sufficient in the production of energy and most primary staples. Argentina was thus less vulnerable to possible economic sanctions in case of a default on its external obligations.[34] MIT economist Rudiger Dornbusch corroborated this point of view in testimony before the Joint Economic Committee of Congress, arguing that Argentina "because of [its] strong position in terms of reserves, trade surpluses, [and] ability to sell wheat to Russia can in fact play games with the banks [and] hold out for better terms. It is quite obvious that Argentina now is in a much better position than the banks to which she owed the debts."[35]

The Argentine government also believed it had a strong hand against creditor banks because unilateral debt repudiation would endanger the very survival of the banks.[36] The financial costs for Argentina, by contrast, appeared limited, and some observers even held that debt repudiation might benefit the country. Philip O'Brien argued that it was beneficial for a country to default on its external obligations if expected capital inflows were lower than the payments on existing loans as long as the cost of possible sanctions was not excessive.[37] In the case of Argentina, interest payments exceeded capital flows by 2 to 4 percent of GDP per year. This made default a tempting proposition.[38]

Raúl Alfonsín was also convinced that the recent transition to democracy significantly improved his bargaining position because Western democracies

32. "Al margen de la semana," *La Nación*, February 19, 1984.

33. "Alfonsín criticó al Fondo Monetario," *La Nación*, June 4, 1984.

34. Stiles, "Argentina's Bargaining with the IMF," 65.

35. U.S. Congress, Joint Economic Committee—Subcommittee on Economic Goals and Intergovernmental Policy, Rudiger Dornbusch's statement, 98th Cong., 2nd sess., March 28, 1984.

36. "Argentina's Game of Chicken," *Newsweek*, June 25, 1984.

37. O'Brien, "The Debt Cannot be Paid," 59.

38. Author's calculations based on Economist Intelligence Unit database, CountryData, annual time series for nominal GDP (U.S.$) and total interest payments due (accessed June 2, 2005), and World Bank, World Development Indicators database for external debt (DoD, current U.S.$) and foreign direct investment and net inflows (BoP, current U.S.$) (accessed May 30, 2006).

would not want to see a new democracy falter under the burden of the external crisis. Raúl Prebisch expressed this view most clearly when he stated in November 1983 that "democracy will help obtain better conditions for the refinancing."[39] Alfonsín and Grinspun repeatedly invoked the importance of defending democracy and pleaded with the governments of industrial countries for help in this moment of crisis. At a conference in Punta del Este in late March 1984, Grinspun made a dramatic appeal. "We are going through a very difficult situation and we need the cooperation of our financial partners. The Argentine democracy needs and demands it. You cannot extort from a democratic government what you didn't ask from an unconstitutional government."[40] In mid-April Alfonsín made an even more desperate appeal for help. Alluding to the civil war in Lebanon, he warned that Argentina could enter into a process of "Lebanization" if they failed to receive external help.[41]

The perception that the foreign debt was impossible to repay and that creditors would eventually have to grant a substantial reduction of its external obligations together with the belief that Argentina had a strong bargaining position and held the moral high ground led the Alfonsín government to adopt an extremely confrontational strategy in their negotiations with international banks and the IMF. Grinspun summed up his strategy in this famously candid statement in January 1984: "We have to get everything until the last cent that we can legally get from the IMF or from whomever else, and if there remains a coin on the rug, we are going to come back to look for it."[42]

The actual events resembled Grinspun's blunt comments. Argentina systematically delayed interest payments—forcing the IMF, creditor banks, and foreign governments to come to the rescue with a combination of bridge loans and rescheduling. The *New York Times* described negotiations between banks and Argentine government as "Argentine Roulette" and complained that "Argentina and its creditors . . . are playing chicken with this country's imminent default on interest payments. They may think its shrewd bargaining, but they're not the only ones that stand to be seriously hurt."[43] In Washington, the IMF staff grew increasingly frustrated with the fact that the Argentine authorities were spending too much time trying to blame the multinational banks and the IMF

39. Schvarzer, *Implantación de un modelo económico*, 92.
40. Kannenguiser, *La maldita herencia*, 55.
41. "La palabra presidencial," *La Nación*, April 12, 1984.
42. "Hay que sacarle hasta el último centavo que podamos legalmente sacarle al Fondo Monetario y a quien sea, y si queda en el tapete una chirola vamos a volver a buscarla," *La Razón*, January 13, 1984; quoted in Zlotogwiazda and Balaguer, *Citibank vs. Argentina*, 138.
43. "Argentine Roulette," *New York Times*, March 30, 1984.

for their difficulties and too little attacking the root of their economic problems. In particular, they objected to the continued policy of wage increases, artificially low interest rates, and an overvalued peso in the face of capital flight, rampant inflation, and high current account deficits. The relations between the IMF and Alfonsín administration further deteriorated during the first half of 1984 despite the mediation by the eminent Argentine economist Raúl Prebisch.[44]

The unilateral strategy reached its peak on June 11, 1984, when Argentina went public with a draft letter of intent to the IMF that had not been previously discussed with IMF staff. Grinspun explained in the letter that Argentina was determined to limit debt service payments to disposable resources from exports without reducing imports so that it could maintain a required level of economic activity. This was a highly unusual move; normally, letters of intent are the product of a long negotiation between the IMF and the debtor country. It also openly defied the advice of the IMF to restrain wage increases by stating that the government was committed to a real wage increase of 6 to 8 percent during the course of the year. Grinspun publicly stated that he would oblige Managing Director Jacques de Larosière to submit the letter to the Executive Board where he hoped to be able to apply political pressure.[45] The timing of this move was carefully chosen; the letter was made public just weeks before a large part of the Argentine external debt was coming due.[46] Grinspun wanted to pressure the IMF to give Argentina a seal of approval and thus enable a rollover of commercial debt while accepting their economic policy as a fait accompli.[47]

However, the IMF did not yield to Argentine pressure. The IMF gave the draft letter of intent a cool reception, and de Larosière insisted on additional consultations.[48] The director of the Western Hemisphere Department of the IMF, Eduardo Wiesner Durán, was more outspoken. He reportedly said, "A country can describe in the Letter of Intent that it wants to go to Mars on a plane and in the Memorandum of Understanding it has to explain how it is going to do it. The specialists are going to revise it: 'Let's see . . . the numbers don't add up, you can't go to Mars on a plane.' Now the country will say: 'Okay, then to the

44. Raúl Alfonsín to Raúl Prebisch, March 21, 1984, folder 7: Argentina, 1984, box 102: Subject Files, Donald T. Regan Papers.
45. Boughton, *Silent Revolution*, 391.
46. "La deuda externa; Se firmó la carta de intención con el FMI; Lo hizo el Presidente después de una reunión del Gabinete; mañana será enviada al organismo internacional, previo conocimiento del Parlamento y partidos políticos," *La Nación*, June 10, 1984.
47. "Defying I.M.F., Argentina Sets Austerity Plan; Argentina Defies Fund on Austerity," *New York Times* June 12, 1984.
48. Minutes of Executive Board Meeting, June 13, 1984, EBM/84/92, IMF Archives.

Moon.' It's going to turn out this won't work either and in this form the two sides continue until the government's goals coincides with its possibilities."[49]

U.S. officials also grew progressively exasperated with Argentine policies in general and Bernardo Grinspun's abrasive personality in particular. Many anecdotes surround the famously strained relationship between Bernardo Grinspun and the chairman of the Federal Reserve, Paul Volcker. On one occasion, Paul Volcker asked Grinspun what it meant to increase the real salary by 6 percent in a country with an annual inflation rate of 500 percent. Grinspun answered "506 percent."[50] Toward the end of 1984, the incompetence of Grinspun was so obvious that Paul Volcker even asked Raúl Alfonsín during a meeting whether he intended to keep Grinspun much longer as minister of the economy.[51]

Over time, it became obvious that the Argentine government had overestimated the political clout it had in Washington. In fact, the U.S. government's reaction to successive calls for help was lukewarm at best. Ronald Reagan eagerly embraced Alfonsín as a champion of democracy and gave him the rare opportunity to address a joint session of Congress during his state visit in March 1985. In a letter to Thomas (Tip) O'Neill, Speaker of the House of Representatives, Ronald Reagan stressed, "President Alfonsín has become a symbol of democracy and respect for human rights. His visit here presents an opportunity to demonstrate our support for democracy and is a chance to hear the views of the most prominent and influential leader in Latin America."[52] However, in practical terms, the U.S. government did little to answer Alfonsín's plea for help to cope with the mounting debt burden, which, as he exclaimed, "conspire[d] against the democratic system."[53] Alfonsín had also underestimated the banks' determination to resist substantial concessions. Major U.S. banks were not as vulnerable to unilateral action as Argentine authorities believed. Debt repudiation by Argentina alone would not have been a vital threat to any of them. Manufacturers Hanover, Argentina's largest U.S. creditor bank, had only US$1.3 billion in outstanding loans to Argentina. Citicorp's exposure was just below US$1.1 billion. While these numbers were substantial, loans to Argentina amounted to less than 2 percent of these banks' entire loan portfolios. When

49. Quoted in Kannenguiser, *La maldita herencia*, 60.

50. Ibid., 61.

51. Adolfo Canitrot, interview, Buenos Aires, May 24, 2004.

52. President Reagan to Thomas P. O'Neill, "Address by Argentine President Raúl Alfonsín to a Joint Meeting of Congress," March 8, 1985, case file 271131 CO008, WHORM Subject File, Ronald Reagan Presidential Library.

53. Remarks at the Welcoming Ceremony for President Raúl Alfonsín of Argentina, March 19, 1985, Public Papers of President Ronald W. Reagan, Ronald Reagan Presidential Library.

Argentina seemed close to a unilateral default on its debt during the critical months of June–September 1984, major U.S. banks already began reporting Argentine loans as nonaccrual items. An internal memorandum of the U.S. Treasury suggested that potential losses were limited for most of the banks, which would see their profits reduced by between 5 and 10 percent. Only Manufacturers Hanover would face a reduction of profits by as much as a 25 percent.[54] The banks' exposure to Mexico and Brazil was much higher. Citibank had lent almost three times as much to Mexico as to Argentina and had lent almost five times as much to Brazil.[55] Since creditor banks were simultaneously negotiating with the other countries as well, granting concessions to Argentina would have led to similar demands from other heavily indebted countries. The banks therefore felt that they had to hold their ground at all costs in order to avoid creating an unfavorable precedent.[56] The banks' bargaining position also significantly benefited from the commitment of the IMF not to lend into arrears. An IMF drawing could only proceed if the authorities had previously reached an agreement with the creditor banks to roll over existing loans and to finance the payment of overdue interest and capital payment. This meant that banks had effective veto power over official financial flows to heavily indebted countries.

The political costs of debt repudiation were much harder to estimate, and Argentine negotiators feared they might include trade sanctions, which would prevent Argentina from acquiring new technology or attracting foreign direct investment. Not very subtly, the U.S. government threatened debtor countries with sanctions if they tried to take unilateral action. On October 12, 1983, Richard T. McNamar, deputy secretary of the treasury, explained that if a country unilaterally repudiated its foreign debt, it would have to pay a heavy price. "The foreign assets of a country would be attached by creditors throughout the world; its exports would be seized by creditors at each dock where they landed; its national airlines unable to operate; and its sources of desperately needed capital goods and spare parts virtually eliminated. In many countries, even food imports would be curtailed. Hardly a pleasant scenario."[57]

54. Memorandum, Bob Bench to Rodd Conover, "Argentina," September 5, 1984, folder 7: Argentina, 1984, box 102: Subject Files, Donald T. Regan Papers.

55. "A War of Nerves over Latin Debt," *Business Week,* June 18, 1984.

56. John Reed, interview, New York, July 23, 2004.

57. R. T. McNamar, deputy secretary of the treasury (address, International Forum, U.S. Chamber of Commerce, Washington, October 12, 1983); quoted in U.S. Congress, Joint Economic Committee—Subcommittee on Economic Goals and Intergovernmental Policy, Rudiger Dornbusch's statement, 98th Cong., 2nd sess., March 28, 1984.

·One way a debtor country could reduce the cost of debt repudiation and increase its bargaining power was to seek close cooperation with other debtor countries. The possibility of such a "debtors' cartel" created strong reactions on both sides during the early years of the debt crisis. Banks were intensely preoccupied with the possibility of such a cartel, which they considered much more dangerous than an isolated default by a single country.[58] Economists and political scientists in heavily indebted countries believed that a debtors' cartel offered the best solution for the crisis because it could force banks and industrial countries into making real concessions.[59]

The first attempt to reach a coordinated strategy for debt negotiation took place in September 1983 at the summit of the Organization of American States in Caracas in defiance of open U.S. opposition.[60] However, Latin American countries were unable to come to an agreement. The second summit meeting took place in Quito, Ecuador, in January 1984 and resulted in a nonbinding declaration that stressed that debt service payments should be subordinated to the countries' goal of achieving economic development.[61] In late June 1984, representatives of eleven heavily indebted Latin American countries met for a third time in the Colombian coastal town of Cartagena. The Argentine delegation, which consisted of Minister of Foreign Affairs Dante Caputo and Minister of the Economy Bernardo Grinspun, was the most vocal advocate of joint action to alleviate the debt burden.[62] However, they failed again in their efforts. The "Cartagena Consensus," which called for drastic and immediate measures to ease the burden of the foreign debt for developing countries, was a mere nonbinding statement of intent.[63]

Efforts to form a debtors' cartel continued on a bilateral basis especially with Mexico and Brazil. They all failed even though they might have strengthened the bargaining power of heavily indebted developing countries. Theoretically, debtor countries would have been better off confronting their creditor banks together rather than singly, because together they could pose a more credible threat to creditor banks. Governments in industrial countries would also find it much more difficult to impose tough sanctions against a substantial part of

58. "Brazil Could Make or Break a Latin American Debtors' Cartel," *Business Week*, September 5, 1983; "Birth of a Borrowers' Cartel?" *Newsweek*, September 5, 1983.

59. O'Donnell, "External Debt."

60. "Brazil Could Make or Break a Latin American Debtors' Cartel," *Business Week*, September 5, 1983.

61. Boughton, *Silent Revolution*, 479.

62. Acuña, *Alfonsín y el poder económico*, 75.

63. "After Cartagena: Latin Debtors Hope for New Remedies," *Wall Street Journal*, June 25, 1984.

the Third World. In practice, however, each country had incentives to "cheat" on the other potential members of the cartel and reach an individual deal.[64] Creditor banks and the IMF recognized and exploited this inherent instability in the cooperation between debtor countries. They created conditions under which each of the three main debtor countries—Mexico, Brazil, and Argentina—had more to gain from reaching individual agreements than from collaborating with one another. José Luis Machinea, at the time a close adviser of Secretary of Planning Sourrouille, explained that the IMF and the U.S. Treasury made sure to reach an agreement with at least one of the three main debtor countries at a time so that the countries had never the same interest in forming a debtors' cartel.[65] Paul Volcker later elliptically described the reason for the failure of Latin American countries to form a debtors' cartel: "By good fortune or *otherwise* [emphasis added], there always seemed to be one important country that was doing fairly well and sensed it had a lot to lose from joining others in a strong confrontation with their creditors."[66] At the same time, the mere threat of a debtors' cartel had already strengthened the bargaining position of individual countries. Mexico and Brazil in particular used Argentina's eagerness to form a debtors' cartel as leverage to reach better individual deals with the banks. Machinea explained that they came very close to an accord on two occasions but both times the temptation to use the threat of the formation of a cartel as a bargaining tool to achieve individual concessions was stronger. In 1985, an Argentine delegation traveled to Brazil in great secrecy to negotiate a common debt strategy at a time when Brazil was involved in very difficult negotiations with the IMF and creditor banks. The Argentine delegation was very surprised to find a large number of journalists waiting for them at the house of the Brazilian minister of the economy for the supposedly secret meeting.[67]

After several dramatic showdowns with the IMF and creditor banks during the first half of 1984, Argentina and the international creditors reached an uneasy truce. On July 1, Argentina paid the banks US$350 million, which had been ninety days past due. This cleared the way for future loans and new negotiations with the IMF. In a surprising turnaround, Alfonsín, who had long held that the Argentines could not accept another austerity program, publicly announced that they should brace for more hardship if they wanted to overcome the acute

64. Stigler, "Theory of Oligopoly."
65. José Luis Machinea, interview, Santiago, Chile, February 27, 2004.
66. Volcker and Gyohten, *Changing Fortunes*, 209.
67. José Luis Machinea, interview, Santiago, Chile, February 27, 2004.

economic crisis.[68] In late September, Argentina reached a preliminary agreement with the IMF and international banks. Under the agreement, Argentina would receive more than US$4 billion in new loans, and banks would roll over more than US$13 billion in outstanding loans, which would fall due in 1984 and 1985. Argentina in turn committed itself to pay at least US$750 million of more than US$1 billion in arrears with commercial banks by the end of the year.[69] However, it would take until December for all the details to be worked out.[70] The agreement involved exactly the measures the Alfonsín administration had long tried to avoid, namely a drastic reduction of inflation with the help of tight monetary policy, a sharp cut in government spending, wage restraint, deregulation of domestic interest rates, limits on the total external debt of the public sector, and liberalization of foreign exchange markets, especially for the purpose of transfer of profits and dividends.[71]

The agreement provoked outrage among the Peronist opposition, which unleashed all its pent-up anger against the Alfonsín administration. The Peronists attacked Alfonsín for pursuing an antinational policy and accused him of continuing the same economic policies that Martínez de Hoz had introduced.[72] In Congress, Peronists refused even to attend a plenary session where Grinspun explained the deal, and union leaders ominously warned of a "social explosion" if workers were made to pay for the foreign debt.[73]

The agreement was not the result of a fundamental reorientation of Alfonsín's economic strategy but rather the product of necessity. Since Argentina was unable to reduce the debt burden unilaterally and feared the consequences of a unilateral default, the economic team considered it advantageous to play along as if the crisis were a mere problem of liquidity. Argentina tried to minimize debt service payments in an effort to force creditor banks to roll over existing loans and extend new credit to pay for a large part of the interest payments. Alfonsín was never willing to make debt payments that would have reduced the outstanding capital because he wanted to postpone recessionary economic adjustment as long as possible.[74] The strategy revolved around fictional accounting,

---

68. "Argentina Avoids the Brink Again," *New York Times*, July 1, 1984.

69. "Argentine Accord on Austerity Plan Accepted at IMF," *New York Times*, September 26, 1984.

70. Manzetti, *International Monetary Fund and Economic Stabilization*, 142.

71. Argentina—Request for Stand-by Arrangement, December 3, 1984, EBS/84/251, IMF Archives.

72. "El Partido Justicialista de la Provincia de Buenos Aires a todos los Argentinos," in Instituto de Estudios Latinoamericanos (Argentina), *Argentina 1984*, 21.

73. "IMF Deal Sparks Sharp Backlash," *Latin American Regional Reports: Southern Cone*, December 21, 1984.

74. Juan V. Sourrouille, interview, Buenos Aires, June 9, 2004.

whereby debtors and creditors agreed to pretend that the debtor country was current on its service payments when this really was not the case. The indebted country paid the creditor banks with freshly borrowed money from the very same banks.[75] The consequence was that the debt kept growing throughout the 1980s while net resource transfers turned sharply negative.

This strategy only made sense under one of two premises. Either the Argentine authorities believed that the country could grow fast enough to make a higher debt burden bearable in the future, or they hoped that—in the face of an ever rising debt burden—the international community and creditor banks would finally recognize the folly of insisting on full repayment and agree to a large reduction of the outstanding debt. Juan Sourrouille, Grinspun's successor in the Ministry of the Economy and at the time the secretary of planning, explained that the Alfonsín administration was convinced that the foreign debt was impossible to pay. The negotiation strategy therefore only sought to gain time during which they hoped to convince foreign creditors and the IMF to agree to a large debt reduction.[76]

Since the Argentine government displayed little resolve to tackle the root of inflation, namely the uncontrolled budget deficit and external disequilibrium, economic conditions continued to deteriorate in late 1984. At the end of the year, the Argentine public realized that tough bargaining with the IMF was not a guarantee for economic success and that they could not fully control their economic fate. In December 1984, the Argentine newspaper La Nación printed a political cartoon showing Bernardo Grinspun as a helpless technician unable to control the mechanics of the economy who was slowly realizing that rapid economic growth, interest rates, inflation, and the exchange rate were closing linked (see fig. 5).

When the IMF refused to disburse the next credit tranche for lack of progress in February 1985, Bernardo Grinspun was forced to resign. His ideological stance and abrasive negotiation style had become too closely associated with the economic chaos and diplomatic failure during the first year of the Alfonsín administration, and had made him a political liability.[77]

During its first year in office, the Alfonsín administration's policies were guided by the desire to eliminate the legacy of the military dictatorship.[78] Alfonsín had

75. José Luis Machinea, interview, Santiago, Chile, February 27, 2004.
76. Juan V. Sourrouille, interview, Buenos Aires, June 9, 2004.
77. Frenkel and Fanelli, "Argentina y el FMI," 152.
78. Cavarozzi, "Beyond the Transitions to Democracy in Latin America," 670.

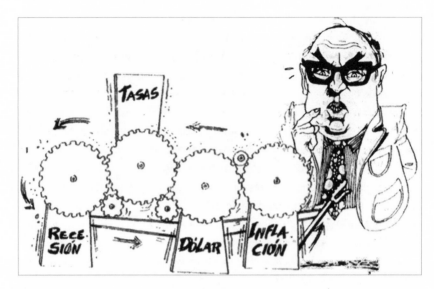

Fig. 5   Bernardo Grinspun helpless in the face of economic mechanics. Cartoon from
La Nación, December 1984

a strong sense of justice and mission and believed in the transformative power
of democracy. Unfortunately, he and his cabinet had to learn the hard lesson
that their domestic political power was more limited than they had expected
and that their bargaining power in the international arena was not sufficient to
reduce the debt burden unilaterally. The economic legacy of the military dictatorship weighed heavily on the incoming democratic government.[79] The country
was severely impoverished, yet countercyclical, "Keynesian" economic policies
were impossible to implement because the government was already running an
unsustainably large fiscal deficit. The large public foreign debt worsened Argentina's predicament because it represented a large drain on the treasury and made
it impossible to access world financial markets for voluntary lending. However,
the foreign debt was more than just an economic burden for the new democracy. The large foreign debt, which was closely associated with the hated military dictatorship and their supposedly neoliberal economic policies, created a
severe problem of incentives for the new constitutional government.

The transition to democracy did not significantly strengthen Argentina's
bargaining power with international creditors. The unilateral strategy was as
much of a failure as the attempts to create a debtors' cartel. International banks

79. Haggard and Kaufman, "Political Economy of Democratic Transition," 277.

fiercely resisted giving any special privileges to Argentina, fearing the precedent it would create. At the same time, they used their influence over the U.S. government and the IMF to make sure the interests of the three largest Latin American debtor countries—Mexico, Brazil, and Argentina—never coincided in such a way that creating a debtors' cartel became a real possibility. After several months of extreme tensions and repeated last-minute deals to avoid an imminent Argentine default on its external obligations, the country and its creditors settled into an uncomfortable stalemate during the second half of 1984.

7 FALSE DAWNS: FAILED STABILIZATION PLANS, 1985–1991

Following economic chaos and military defeat in 1981–82 and the turbulent transition to democracy in 1983–84, Argentines longed for personal security as well as political and economic stability. Governments soon discovered that these concerns were intimately linked. Political success and legitimacy critically depended on success in reining in the economic chaos, which left the population increasingly weary and traumatized. This "quest for stability" took place in a highly politically and ideologically polarized situation that resembled the struggles a decade earlier. Would Argentina confront the United States and the IMF and try to reduce its dependence on international capital and trade or would it align itself with the West and embrace the new opportunities the global economy offered? The ideological discussion did not play out along party lines but instead divided both the Radical Party of President Alfonsín and the Peronist opposition. The tension between the desperate need to produce immediate economic results and the lack of a consensus on the general direction the country's economy was to take paved the way for the implementation of more than a dozen emergency programs, which were often announced just before critical elections and faltered shortly thereafter. The results were disastrous. Not only did the programs fail to lower the high rate of inflation and restore investor confidence, which would have been essential for sustainable growth; each failed attempt to set the economy on a sound footing made the population increasingly skeptical of the government's ability and willingness to live up to its commitments, which made subsequent stabilization efforts more difficult. The lack of trust was reflected in high sensitivity of capital flows to changes in economic policy, the demonetization of the economy, and a sharp drop in private investments.

The conflict over the future direction of the Argentine economy needs to be understood in the context of a rapidly changing world economy. The first half of the 1980s was a contradictory period. On the one hand, the 1980s represented a revival and reassertion of Western capitalist values, which manifested themselves in the person of Ronald Reagan. On the other hand, industrial countries experienced the sharpest economic downturn of the postwar years, and developing countries suffered through a decade of slow or negative growth caused by the fallout of the debt crisis, which severely undermined confidence in the viability of the existing world economic order.

The first year of Raúl Alfonsín's presidency had been dominated by intense conflicts between the government, the Peronist trade unions, and the military on the domestic front and between Argentina and its creditors on the international front. The conflictual nature of policymaking was symbolized by the abrasive Bernardo Grinspun, who served as minister of the economy between December 1983 and February 1985. The replacement of Grinspun with Juan Vital Sourrouille, an aristocratic and soft-spoken technocrat, whose hallmark was his large tinted glasses, represented an important departure on a practical as well as on a symbolic level. The new economic team would try to mend fences with external creditors and the Peronist opposition in an effort to forge a new social consensus on which to build a stable economic future. The consensus, which Alfonsín envisioned in the mid-1980s, assigned a large role to the state as an arbiter and economic planner.

The economic thinking that dominated policymaking in Argentina for the subsequent four years had its origins in a small group of Argentine economists— Adolfo Canitrot, Roberto Frenkel, Juan Sourrouille, José Luis Machinea, Roberto Lavagna, and Jorge Katz—who had met at the CEDES (Centro de Estudios de Estado y Sociedad) in Buenos Aires during the late 1970s. They developed the ideas that would later form the basis for the Austral Plan partially as a reaction against the economic policies pursued by José Martínez de Hoz.[1] These

---

1. "La historia secreta del plan 'Austral,'" *Prensa Económica*, August 1985, 22.

self-described heterodox economists—as opposed to the "orthodox" ones close to Martínez de Hoz—believed that defeating inflation was more than just a means to an end but rather an end in and of itself. They stressed that the high rates of inflation that Argentina had experienced during the postwar decades were among the main reasons for its lackluster economic performance.[2] The heterodox strategy was based on a structuralist interpretation of inflation, which had also guided the Social Pact of the Peronist government in the mid-1970s. It rejected the focus on monetary policy and instead argued that inflation reflected structural deficiencies of the economy and was caused by a distributional struggle between different groups in society.[3] The main driving force of inflation was the desire of each social group to defend or enlarge its share of the national income. Under these premises, stabilization could only be achieved if the government succeeded in convincing social actors to moderate their demands in the short and medium term in the expectation that the overall size of the economic pie would increase with successful stabilization. The second factor driving inflation was inertia—the carry-over of past inflation through the indexation of wages and prices, or through inflationary memory—which could make inflation self-perpetuating.[4]

The group of economists surrounding Sourrouille sharply criticized orthodox anti-inflationary programs for failing to address the inertial aspect of inflation and ignoring the long-term political problems. They argued that orthodox programs tended to lead to a drawn-out recession, which made them politically unsustainable. The consequence was a premature abandonment of the anti-inflationary program.[5] Instead of the traditional anti-inflationary medicine, the *heterodoxos* proposed a "heterodox shock program," which aimed at eliminating inflationary expectations almost instantaneously.[6] At the heart of the heterodox shock program was a monetary reform with the creation of a new and more stable currency, which would eliminate expectations of permanent devaluations. The second element were "incomes policies"—controls of prices, wages, and contracts—which would coordinate the expectations of economic actors and break the vicious circle of inertial inflation. The combination of these two measures, the theory went, would help move the economy from

---

2. "Comisión de asuntos económicos," UCR, Comité Nacional, September 1985, Collection of ephemera from the Argentine national elections, 1989, Princeton University Library.

3. Pereira and Nakano, *Theory of Inertial Inflation*, 10.

4. Dornbusch and Simonsen, "Inflation Stabilization with Incomes Policy Support," 7.

5. Machinea, "Stabilization Under Alfonsín," 125.

6. Smith, "Heterodox Shocks," 141.

an equilibrium of high inflation to one of low inflation without a reduction in real wages or profits.[7]

When Sourrouille moved from his post as planning secretary to the top post in the Ministry of the Economy following the resignation of his predecessor Bernardo Grinspun in mid-February 1985, the moment had finally arrived for the *heterodoxos* to prove their theories in practice. Argentina was again in external and internal crisis. The country was in deep recession, inflation was rising uncontrollably, and negotiations with the IMF and international banks had broken down. The new economic team was aware that drastic measures were needed to pull the economy back from the brink, stop the inflationary spiral, and solve the external crisis.[8] In order for this plan to succeed, it had to inspire confidence at home and abroad as soon as it was announced. This required months of secret preparation, both to finalize domestic legislation and to line up external support. Sourrouille approached the IMF and the Federal Reserve in an effort to win their confidential approval. The first contacts took place during Alfonsín's state visit to the United States in March 1985. By mid-April, two months before it became effective, Sourrouille, Mario Brodersohn, and José Luis Machinea presented the project to the IMF, the U.S. Treasury, and the Federal Reserve Bank in the managing director's office at the IMF in Washington.[9] The IMF staff was initially skeptical about the feasibility of such an ambitious program and opposed some of the measures such as price controls and a fixed exchange rate as interventionist.[10] Paul Volcker was finally the one who helped to break the ice between the Argentine negotiating team and the IMF. He argued that the plan, while risky, deserved international support because it bore the stamp of "Made in Argentina" and represented the best chance of achieving stabilization.[11] De Larosière agreed that given the desperate situation in which Argentina found itself, the IMF should support the program, even though it looked only vaguely promising.[12] In order to help the Argentine authorities conceal the real nature of the Austral Plan, the IMF even agreed to negotiate a mock stand-by agreement to be signed on June 11, which would be superseded by the new one as soon as it was announced.[13]

7. Dornbusch and Simonsen, "Inflation Stabilization with Incomes Policy Support," 10.

8. Acuña, *Alfonsín y el poder económico*, 138.

9. Boughton, *Silent Revolution*, 399.

10. Adolfo Canitrot, interview, Buenos Aires, May 24, 2004.

11. Volcker and Gyohten, *Changing Fortunes*, 207.

12. Jacques de Larosière, interview, Princeton, April 20, 2004.

13. Boughton, *Silent Revolution*, 399.

On Friday, June 14, Sourrouille introduced the new economic plan (which was launched prematurely because of leaks in the press) with a dramatic appeal to the Argentine people. "If we don't reduce the current rate of inflation drastically, all of our hopes, all of our projects will lead to nothing, and the recently born Argentine democracy will suffer a setback of unpredictable consequences."[14] The plan consisted of three interrelated elements. The government announced that it would reduce the fiscal deficit with the help of sharp cuts in expenditures, new temporary taxes, and an increase in real tax receipts, which would be achieved with the help of better tax administration and the lower inflation rates themselves. With the fiscal deficit reduced to levels that could be financed on domestic or international capital markets, the Central Bank committed itself to stop financing the fiscal deficit either through money creation or through discount loans. Wages and prices were frozen in order to de-index the economy and break the inflationary inertia. Finally, the peso was replaced by a new currency, the *austral*, at 1,000:1, and the latter would be fixed to the dollar at 0.80 australes per dollar.[15] Since an abrupt end of high inflation would cause massive redistribution of income from debtors to creditors, Sourrouille enacted a delayed conversion scheme for contracts in old pesos.[16]

The initial results of the Austral Plan were promising. It eliminated inflation virtually overnight, which led to an increase in the real value of tax receipts of around 4 percent of GDP for the combined central and provincial governments. Public enterprises also enjoyed a considerable improvement of receipts of around 1.6 percent of GDP.[17] The government also unveiled a compulsory savings plan, doubled the tax on bank transactions, and raised export and import duties. In addition to sharply higher fiscal revenues, the Alfonsín government significantly reduced fiscal outlays during the initial phase of the program. Between 1983 and 1986 spending was cut from 35 percent of GDP to 28.8 percent, most of which was absorbed by the central government and by reduced losses of public enterprises.[18]

The Austral Plan also succeeded in creating confidence among important business sectors and the international financial community. In October 1985, the U.S. Embassy noted that the business executives they were in contact with

14. Mensaje dirigido a todo el país por el señor Ministro de Economía, Dr. Juan V. Sourrouille por radio y televisión el 14 de junio de 1985—Anuncio del Plan Austral, Centro de Documentación del Ministerio de Economía, Buenos Aires.

15. Heymann, "Austral Plan," 285.

16. Bruno, *Crisis, Stabilization, and Economic Reform*, 178.

17. Machinea, *Stabilization Under Alfonsín's Government*, 30.

18. "Argentina—Recent Economic Developments," July 15, 1987, SM/87/162, 31, IMF Archives.

had a "very favorable perception of the Austral Plan and its effects on their operations in 1985."[19] The first meeting of the IMF Executive Board after the beginning of the Austral Plan reflected the initial optimism that this time the stabilization might be successful. In the concluding remarks, the acting chairman called the Austral Plan "bold, courageous, and imaginative" and concluded that this radical program was also "radically needed in view of the risk that Argentina would slide into a situation of both hyperinflation and deep recession."[20] The success of the Austral Plan was also reflected in an—albeit fleeting—resurgence of economic growth. The year 1986 became the most economically successful year of the 1980s as GDP grew by more than 5 percent while consumer price inflation reached the lowest rate since 1974 (though it still exceeded 80 percent annually).[21]

Contrary to the technocratic rhetoric of the economic team around Sourrouille, the design and timing of the Austral Plan was not exclusively determined by technical factors. The Austral Plan also had an important political element. The government made a conscious effort to reduce inflation before the midterm congressional elections in November in order to appear competent in the eyes of voters. At the same time, they sought to postpone the costs of adjustment until after election day.[22] They succeeded. Alfonsín expanded his hold on power, and the Radical Party successfully penetrated traditionally Peronist districts.

The initial success of the Austral Plan coincided with a fundamental rethinking of the industrial countries' strategy for dealing with the debt crisis. The original strategy had aimed at preventing a general breakdown of the world financial system and a retreat by debtor countries into autarky. To achieve these immediate goals, the international community led by the IMF and the Federal Reserve called for firm adjustment programs in debtor countries and new "involuntary" lending from official and commercial sources. By 1985, it became clear that this strategy, while succeeding in avoiding a financial meltdown, had reached a dead end. Lenders were growing increasingly reluctant to increase their exposure to heavily indebted developing countries. Especially smaller banks, which had limited exposure, tried to leave the concerted lending process. In June 1985, the IMF warned in a confidential document titled "The Role of the Fund in Assisting Members with Commercial Banks and Official Creditors"

19. Telegram, Buenos Aires to State Department, "Businesses Modestly Hopeful for 1986," October 22, 1985.

20. Minutes of Executive Board Meeting, August 9, 1985, EBM/85/125, 8, IMF Archives.

21. Banco Central de la República Argentina, *Memoria annual*, 1986, 3.

22. Stein and Streb, "Political Stabilization Cycles in High-Inflation Economies."

that it was becoming increasingly difficult to orchestrate the restructuring programs, which involved a large number of commercial banks with oftentimes
very different interests. "It has to be recognized that occasions could arise in
which the payment outlook is so adverse that it will be difficult for banks whose
interests may well be divergent to hold together in a common approach."[23]
Heavily indebted countries, suffered from "adjustment fatigue." After years of
slow or negative economic growth and with external circumstances increasingly
adverse because of falling commodity prices, politicians in the affected countries found it more and more difficult to convince voters that more painful
measures were both necessary and promising for the country's future.[24] At the
same time, it became clear that the hope that countries would be able to "grow
out of the debt," that is to say, reduce the burden of it by strengthening their
economies, was unfounded. Growth rates remained disappointing during the
1980s, and most heavily indebted countries also failed to increase their exports
substantially.[25]

The failure of the initial strategy to solve the debt crisis coincided with increasing domestic political pressure in the United States to reduce the large and
growing trade deficit, whose origins were the overvaluation of the U.S. dollar
and the large and growing fiscal deficit. Even though almost half of the U.S.
trade deficit had its origins in trade with the most advanced developed countries—especially Japan and West Germany—agricultural and manufacturing
sectors openly called for protectionist measures against what they considered
unfair competition from developing countries, many of which were the very
countries struggling with the debt crisis.[26] In early 1984, U.S. Deputy Secretary
of the Treasury Richard T. McNamar seemed to be endorsing the case for protectionism when he explained at the Davos Meeting, "In an interdependent
world, exporting developing countries cannot pursue 'beggar-thy-neighbor'
policies and expect continued financing by importing countries with the highest unemployment in over a generation."[27]

It was in the context of a growing perception of the failure of the existing
strategy to solve the debt crisis and increasing domestic pressure to rein in competition from developing countries that U.S. Secretary of the Treasury James A.

---

23. "The Role of the Fund in Assisting Members with Commercial Banks and Official Creditors," July 23, 1985, EBS/85/173, 3, IMF Archives.
24. Boughton, *Silent Revolution*, 418.
25. Krueger, "Debt, Capital Flows, and LDC Growth," 162.
26. Bogdanowicz-Bindert, "Debt Crisis," 33.
27. R. T. McNamar, "The International Debt Problem: Recent Progress and Future Ideas"
(speech delivered at the Davos Symposium, Davos, Switzerland, January 30, 1984).

Baker III unveiled a new strategy for dealing with the debt of developing countries to the governors of the IMF and the World Bank in Seoul, South Korea, on October 8, 1985. The goal of the Baker Plan was to induce heavily indebted developing countries to enact sweeping promarket economic reforms that would integrate them more tightly into the world economy. In exchange, multilateral development agencies and commercial banks would increase loans by roughly US$26 billion over the next three years.[28] The Baker Plan was a mixed bag for Argentina. It gave legitimacy to Argentina's claim that it would be impossible to overcome the crisis without concessions on the part of the banks and easier access to new loans. At the same time, by making market-oriented reform a precondition of these loans, it aroused suspicion concerning the motives behind it. The financial press in Buenos Aires asked in late 1985 whether the Baker Plan was a victory for debtor countries or just another imposition of conditions by the creditor countries.[29] The U.S. Embassy also reported that large segments of the ruling UCR and the opposition Peronists opposed the Baker Plan because of the provisions to liberalize the economy as a precondition for renewed lending.[30]

The success of the Austral Plan, while boosting the popularity of Alfonsín and Sourrouille, also united the political opposition inside and outside government. The Austral Plan was particularly vulnerable to political pressure because the taxes, forced savings, and freezes in prices and wages that it mandated were all temporary measures. Making them permanent would require congressional approval. The Austral Plan faced opposition from Peronists in Congress and from the trade unions, who blamed it for causing a recession. The period from January to April 1986 saw two major general strikes; a third was called off only after the government promised to revise the strict wage guidelines.

Important elements of the governing Radical Party were also disgruntled by measures they perceived as going against the traditional ideological position of their party of improving real wages.[31] Indeed, despite efforts to minimize the distributive impact of the stabilization program, the Austral Plan initially resulted in an erosion of the purchasing power of salaried workers. Official estimates showed that in 1985 the real income of white-collar workers fell by

28. James Baker (statement before the Joint Annual Meeting of the International Monetary Fund and the World Bank, October 8, 1985), case files 578791, 587892, and 578793, FG012, WHORM Subject File, Ronald Reagan Presidential Library.

29. "El plan Baker: ¿conquista o imposición?" *Prensa Económica*, November 1985, 7.

30. Telegram, Buenos Aires to State Department, "Meeting Between Deputy Secretary Whitehead and Argentine Finance Secretary Brodersohn—The Need for More In-depth Dialogue," December 31, 1985.

31. Damill and Frenkel, *Malos tiempos*, 28.

23.9 percent, that of blue-collar workers by 21.8 percent.[32] Adolfo Canitrot, one of Sourrouille's closest advisers remembered, "An important reason for the failure of the Austral Plan was that the economic team lacked support within the UCR. It was a small group of seven people. The large majority of the UCR hated us." Even the president of the Central Bank, Juan Concepción, was vigorously opposed to the Austral Plan.[33]

The military was a third destabilizing factor. Alfonsín, who was intensely preoccupied with the possibility that disaffected members of the military might end the democratic experiment, was particularly vulnerable to their pressure. In late 1985, wage concessions to the armed forces triggered a rupture with the policy of wage restraint, which had been an integral part of the Austral Plan. Wages of military personnel were increased by 20 percent. However, since Alfonsín did not want to appear to be favoring the military over other public servants, he extended the wage increase to all public employees.[34] This opened the floodgates for wage demands from private and public sector trade unions, which became increasingly difficult to ignore.

Despite these setbacks, the Austral Plan still enjoyed popular support in late 1985. A poll completed in December 1985 showed that 68 percent of all respondents supported the continuation of the Austral Plan, while only 18 percent wanted to abandon it.[35] However, the IMF and the U.S. government started to doubt its sustainability. The IMF mission that visited Argentina in December 1985, concluded that Alfonsín's government had been unable to reduce the fiscal deficit by as much as had been promised in the initial stand-by agreement.[36] While inflation was falling substantially, at 2 to 3 percent per month, it still remained high by international standards and, together with a fixed exchange rate to the U.S. dollar, would necessarily lead to a substantial overvaluation of the austral and a growing external disequilibrium. The IMF concluded that the Alfonsín administration lacked the necessary political will to follow through on the program and denied Argentina's drawing under the stand-by agreement of June 1985. However, negotiations resumed in early 1986, which culminated in a new Argentine letter of intent sent to the IMF in late February.[37]

32. Epstein, "Recent Stabilization Programs in Argentina," 1002.
33. Adolfo Canitrot, interview, Buenos Aires, May 24, 2004.
34. Juan Carlos Torre, interview, Buenos Aires, June 28, 2004.
35. Telegram, Buenos Aires to State Department, "Economic Notes: Number 62," March 6, 1986.
36. "Argentina—Staff Report for the 1985 Article IV Consultation and Review of Stand-By Arrangement," February 21, 1986, EBS/86/39, 5, IMF Archives.
37. Boughton, Silent Revolution, 461.

Adverse circumstances beyond the government's control added to the fragility of the economic situation. A large part of the fertile pampas was affected by severe flooding, which substantially reduced the harvest. In addition, international prices of commodity exports fell sharply, which contributed to a deterioration of Argentina's terms of trade by some 40 percent between 1984 and 1986–87. The decline in export receipts hit Argentina hard not only because it contributed to a growing current account deficit but also because it reduced tax receipts, since the government relied on export taxes for a large part of its total revenues.[38] This effect added to the structural weakness of Argentina's finances, something the Austral Plan failed to address. Even though the tax rates were high with a value-added tax at 18 percent and the income tax rate in the highest tax bracket reaching 45 percent, tax receipts from these two taxes remained negligible and amounted to only about 4 to 5 percent of fiscal receipts.[39]

The central government also enjoyed only limited control over public expenditure. The two most important sources of the deficit were provincial governments and public enterprises. Despite the fact that the government nominally controlled the public enterprises, it oftentimes appeared that the real power dynamic was exactly the opposite. The U.S. Embassy reported that the president could appoint the managers of state enterprises but "once in place each tends to be caught up in protecting its fiefdom and becomes resistant to outside efforts which would in effect limit his financial power, or diminish the size of his domain."[40] In addition, trade unions directly threatened managers and members of the economic team who wanted to rein in their activities. Not only were public enterprises responsible for a large source of the public deficit, they also failed to provide the services the population expected. A *New York Times* reporter recounted that "the electricity fails when the weather is hot, and heating gas does not flow in the winter. You can wait 10 minutes for a dial tone to make a local call during business hours or all day to call the outside world. Mail is delivered when postal employees are not conducting one of their slowdowns, which have variously been called working 'with fallen arms,' 'in sadness' or 'with displeasure.'"[41]

Over time, Sourrouille's economic team concluded that the privatization of inefficient public enterprises was one of the few solutions to this seemingly

38. Damill and Frenkel, *Malos tiempos*, 30.

39. Bruno, *Crisis, Stabilization, and Economic Reform*, 180.

40. Telegram, Buenos Aires to State Department, "GOA Raises Pressure on State Enterprises to Become More Efficient and Illuminates a Major Struggle Within the GOA," September 6, 1985.

41. "Argentina's Woeful Services," *New York Times*, October 13, 1987.

intractable problem.[42] However, privatization faced almost insurmountable political hurdles from not only Peronists but also large sectors of the Alfonsín's own party, both of which believed that public companies were an integral part of the national patrimony and privatizing them amounted to selling out the country. The management and trade unions of the affected public enterprises also tried their utmost to undermine the government's efforts. Government officials denounced the management of the steel conglomerate SOMISA for deliberately sabotaging an effort to privatize the company in early 1986 by raising unrealistic expectations about the value of the company. While the Ministry of the Economy assessed the real value of the company to be less than US$800 million, the president of SOMISA publicly declared that the company was worth at least US$4 billion! This made it much more difficult to convince an already hostile Congress that the sale would be in the best interest of the country because selling it for a realistic price would immediately have been condemned as "giving away for free" the national patrimony.[43] Public expenditure in the provinces was also beyond control of the central government. Most of the provinces were governed by Peronist or independent provincial parties. The provincial governments were unwilling to pay the political cost of austerity and at the same time gambled that the central government ultimately could not allow them to fail.[44]

By early 1986, Sourrouille had to resort to increasingly costly short-term measures in order to keep up the image that the Central Bank was not financing the fiscal deficit with the printing press. One measure was the emission of new dollar-denominated bonds, which the Central Bank purchased immediately and accounted for as additional reserves for the emission of australes. A second measure included borrowing from provincial banks and public enterprises with the help of short-term credit lines.[45] The faltering of the Austral Plan was also reflected in increasingly tense negotiations with the IMF, which sharply criticized the authorities for failing to live up to the agreed-upon criteria. However, under heavy pressure from the U.S. Treasury, the IMF was afraid to create a negative precedent by letting Argentina fall. The Board of Executive Directors thus repeatedly granted exceptions and extensions to Argentina.[46] Instead

42. Daniel Heymann, interview, Buenos Aires, May 27, 2004.
43. José Luis Machinea, interview, Santiago, Chile, February 27, 2004.
44. Acuña, *Alfonsín y el poder económico,* 190.
45. Rodríguez, "Comentarios a la segunda parte," 246.
46. Juan V. Sourrouille, interview, Buenos Aires, June 9, 2004.

of tightening the program to maintain stability, the Alfonsín administration opted for a "flexibilization" of the Austral Plan in early April 1986 in order to reduce the severe distortions of relative prices caused by price controls and the growing political pressure to increase wages. This move further undermined the credibility of the government's commitment to price stability. A poll in June showed that support for the Austral Plan had fallen to only 20 percent and that a mere 14 percent of the respondents believed that their living conditions had improved during the previous year.[47]

By mid-1986, the conflict over the future of the Austral Plan deeply divided the ruling UCR. The populists under the leadership of former minister of the economy and now planning secretary Bernardo Grinspun and Central Bank president Juan Concepción favored lowering interest rates to stimulate the economy, but Sourrouille argued that a tight monetary policy was an essential element of the anti-inflationary program. The conflict reached its climax when Sourrouille told President Alfonsín in August 1986 that he would resign if the president of the Central Bank stayed in power.[48] The power struggle ended with a resounding victory for Sourrouille. Concepción resigned on August 22 to be replaced by José Luis Machinea, one of Sourrouille's closest allies.[49] The new president of the Central Bank significantly tightened monetary policy in an effort to reverse the rising trend of price inflation and to regain the high ground of confidence and relative price stability necessary to encourage productive investment.[50]

The year 1986 also saw the disintegration of the Baker Plan. Conservatives inside the Reagan White House had been opposed to what they saw as undue political intervention in the market mechanism from the very beginning. Pat Buchanan, the White House communications director, expressed his deep reservations directly to the secretary of the treasury. He argued that "the 'bailing in' of the Big Banks for an extra US$20 billion is not going to happen" because banks were finally recognizing the "idiocy of what they were doing in the decade lately ended." He then challenged Baker directly: "As a former banker, ask yourself: If your bank were not steeped in Mexican paper, would you lend your

47. Telegram, Buenos Aires to State Department, "The Austral Plan at Two Years—A Second Chance Coming," June 23, 1987.
48. Telegram, Buenos Aires to State Department, Treasury, "Economic Team Searches for Policy Fixes," August 14, 1986.
49. Telegram, State Department to all American Republic Diplomatic Posts, "ARA Economic Highlights, August 20–26," August 27, 1986.
50. Telegram, Buenos Aires to State Department, Treasury, "Tight Monetary Policy, How Effective for How Long," September 3, 1986.

depositors' funds to the Government in Mexico City because a Treasury Secretary urged you to do so? If the answer is no, then, what the Reagan administration is now recommending is the *political* allocation of capital, something free market governments are supposed to abhor" (emphasis original).[51]

As Buchanan correctly predicted, commercial banks were not sanguine about the Baker Plan. They hoped that stronger involvement of multilateral financial institutions would help reduce their burden and convince heavily indebted countries to pursue more thorough economic reforms. However, they were unwilling to contribute to new loans because this would only draw them deeper into the quagmire. In an internal memorandum the executive director of the World Bank, Ferdinand van Dam, warned the president of the World Bank, B. B. Conable, that the Baker Plan was likely to fail. He argued, "On the one hand, the proposal is not attractive for the major debtor countries as the suggested amount of fresh money for new investments is too small to ensure reasonable economic growth, taking into account the high debt service of those countries. On the other hand, the proposal is not attractive for the commercial banks as it fails to guarantee the servicing of debts by the major debtor countries in the years ahead."[52]

The results of the Baker Plan were therefore disappointing. One study found that exposure of U.S. banks to the fifteen most heavily indebted countries actually fell, from US$90.5 billion to US$89.2 billion, in the six months following the announcement of the Baker Plan.[53] While developing countries enacted economic reform only halfheartedly, they continued to be excluded from voluntary commercial lending. In early 1987, the IMF concluded that banks were in a more secure position than at the beginning of the debt crisis because they had increased their capital more rapidly than their exposure to developing countries' loans. Heavily indebted developing countries, by contrast, had made little progress and continued to suffer from the consequences of the debt crisis.[54]

Two additional events in 1987 exposed the failure of the Baker Plan. First, Brazil declared a moratorium on paying the interest on the US$78 billion it owed

·

51. Memorandum, Pat Buchanan, White House Communications Director to the Secretary of the Treasury, "World Bank/IMF Meeting in Soul," October 14, 1985, 34000–360820, IT023, WHORM Subject File, Ronald Reagan Presidential Library.

52. The World Bank, memorandum, Ferdinand van Dam to President B. B. Conable, "Implementing Secretary Baker's Proposal," July 28, 1986, Pasta VII, Dossiê Divida Externa, Serie Embaixador em Washington, Arquivo Marcilio Marquez Moreira.

53. Bogdanowicz-Bindert, "Debt Crisis," 41.

54. "Implementation of the Debt Strategy—Current Issues," February 20, 1987, EBS/87/38, 23, IMF Archives.

to commercial banks. This shattered the illusion that the debt crisis would somehow disappear and countries could grow out of their debt without a major debt reduction.[55] Second, in May 1987, John Reed, chairman of Citicorp, declared that his bank would increase its bad-debt reserves by US$3 billion in order to provision for possible losses from lending to heavily indebted developing countries. Consequently, Citicorp declared a loss of almost US$1 billion for all of 1987. Baker publicly praised Reed's decision as a "positive step";[56] however, behind closed doors, both Baker and Federal Reserve Chairman Volcker vigorously opposed Reed's decision, which they perceived as an attack on their authority. Reed argued that he was primarily interested in presenting a faithful picture of the bank's financial situation to its stockholders. However, bad-debt reserves were not tax-deductible under U.S. tax law, and therefore strengthened the financial position of the bank only as far as they justified a reduction in dividends to be paid to shareholders at the end of the year. Increasing the bad-debt reserves was therefore primarily a strategic move, the immediate result of which was to strengthen the bank's bargaining position vis-à-vis the Federal Reserve and the Treasury, which had pressured them to make new loans to heavily indebted countries. How could banks be asked to make new loans if they had just declared that a large part of their earlier loans were nonperforming?[57] John Reed's decision forced competing U.S. commercial banks to make similar provisions in order not to appear less responsible in the eyes of their shareholders and depositors. It thus triggered a chain reaction of banks making provisions against losses and at the same time reduced the banks' willingness to participate in internationally coordinated lending in the future, which spelled the end of the Baker Plan.[58]

Nineteen eighty-seven became the defining year of Raúl Alfonsín's presidency. All provincial governments were up for election, together with a large number of the seats in Congress. The electoral strategy of the Radical Party was based on the notion that instead of distancing themselves from the Peronists and providing a clear alternative, they would try a rapprochement, the *concertación*, with some trade unions. As part of this strategy, a powerful trade union leader, Juan Carlos Alderete of the Light and Power Union, was named minister

55. Telex do ministro de fazenda aos bancos credores, secreto, February 20, 1987, Pasta II, Dossiê Divida Externa, Serie Embaixador em Washington, Arquivo Marcilio Marquez Moreira. For reactions, see "The Burden Shifts Back to Debtors," *Washington Post*, August 16, 1987.

56. "Citicorp Faces Reality—and Finds It Doesn't Hurt," *Newsweek*, June 1, 1987.

57. John Reed, interview, New York, July 23, 2004.

58. Boughton, *Silent Revolution*, 482.

of labor.[59] This resulted in even more internal tensions within the Alfonsín government and strengthened the hand of anti-Sourrouille forces.[60] To break the political deadlock, Sourrouille launched a new stabilization program, the so-called *Australito* (little Austral), in the midst of the electoral campaign in February 1987. However, the plan contained little to convince skeptical international investors, the IMF, and a weary Argentine population that it would succeed.[61] Nevertheless, under intense pressure from the U.S. Treasury Argentina and the IMF reached a new agreement in February 1987, in which Argentina committed itself to reducing the rate of inflation to 40 percent and the balance of payments deficit to less than US$1.7 billion annually for the year 1987. In April 1987, commercial banks agreed to a rescheduling and new money loans amounting to US$1.95 billion and by the end of June, most creditor banks had agreed to participate in it. However, in an increasingly volatile and politically unstable environment, the Argentine authorities failed to live up to any of their main commitments. By June 1987, the year-to-date inflation exceeded the limit set for the entire year, which would ultimately amount to close to 200 percent, almost three times the rate of the previous year. The fiscal deficit almost doubled to 7 percent of GDP, and the current account deficit was US$4.2 billion, more than twice as high as foreseen under the stand-by agreement.[62]

The elections in early September were surrounded by the intense atmosphere of a plebiscite on the Alfonsín administration. The Justicialist Party won with 42 against 37 percent of the vote for the Radicals in Congress. Even more important, Peronist candidates won most of the provincial elections. This defeat led to a profound crisis of legitimacy for the government. Juan Carlos Torre argued that Alfonsín would probably have resigned if Argentina had been parliamentary democracy because he knew that he now lacked the political power to implement the difficult reforms that still lay ahead during the remaining two years of his administration.[63]

With the breakdown of the Austral Plan and the defeat in the congressional and provincial elections in September 1987, the disintegration of Alfonsín's presidency started to pick up speed. The last year of his administration in many ways resembled the final throes of Isabel Perón's in late 1975 and early 1976.

59. Machinea, *Stabilization Under Alfonsín's Government*, 62.

60. Torre, "Conflict and Cooperation," 81.

61. Acuña, *Alfonsín y el poder económico*, 242; Minutes of Executive Board Meeting, February 18, 1987, EBM/87/29, 3, IMF Archives.

62. Argentina—Staff Report for the 1990 Article IV Consultation and Review and Modification of Stand-By Arrangement, November 12, 1990, EBS/90/191, 39, IMF Archives.

63. Torre, "Conflict and Cooperation," 81.

Powerless to implement any drastic measures to halt the disintegration, Alfonsín's government chose policies that helped gain time but ultimately proved harmful for the country. The spiral of political disintegration added another dimension to the crisis. While inflation soared beyond 10 percent per month from February 1988 on, the precariousness of Alfonsín's hold on power became evident with another military uprising, this time at Monte Caseros.[64] The Peronist opposition saw in Alfonsín's desperate economic measures nothing but efforts to manipulate the economy in the short term in order to secure an electoral victory for the UCR's presidential candidate in the 1989 election.

The years 1987–89 were a difficult political and economic transition period in the international arena as well. The breakdown of the Baker Plan in early 1987 coincided with a change in the leadership of the IMF. Michel Camdessus, who succeeded de Larosière, advocated debt reduction for the most heavily indebted countries. However, the U.S. government and the Federal Reserve were opposed to this new strategy. Paul Volcker believed that debt relief actually hurt heavily indebted countries because it further delayed the normalization of their relationship with international banks. The nomination of Alan Greenspan to succeed Paul Volcker in August 1987 removed one obstacle to a new approach to the debt crisis. However, Secretary of the Treasury Baker continued to oppose debt relief to developing countries before the presidential election in November 1988. Baker was convinced that it was politically impossible to justify debt relief for developing countries while denying it to heavily indebted American farmers.[65] Serious preparations for a U.S.-sponsored debt relief program therefore only started after the presidential elections in November in which George H. W. Bush defeated the Democratic challenger, Michael Dukakis. The new secretary of the treasury, Nicholas F. Brady, who had replaced Baker in August 1988 and continued to serve under President Bush, presented an early version of his plan to the U.S. State Department on March 10, 1989. The Brady Plan envisioned achieving a reduction of the present value of the foreign debt of heavily indebted countries with the help of voluntary and market-based measures such as debt buybacks, exchange of old debt at a discount or at par value but with reduced interest rates for new collateralized bonds (the "Brady Bonds"), exit bonds, and debt-equity swaps.

The political deadlock in Washington cost Argentina dearly. By the time the Bush administration unveiled the Brady Plan, Argentina was already virtually

---

64. Huser, *Argentine Civil-Military Relations,* 109.
65. James Boughton, interview, Princeton, February 7, 2005.

ungovernable and the economy at the verge of hyperinflation. In early 1988, Argentina and the IMF had come close to a comprehensive agreement, which included debt reduction—a key Argentine demand—and at the IMF's insistence, a tough adjustment program. Sourrouille recalled Camdessus as having given him a firm promise that debt relief was forthcoming during a secret meeting in Madrid in February.[66] While the details surrounding these negotiations remain obscure because pertinent IMF documents have not been released, it is clear that the debt reduction never materialized primarily because of opposition from the U.S. government. Ultimately, the IMF and Argentina only agreed on new and tougher adjustment program and a reduction of the fiscal deficit to 2 percent of GDP in 1988.[67] It soon became obvious how unrealistic even these goals were. Faced with low and falling international reserves and unable to convince commercial banks to supply additional loans to finance the current account deficit, Argentine authorities concluded that they had no choice but to stop servicing their foreign debt. Sourrouille tried to keep a low profile with respect to this de facto moratorium. In April 1988, he called William Rhodes, vice chairman of Citicorp and president of the international creditor banks' advisory committee on Argentina, and told him: "Look, Bill, we are not going to pay tomorrow. We are giving you this notification. And I'm telling you that I won't publicly announce it. If you want to do it, I'm going to talk as well, but if you keep quiet, we won't talk either."[68] At the same time, members of the economic team repeatedly pointed out that the moratorium did not reflect the Argentine government's unwillingness to honor its obligations but rather a mere lack of international reserves.[69]

The moratorium ushered in the end of the long and tortuous period of cooperation between the IMF and the Alfonsín administration. In June 1988, the IMF declared Argentina noncompliant with the agreement and suspended all further disbursements.[70] Argentina would not regain access to IMF funds until after Carlos Menem had assumed the presidency a year later. Cut off from additional lending from the IMF and commercial banks, the only source of international finance remained the World Bank, which was under heavy pressure to help Argentina from Secretary of the Treasury Baker. When Baker resigned his

66. Juan V. Sourrouille, interview, Buenos Aires, June 9, 2004.
67. Boughton, *Silent Revolution*, 473.
68. Juan V. Sourrouille, interview, Buenos Aires, June 9, 2004.
69. José Luis Machinea and Juan Sommer, *El manejo de la deuda externa*, 20.
70. Boughton, *Silent Revolution*, 475.

post in August to manage George H. W. Bush's presidential campaign, Argentina lost her most important ally in the U.S. government.[71]

In mid-1988, the Alfonsín administration faced an economic and political challenge of monumental proportions. While the budget deficit again exceeded 8 percent of GDP, and inflation soared beyond 30 percent a month, the Alfonsín administration made a new attempt to stop the spiraling inflation and bring the fiscal deficit under control. The Primavera (Spring) Plan represented a high-risk, last-ditch effort to control inflation before the presidential elections of mid-1989.[72] The plan consisted of two elements: a split exchange-rate system and a complicated system of price and wage controls. The split exchange-rate system consisted of a fixed and significantly overvalued "commercial" rate for agricultural exports, an intermediate exchange rate for industrial exports, and a free exchange rate for most imports and financial transactions. The overvalued "commercial" rate would serve as an export tax on agricultural exports and was expected to yield more than 1 percent of GDP in additional revenues. The very high free exchange rate for imports and financial transactions was supposed to protect domestic industry and reduce imports while at the same time discourage capital flight.[73] The incomes policies were not unlike those pursued in previous occasions. Leading firms agreed to restrict price increases until the end of September. The government committed itself to freezing utility rates, public salaries, and the exchange rate. The pact was then extended until February 1989 with the understanding that "leading companies could adjust prices in unison with the exchange rate and utility rates."[74]

The immediate effect of the stabilization program was a significant reduction of the rate of inflation from 25 percent in July to only 6.8 percent in December. The U.S. government initially fully supported the Primavera Plan because it feared the repercussions of the election of the Peronist candidate, Carlos Menem, who was seen as an irresponsible populist.[75] However, Sourrouille failed to reproduce even the partial success of the Austral Plan. By late September, the U.S. Embassy noted that credibility of the Primavera Plan had completely evaporated. Embassy sources in the banking and business sectors explained that investors were "taking their profits while they can, ever vigilant for the first indicator—

71. James Boughton, interview, Princeton, February 7, 2005.
72. Heymann, "From Sharp Disinflation to Hyperinflation, Twice," 105.
73. Damill and Frenkel, *Hiperinflación en Argentina*, 3.
74. "Argentina—Staff Report for the 1989 Article IV Consultation and Request for Stand-By Arrangement," October 17, 1989, EBS/89/199, 3, IMF Archives.
75. Telegram, Buenos Aires to State Department, Treasury, "My Meeting with Economic Minister Sourrouille, August 27," August 29, 1988.

an upturn in inflation, problems on the debt front, a political crisis, etc.—that the tide has changed."[76] International financial markets had very little confidence in Alfonsín and his efforts to bring the economy under control. After five years of continuous struggle and a series of disappointments, they refused to give Alfonsín another chance. The *Economist* argued that "Argentina's economy is a mess" and the only reason why international creditors might continue to support Alfonsín was the fear that his successor might be even worse.[77]

With a string of bad news, the situation became critical for the embattled Alfonsín administration in January 1989. A left-wing guerrilla group attacked a military base near Buenos Aires. Around the same time, the World Bank communicated to the government that it would be unable to disburse US$350 million scheduled for the end of February because the government had failed to fulfill all the requirements of the loan. Only days later, the "steering committee" of commercial banks informed the Ministry of the Economy that further negotiations were useless without an agreement with the IMF, and they openly threatened to break off negotiations and suspend short-term trade credit if Argentina failed to pay US$300 million immediately.[78]

In the run-up to the elections, the Argentine authorities had become trapped in the logic of their election-oriented stabilization program. On the one hand, they feared that devaluing the exchange rate would invariably lead to a sharp rise in inflation. On the other hand, the defense of the overvalued exchange rate became an increasingly costly and hopeless endeavor. Interest rates were raised sharply in order to attract sufficient capital to finance the widening current account deficit and to stop capital flight. This led to a massive buildup of domestic debt. At the same time, capital flight set in and resulted in a rapid reduction of international reserves. Between January and February, the Central Bank lost some US$900 million in a futile effort to stabilize the exchange rate.[79]

With reserves running out, Argentina approached an impasse in February 1989. The precarious economic situation further worsened because of growing political insecurity surrounding the political transition. Alfonsín became a "lame duck" months before the election because he was unable to introduce new legislation. The Peronists were not the only opponents of economic reform; the

76. Telegram, Buenos Aires to State Department, Treasury, "GOA Economic Program: Monetary Policy Tested," September 28, 1988.

77. "Awaiting the Receivers," *Economist*, August 6, 1988.

78. Machinea, *Stabilization Under Alfonsín's Government*, 85.

79. "Argentina—Staff Report for the 1989 Article IV Consultation and Request for Stand-By Arrangement," October 17, 1989, EBS/89/199, 4, IMF Archives.

presidential candidate for Alfonsín's Radical Party, Eduardo Angeloz, was also afraid that new measures might undermine his electoral prospects. To make matters worse, the IMF and the World Bank insisted that any agreement needed the endorsement of both presidential candidates. This was an impossible task in a country where a large part of the political spectrum (both Left and Right) blamed the IMF for all the ills of the economy and branded ministers of the economy who negotiated with the IMF as traitors. The Peronist opposition also did its utmost to discredit the Alfonsín administration in the run-up to the elections. During a visit to the United States in late January 1989, the president of the Central Bank, José Luis Machinea, was supposedly told that Domingo Cavallo, at the time a member of Congress for the Justicialist Party and their spokesman for economic affairs, had threatened banks that a Menem administration might not honor new debt extended to the outgoing Alfonsín administration.[80] This implicit threat reinforced the populist discourse by Carlos Menem, the unpredictable "caudillo" from the northern Province of La Rioja, who talked about "wage explosions" (*salariazo*) and promised to free Argentina from subjugation to the IMF.

The uncertainty surrounding future economic policies led to a financial panic in early February 1989, often referred to as a *golpe de mercado*, a "market coup," implying that the Alfonsín government was brought down by a conspiracy of the market.[81] On February 6, 1989, the Central Bank had to abandon the defense of the austral. Within a period of five days, the dollar jumped 45 percent in the free market and the Central Bank continued to lose foreign exchange despite the fact that it had discontinued exchange intervention. Exporters were holding back receipts anticipating a sharp devaluation of the commercial rate.[82] During the subsequent days the run on banks and the austral continued. The sharp devaluation of the austral led to an explosion of the austral-value of the internal and external debt and threatened to bankrupt the Argentine government. This effect resulted from the fact that the external debt was dollar-denominated and a large part of the internal austral-denominated debt consisted of bonds, which were adjustable with respect to the unregulated austral-dollar exchange rate. While the internal debt was thus nominally in australes, effectively it had become a dollar-denominated obligation.[83] The sharp devaluation also started another vicious circle because higher prices for tradable goods spilled over into

80. Zlotogwiazda and Balaguer, *Citibank vs. Argentina*, 163.
81. Acuña, *Alfonsín y el poder económico*, 346.
82. Machinea, *Stabilization Under Alfonsín's Government*, 86.
83. Damill and Frenkel, *Hiperinflación en Argentina*, 13.

higher domestic inflation. Higher inflation, in turn, reduced the value of tax receipts. This caused a widening fiscal deficit, which reached almost 8 percent during the first quarter of the year, which fed back into higher inflation. The collapse of the austral also led to a financial crisis of the banking system, which the Central Bank sought to accommodate. Consequently, the money supply rose rapidly. The money supply M-1, which includes currency in circulation and demand deposits, increased by more than 50 percent in May alone.[84] The devaluation of the austral, far from helping the struggling economy recover, brought the country closer to the brink of economic collapse.

The breakdown of the Primavera Plan was the final blow to the credibility of Alfonsín's economic team. They lost support not only abroad but at home. Sourrouille, with an approval rating hovering around 2 percent, had become a severe liability for UCR's presidential candidate Eduardo Angeloz, who tried to distance himself from the now luckless minister.[85] Sourrouille finally resigned on February 30, 1989. The new economic team under the leadership of Minister of the Economy Juan C. Pugliese and the new Central Bank president Enrique García Vázquez was little more than a group of caretakers who hoped to keep the "the lid on the situation" until the presidential elections in May. The new secretary for economic coordination Mario Vicens declared publicly on April 16 that the present administration was not trying to lower inflation anymore but rather simply to contain it. However, the time until the elections proved to be too long and insecurity too high to avoid an economic meltdown before the polls. The austral lost more than 70 percent of its value in April and fell by another 60 percent in May. Inflation followed the exchange rate with some delay. After an inflation rate of 33 percent in April, consumers started to hoard basic staples.[86]

Pugliese's public attack against "economic terrorists" who supposedly circulated negative rumors in order to create economic chaos epitomized the desperation of the new economic team. Alfonsín allegedly even ordered the Argentine intelligence service, the Servicio de Inteligencia del Estado (SIDE), to launch a formal inquiry into the alleged conspiracy.[87] At the same time, the Argentine government repeatedly approached the U.S. government and asked it for direct

84. "Argentina—Staff Report for the 1989 Article IV Consultation and Request for Stand-By Arrangement," October 17, 1989, EBS/89/199, 6, IMF Archives.

85. Telegram, Buenos Aires to State Department, Treasury, "Sourrouille's Resignation: Political Backdrop," April 3, 1989.

86. Telegram, Buenos Aires to State Department, Treasury, "Economic Crisis Takes a Turn for the Worse," April 18, 1989.

87. Acuña, *Alfonsín y el poder económico*, 355.

aid. However, U.S. authorities did not believe lending to Argentina at this juncture would be prudent. The U.S. ambassador noted that even though Argentina asked for financial help it was unwilling or unable to adopt the economic policies needed to restore stability and a working relationship with the IMF.[88] Direct U.S. intervention also appeared politically inopportune. While the U.S. Embassy argued that U.S. interests would be best served by an Angeloz victory, it held that any interference during the electoral campaign could be used against the candidate of the UCR and therefore urged U.S. officials to proceed with the utmost care and to avoid making this stance known even as confidential background to the media.[89]

Menem's populist campaign rhetoric further heightened the sense of insecurity that permeated Argentine society in the weeks before the elections. Menem's campaign accused Alfonsín of having "definitely subjugated Argentina to the IMF, to whom we are more enslaved than ever before." It further explained that Argentines had become "morally pauperized, defrauded of its right to work, its dignity and social peace."[90] What would Menem do in case of an electoral victory? He promised to work toward a "production revolution," which would imply a change in political culture from a "culture of speculation" to a culture that fosters work and production."[91] What exactly this "production revolution" entailed, however, remained unclear. The *Economist* argued that Menem's production revolution probably amounted to little less than "pouring more money on a hyperinflation," because he promised to give employers cheap credit while raising wages for workers.[92] The U.S. Embassy called the program "irrational and confused" but was hopeful that if Menem was elected, the U.S. government would be able to convince him to adopt more responsible measures.[93]

In the weeks leading up the elections, Argentina slipped into economic chaos. The *Review of the River Plate* reported:

As we write, a number of industrial companies in different lines of business have suspended delivery of their products and a great many shopkeepers

88. Telegram, State Department to Buenos Aires, "Official—Informal," May 2, 1989.

89. Telegram, Buenos Aires to State Department, US Mission to UN, New York, "Prospects for Bilateral Relations in 1989: An Overview," January 18, 1989.

90. "Menem," *Todos,* Año 1, No 1 del 18/3 de 1988, Collection of ephemera from the Argentine national elections, 1989, Princeton University Library.

91. "Plataforma Electoral 1989: Menem Duhalde," Partido Justicialista, Collection of ephemera from the Argentine national elections, 1989, Princeton University Library.

92. "Perón with Sideburns," *Economist,* May 20, 1989.

93. Telegram, Buenos Aires to State Department, US Mission to UN, New York, "Prospects for Bilateral Relations in 1989: An Overview," January 18, 1989.

have chosen to close down because of their uncertainty about the replacement price of goods they sell. The social problem has gone beyond
the limits of the tolerable, since wages have fallen far behind soaring
prices. . . . The basic reason for this is the lack of confidence generated by
the figure of the probable future president, candidate Menem.[94]

After Menem's decisive victory at the polls, the disintegration of political
power only accelerated. The transition was scheduled to take place in early
December, almost seven months after the elections. The power vacuum in May
1989 was such that it was difficult for Alfonsín to find a new minister of the
economy to replace Pugliese. A joke circulated in Buenos Aires that President
Raúl Alfonsín had placed an advertisement that read: "Wanted. Emergency care-
taker cabinet. Previous experience unnecessary."[95] Jesús Rodríguez, who finally
assumed the post of minister of the economy, was a young congressman of the
Radical Party who fit the description. He had little previous political experience and accepted the position out of a sense of loyalty to Alfonsín and in full
awareness that he would be unable to do much to stabilize the economy.[96] The
U.S. Embassy commented that the "Alfonsín administration has a figurehead
economic team in place which is merely able to apply Band-Aids to economic
ills when radical surgery is required."[97]

Amid economic chaos and a wave of lootings of supermarkets, Alfonsín tried
to negotiate an orderly transition; however, the Peronists were hesitant to accept
the responsibility of government. The outgoing Alfonsín administration was
convinced that the delay was partially motivated by the desire on the part of the
Menem team to let the crisis "bottom out" in order to inflict the largest possible
damage on Alfonsín and to have an easier starting point for the implementation
of painful measures.[98] A worsening of the crisis was politically expedient for
the Peronists because it helped put the blame for all the economic problems on
Alfonsín, allowing the new authorities to start with a clean slate. And worsen the
crisis did. A reporter from the London *Times,* reported at the end of May 1989:

> Relatively well-off Argentines have been forced to switch their children
> to cheaper schools. Their credit cards are useless because nobody accepts

94. "Chaos Is Here," *Review of the River Plate,* April 28, 1989.
95. "Argentina Cries for an Economic Miracle," *Times* (London), May 28, 1989.
96. Jesús Rodríguez, interview, Buenos Aires, June 14, 2004.
97. Telegram, Buenos Aires to State Department, Treasury, "Argentine Economic Officials Comment on Economic Situation," June 13, 1989.
98. Jesús Rodríguez, interview, Buenos Aires, June 14, 2004.

them. Last week banks opened for two days, permitting withdrawals of only US$100 a day. For poorer Argentines, the crisis has been more painful. Many have suddenly become unable to pay rent. If evicted, their chances of finding a home are slim; landlords are demanding two years' rent in advance. In poor districts, small shops sell sugar by the spoonful and eggs in ones or twos. Muggings have increased and beggars have multiplied, as have the part-time prostitutes touting for business on the highways leading out of Buenos Aires.[99]

With an economy in disarray, Alfonsín declared martial law on May 29, suspending civil liberties for thirty days in an effort to stop the lootings and restore order in the country.[100] However drastic this step might have been, it did little to bring the economy under control. Unable to enact new policies or to come to a negotiated early transition to a Menem government, Raúl Alfonsín resigned from office and thus opened the way for the Peronists to assume the presidency on July 8, 1989.

Carlos Menem, who had run for president on a populist platform promising a confrontation with creditor banks and a "wage explosion" for workers, surprised critics and supporters alike by assuming a conservative and pro-business attitude. His first two ministers of the economy were former directors of the powerful company Bunge & Born, a symbol of aristocratic power, which had always been stigmatized by Juan D. Perón.[101] Menem's departure from the Peronist legacy went beyond the symbolic alliance with the former archenemy. He set out to dismantle the corporatist state with the help of far-reaching privatizations of public enterprises and a sharp reduction of public employment. This choice was symbolized by the selection of Jorge Triaca, the head of the plastic workers union, who had closely cooperated with the military authorities during the dictatorship, as the new minister of labor.[102] The alliance with conservative forces and the military was finally cemented at the end of December 1990, when Menem issued a presidential pardon for the leading generals of the military dictatorship, who had been imprisoned for human rights abuses.[103]

99. "Argentina Cries for an Economic Miracle," *Times* (London), May 28, 1989.
100. "State of Siege as Crowds Take to Looting Food Stores," *Latin American Weekly Report,* June 8, 1989.
101. Acuña, "Politics and Economics in the Argentina of the Nineties," 51.
102. Smith, "State, Market, and Neoliberalism in Post-Transition Argentina," 52; Jorge Triaca, interview, Buenos Aires, February 25, 2004.
103. "Menem to Pardon Former Army Rulers for Human Rights Abuses," *Financial Times,* December 29, 1990.

How could Menem, a Peronist who won the presidency on a populist platform, depart so radically from Argentine economic and political traditions?
Some observers have argued that the experience of hyperinflation made a continuation of previous policies impossible and created the political and economic
context for a sharp break with the postwar political and economic order.[104]
According to this view, hyperinflation was a "Malvinas Económicas," a turning
point for economic policymaking equivalent to the military defeat in the South
Atlantic War for military involvement in the political process. What had previously been seen as unshakable—the military's influence in politics before 1982
and the statist orientation of economic policy before 1989—suddenly appeared
indefensible.[105] According to this theory, the hyperinflation was a blessing in
disguise because it helped break the political stalemate and open the possibility for deep structural reforms.[106]

This theory has important explanatory power for the case of Argentina in
1989. The sheer economic and political chaos, which went hand-in-hand with
hyperinflation, created a sense of urgency, which opened a window of opportunity for drastic action. Furthermore, the shock of hyperinflation made it possible for politicians to appeal to patriotism to save the nation from the very
threat of disintegration.[107] These two factors helped to break the political deadlock and noncooperative behavior and created a sense of joint purpose, which
resulted in a coalition of "strange bedfellows" such as the populist Peronists and
the orthodox conservatives. The fact that Menem belonged to the Justicialist
Party, which had been traditionally hostile to economic liberalism and U.S. influence and had controlled the trade union movement, proved to be an additional boon for the incoming president. At least initially, Menem could count
on the support of the trade unions, whose opposition had severely disrupted
Alfonsín's reforms. Even as important elements of the Peronist movement grew
disenchanted with the economic and political programs Menem enacted, his
Peronist affiliation and populist rhetoric divided and weakened this opposition
because any alternative appeared even less desirable.[108]

How would Menem use his opportunity in mid-1989 to stop the hyperinflation and transform the Argentine economy? Many economists in the late
1980s had shifted their focus from seeing hyperinflation as a purely monetary

104. Bruno and Easterly, "Inflation's Children," 214.
105. "Al Lector," *Prensa Economica*, June 1989, 1.
106. Drazen and Grilli, "The Benefit of Crises for Economic Reforms," 598.
107. Corrales, "Do Economic Crises Contribute to Economic Reform?" 627.
108. Starr, "Government Coalitions," 91.

phenomenon to seeing it as more of a credibility problem.[109] They argued that hyperinflation generally coincides with a total breakdown of trust in the state as a sovereign entity. Restoring confidence in the government therefore requires more than a commitment to stop financing the fiscal deficit with the printing press. The population had been deceived too many times by governments to take such a promise at face value.[110] Instead, the government needed to attempt a fundamental reform of state and economy, which would restore trust in the state as an entity and would create the preconditions for a credible anti-inflationary program. Some of Menem's economic advisers—most notably Harvard University's Jeffrey Sachs—declared that Menem had only one opportunity to do so, "Carlos Menem is in front of a tiger with a shotgun, but with only one bullet." If Menem fails, "the possibilities of receiving external assistance will be closed for two decades."[111]

Menem's first economic plan, enacted in July and August by the two ministers of the economy, Miguel Ángel Roig—who died after a few days in office of a heart attack—and Néstor Mario Rapanelli, broadly followed these prescriptions. After a sharp devaluation of the austral from A$300 to A$600 per dollar and a series of fiscal emergency measures, he enacted a price and wage freeze supported by an agreement among labor, government, and industry.[112] The results were encouraging; inflation fell sharply from over 200 percent in July to only 5.6 percent in November, while economic activity started to pick up again. Menem tried to use this respite to achieve lasting stability with the help of the rapid enactment of deep structural reform, through the privatization of inefficient and loss-making public enterprises, and the decentralization and deregulation of economic activity in the country.[113] The Menem administration believed that only special emergency powers would guarantee the rapid enactment of the reform program. The emergency legislation consisted of two parts. The first, the Law for Reform of the State, was passed in August 1989 and gave the executive wide-ranging powers to privatize almost all public companies.[114] The second, the Administrative Emergency Law—better known as the "Dromi

109. Dornbusch, "Stopping Hyperinflation"; Fernández, *What Have Populists Learned from Hyperinflation?*

110. Llach, "La naturaleza institucional e internacional de las hiperestabilizaciones," 554.

111. Telegram, Buenos Aires to State Department, Treasury, "Economist Jeffrey Sachs Signs on with Menem's Economic Team," July 3, 1989.

112. Telegram, Buenos Aires to State Department, Treasury, "Further Details of Menem's Economic Plan," July 6, 1989.

113. Damill and Frenkel, *Hiperinflación en Argentina*, 17.

114. Smith, "State, Market, and Neoliberalism in Post-Transition Argentina," 55.

Law" after Roberto Dromi, Menem's minister of public works and services—was pushed through Congress in September 1989. It suspended all government subsidies for 180 days and allowed the government to impose important economic measures—such as the determination of wages, taxes, and tariffs—by decree.[115] Menem made extensive use of these powers, issuing more than a hundred decrees during his first three years in office—more than four times as many as had been used by all other Argentine presidents over the previous 140 years.[116]

Menem's initiatives were initially greeted with widespread support at home and abroad. The Argentine middle-class and conservative sectors supported Menem, who publicly stressed that the outgoing Alfonsín administration was solely responsible for all the economic woes.[117] One of the most outspoken conservative economists, Álvaro Alsogaray, remarked jubilantly in early January 1990: "We are abandoning the statism, the interventionism, the excessive state control, etc., to begin an economy of freedom. . . . If this measure is confirmed and is successful, it will mark a turning point between two periods. For forty years we have lived one way, and now we are going to have another way of life."[118]

Foreign observers and the U.S. government also wholeheartedly endorsed Menem. MIT economist Rudiger Dornbusch declared exuberantly: "I have to admit that, sincerely, I am fascinated, surprised, really, with President Menem."[119] In a telegram to the U.S. Embassy in early August, Secretary of State James Baker ordered the U.S. ambassador in Buenos Aires to support the Menem administration in every possible way and promised that they were "working hard to set up a Bush/Menem meeting this fall."[120] The IMF was also full of praise for the determination of the new Argentine government and for the direction of the economic reform.[121] A new stand-by agreement between Argentina and the IMF was signed in early November under which Argentina would be able to draw

115. "Economic Emergency," *Review of the River Plate*, September 12, 1989.

116. Munck, "Introduction," 11.

117. Presidencia de la Nación Argentina, Secretaría de Inteligencia de Estado, "Balance de la situación económica y social heredada de la gestión del ex presidente Raúl Alfonsín," U.S. Department of State, FOIA Released Document, July 14, 1989.

118. "Take 3 of 5—'Alsogaray on Economic Measures,' Buenos Aires Argentina Televisora Color Network in Spanish," January 2, 1990, Department of State, Foreign Broadcast Information Service (FBIS), Central Intelligence Agency, FOIA Released Document.

119. "El Diagnostico de Dornbusch: Menem debe ser inflexible pues no tendrá una segunda oportunidad," *Prensa Económica*, August 1989, 14.

120. Telegram, State Department to Buenos Aires, "High Level Treasury/State Visit," August 2, 1989.

121. "Argentina—Staff Report for the 1989 Article IV Consultation and Request for Stand-By Arrangement," October 17, 1989, EBS/89/199, 33, IMF Archives.

US$1.57 billion until the end of March 1991.[122] The Memorandum on Economic Policy stated that the new authorities would pursue an economic shock program to reduce the deficit of the public sector rapidly from 16 percent of GDP in 1989 to 1¼ percent in 1990 and to balance thereafter.[123]

The unconditional support that Menem received during the first few months of his presidency was fleeting. By December, Argentina had fallen back into the old conflictual political dynamics with each interest group defending narrow self-interests. Menem's alignment with conservative forces traditionally hostile to Peronism and his application of free market economic reforms created increasing resentment among rank and file Peronists. In early 1990, graffiti appeared on Buenos Aires walls labeling Menem a "traitor."[124] Menem vehemently defended his vision of a new economic order, which he referred to as "popular market economy."[125] In an interview with the daily newspaper *Clarín*, Menem argued that he had no choice but to reform and open the economy given the changing domestic and international context. "But, my God—what's taking place in East Germany, in Hungary, in Poland? What other path does Argentina have? Socialism? Communism? Please. I represent the Peronism of the present and of the future and they are the leaders of a Peronism that is forty years old. That is the difference."[126]

The honeymoon with the IMF was also short-lived. The staff complained, "Most of the program's performance criteria for end-December 1989 were missed by wide margins." This was particularly the case in the critical areas of growth of money supply and fiscal deficit.[127] The lack of definition of the program led to a gradual erosion of public confidence in the success of the stabilization, which was reflected in a rising black market premium on the exchange market. Between the end of September and the end of November, the exchange-rate premium increased from 10 to more than 70 percent.

The second hyperinflation started on December 10, 1989, when Rapanelli announced a new plan, which included a sharp devaluation of the commercial

122. "Argentina—Stand-By Arrangement," November 16, 1989, EBS/89/199, 2, IMF Archives.

123. "Memorandum on Economic Policy," in "Argentina—Stand-By Arrangement," November 16, 1989, EBS/89/199, 6, IMF Archives.

124. Telegram, Buenos Aires to State Department, Treasury, "The Economic Program—An Analysis," March 22, 1990.

125. Damill and Frenkel, *Malos tiempos*, 41.

126. Telegram, Buenos Aires to State Department, "Menem Reaffirms Policies in Newspaper Interview," April 3, 1990.

127. "Argentina—Review and Modification of Stand-By Arrangement," May 14, 1990, EBS/90/90, 1, IMF Archives.

rate by more than 50 percent, a drastic adjustment of prices public companies charged their customers, and a moratorium on domestic public debt.[128] Prices jumped by more than 40 percent in December alone. Under considerable public pressure from Peronist trade unions as well as agricultural and business interests, Rapanelli resigned a few days later on December 15.[129] Menem replaced him with one of his closest advisers, Antonio Erman González, who had grown up in Menem's home province of La Rioja and had served as provincial minister of the economy between 1985 and 1987 when Menem was governor. Erman González had been a spendthrift as a provincial minister of the economy and was partially responsible for the rapid rise in the number of public employees and the ballooning deficit.[130] In Buenos Aires, however, he disappointed many Peronists who had hoped that Menem would retreat from further economic liberalization. Instead, he enacted two far-reaching reforms within the first two weeks in office. The first was the elimination of price controls and the free floating of the austral, which was announced on December 18. This was widely perceived as an important break with fifty years of Argentine economic history, during which the state had almost constantly controlled either prices, or the exchange rate, or both. The second measure was made public on New Year's Day 1990. Erman González ordered the conversion of time deposits over 1 million australes (around US$550), bank reserves in the Central Bank, and short-term domestic government debt to ten-year dollar-denominated bonds, the "Bonos Externos" (BONEX), at an exchange rate of 1,830 australes per dollar.[131] The BONEX would pay 9 percent interest per year. The plan, which soon became known as BONEX Plan, had been jointly developed by Domingo Cavallo and two conservative economists, Roque Fernández and Guillermo Calvo.[132]

The BONEX Plan had three main intentions. It attempted to stop the run on banks with people withdrawing their austral deposits and converting them into dollars. With Central Bank reserves dwindling rapidly, falling by half from US$2 billion in October to just over US$1 billion in December, the government needed to act rapidly to stop the hemorrhage. When compared to paying out deposits with newly printed money and risking another explosion of hyperinflation, converting austral-denominated deposits into dollar-denominated

128. Damill and Frenkel, *Hiperinflación en Argentina*, 23.
129. Smith, "State, Market, and Neoliberalism in Post-Transition Argentina," 56.
130. Telegram, Buenos Aires to State Department, Treasury, "Provincial Financial Crisis—A Major National Issue," March 28, 1988.
131. Damill and Frenkel, *Hiperinflación en Argentina*, 25.
132. Roque Fernández, interview, Buenos Aires, July 5, 2005.

government bonds appeared to be the lesser evil.[133] The second goal was to consolidate the domestic public debt. With high and highly volatile interest rates ranging from 6 to 40 percent per month during the second half of 1989 and with most domestic financing taking place at very short maturities, the Menem administration hoped that a conversion of austral-denominated debt to long-term dollar-denominated bonds would help reduce financing costs and create predictability, a precondition for long-term budgetary planning. The third objective was to eliminate the large losses of the Central Bank.[134] The losses partially resulted from the so-called *cuenta regulación*. This system stipulated that the Central Bank would pay market interest rates on the reserves commercial banks had to hold with it. When the Central Bank raised interest rates in order to stem the outflow of capital and reduce inflation in late 1989, the side effect was that its interest payments to the banking sector and thus its operating losses soared as well. These losses were monetized and fueled the inflation in a vicious circle.[135] The BONEX Plan attempted to break this vicious circle by eliminating the remunerated reserves and other deposit requirements at the same time as the bank deposits were converted into government bonds.[136] Most immediately, however, the BONEX Plan represented yet another emergency measure that sacrificed citizens' property rights for the purpose of avoiding an imminent crisis. Depositors not only lost access to their savings, at least in the short term the plan also contained an important confiscatory element. BONEX had a substantially lower interest rate; and given Argentina's precarious finances, the BONEX traded at a discount of more than two-thirds in early 1990. This implied a large loss, especially for those who needed the money immediately.[137] This plan created a substantial popular backlash but failed to stop inflation or capital flight. By February 1990, inflation again surpassed 100 percent while the value of the austral fell from two thousand per dollar to almost six thousand.[138]

Reform attempts during the subsequent months concentrated on the privatization of public enterprises. The administration hoped that this could help reduce the fiscal deficit. In the short term, privatization receipts would help

133. Ibid.
134. International Monetary Fund, Independent Evaluation Office, *The IMF and Argentina, 1991–2001*, 78.
135. Starr, "Government Coalitions," 91.
136. Roque Fernández, interview, Buenos Aires, July 5, 2005.
137. Argentina—Recent Economic Developments, November 26, 1990, SM/90/221, 37, IMF Archives.
138. "Argentina—Staff Report for the 1990 Article IV Consultation and Review and Modification of Stand-By Arrangement," November 12, 1990, EBS/90/191, 3, IMF Archives.

finance the current fiscal outlays and reduce some of the foreign debt. In the long term, privatization would eliminate the fiscal burden that the losses of public enterprises represented.[139] Privatizations were presented as an essential part of the structural reform because privatized companies were supposedly more dynamic and would help Argentina modernize. The IMF fully supported these measures and estimated that privatizations would help reduce Argentina's external debt by more than US$7 billion. In addition, it was expected that the newly privatized companies would attract new foreign direct investment of up to US$8.5 billion over the next several years.[140]

Privatizations initially focused on two large public enterprises, namely the telephone company (ENTel) and the national airline (Aerolíneas Argentineas). Privatizations faced many problems. Since Argentina was considered a risky country to do business in and public companies were notoriously badly managed, dominated by powerful trade unions, and in need of large investments, investors were hesitant to bid for them.[141] Not surprisingly, the most important international investors were banks with large outstanding loans to the Argentine government, which hoped to use the instrument of debt-equity swaps in order to convert their loans into equity participations of newly privatized companies. However, banks could not purchase the public enterprises by themselves because they lacked local expertise and technical knowledge.[142] Consequently, most public enterprises were purchased by consortia consisting of one or more international banks, a multinational company with specialized knowledge in the business, and a powerful local *grupo*—such as Pérez Companc, Bunge & Born, Techint, and Macri—many of which had benefited handsomely from the government bailouts during the early 1980s. Aerolíneas Argentinas was purchased by a consortium consisting of Chase Manhattan, First National Bank of Boston, Spain's Iberia, and the Argentine group Cielos del Sur for US$260 million in cash and US$1,610 million in canceled debt.[143] ENTel was split in two parts in order to foster competition in the telecommunication sector. Spanish Telefónica in a consortium with Techint, Banco Río, and Citicorp purchased the part of ENTel that served the southern half of the country, a consortium consisting of the Italian STET, France Telecom, Morgan Guaranty Trust, and the Argentine

139. World Bank, *Argentina's Privatization Program*, 2.
140. Argentina—Recent Economic Developments, November 26, 1990, SM/90/221, 40, IMF Archives.
141. World Bank, *Argentina's Privatization Program*, 3.
142. John Reed, interview, New York, July 23, 2004.
143. World Bank, *Argentina's Privatization Program*, 14.

group Pérez Companc the part that served the northern half of the country.[144] The sales price for ENTel as a whole totaled US$2.27 billion in cash and promissory notes as well as US$5 billion in debt.[145]

When even the far-reaching reforms were insufficient to stabilize the Argentine economy, the World Bank concluded in 1990 that a successful stabilization program required more than a strong commitment to economic reform. Argentina needed a fixed exchange rate as a nominal anchor in order to create sufficient credibility.[146] In late March 1991, Domingo Cavallo, who had moved from the Ministry of Foreign Affairs to the Ministry of the Economy, had come to the same conclusion and presented a weary public with a new exchange-rate-based stabilization program, the so-called Convertibility Plan. The austral would become freely convertible into U.S. dollars at a rate of ten thousand australes to the dollar and would be fully backed by foreign exchange reserves, effectively eliminating independent monetary policy.[147]

The success of the Convertibility Plan, however, was far from assured when it was enacted on April 1, 1991. Previous exchange-rate-based stabilization programs had always failed because the government had been unable to eliminate the fiscal deficit and to follow through on politically difficult reforms. The financial magazine *Review of the River Plate,* which remembered Cavallo for his controversial role in the early 1980s, argued in late March 1991, "Very few people believe that the Cavallo, or Convertibility Plan, will work."[148] The IMF also initially remained skeptical because of Argentina's history of failure to live up to its commitments.[149] The staff report for a stand-by arrangement warned in July 1991 that Cavallo's strategy represented grave risks. "The convertibility scheme can assist the authorities in their search for a rapid deceleration of inflation, but it is also evident that inflation must decline quickly and stay at very low levels if the economy's competitiveness is not to be impaired. This in turn requires that the fiscal objectives of the program be fully met."[150] Only over the course of the following year, after the first severe crisis had been weathered and after

144. Ramamurti, "Impact of Privatization," 103.
145. World Bank, *Argentina's Privatization Program,* 14.
146. World Bank, *Argentina: Reforms for Price Stability and Growth,* xviii.
147. "The Cavallo Stability Plan: Convertibility and the End to Indexation," *Review of the River Plate,* March 27, 1991.
148. "Some Reactions to Cavallo," *Review of the River Plate,* March 27, 1991.
149. Cavallo and Cottani, "Argentina's Convertibility Plan and the IMF"; Mussa, *Argentina and the Fund,* 5.
150. "Argentina—Request for Stand-By Arrangement," July 17, 1991, EBS/91/107, Supplement 1, 34, IMF Archives.

the discredited austral had been replaced by new peso notes, did the initial skepticism give way to exuberance.

During the six years between 1985 and 1991, Argentina saw more than a dozen economic programs, each of which was intended to break the inflationary dynamics, bring lasting stability, and secure a just place for Argentina in the world economy. Why did all of them fail until the introduction of the Convertibility Plan on April 1, 1991? Over the course of this period, officials and economists learned how difficult it was to break the vicious circle of political and economic instability that had given rise to high and volatile inflation in Argentina during the 1980s. For a stabilization program to succeed it needed to create confidence quickly so that the population would not speculate against its success and investors would start investing in the country again. At the same time, the economic team needed to make sure that once the inflation was sharply reduced, the government would follow through with the necessary reforms to make the stabilization permanent. This second step was generally more difficult than the initial stabilization because once at least temporary stabilization had been achieved the government would confront powerful interest groups arguing that they had sacrificed too much and now deserved special privileges. Since the population developed a tendency to second-guess economic measures in an effort to be ahead of the curve on the next devaluation or price freeze, the mere perception of a flagging of determination on the part of the government could lead to bank runs or sudden flight to the dollar. The economic problems were compounded by political instability and a constitutional order with a tendency to produce deadlocks and whose frequent congressional and provincial elections favored short-term measures. The timing and nature of many of the economic programs implemented during the period 1985–91 appeared to be more motivated by electoral considerations than by the long-term interest of the country.

How could a democratically elected government, which could not ignore interest groups and had to defend its record in short intervals at the polls, resist such pressure and create the necessary commitment to break the vicious circle? The Argentine experience during the years 1985–91 suggests that success was not simply a matter of implementing the "correct" program or a mere question of determination on the part of the president or the economic team. Programs using monetary or exchange-rate anchors and promising the elimination of the fiscal deficit and inflationary finances were implemented several times during this period but none was sustainable in the face of conflicting social demands on the government. A new social consensus on the direction in which the government should take the Argentine economy was needed for any such program to succeed. The total collapse of the economy during the hyperinflationary episodes in 1989 and 1990 discredited the old economic model, and the context of the collapse of communism and the perceived triumph of capitalism created an—albeit only temporary—consensus that a radical market-oriented reform was necessary.

8 FROM MIRACLE TO BASKET CASE, 1991–2001

President Menem still has half of his one six-year term to go.
If he and the extraordinarily skilled Minister Cavallo
continue on the path they are on now, Argentina
will truly become an economic miracle.
—CASPAR WEINBERGER, *Forbes,* November 9, 1992

Argentina lived through an unprecedented roller-coaster ride during the last decade of the twentieth and the first years of the twenty-first century. Following political chaos and hyperinflation in 1989 and 1990, the country experienced a spectacular revival starting in early 1991. With inflation disappearing almost overnight and the economy growing at the fastest pace in the twentieth century, the Convertibility Plan was hailed as one of the greatest success stories in Argentine economic history. The Argentine public was euphoric about the plan and trusted Domingo Cavallo to steer the economy in the right direction. Public opinion polls showed that Cavallo was one of the most popular politicians in late 1991, with an approval rating of 67 percent (considerably more than President Menem, who, shaken by a series of corruption scandals, had an approval rating of just over 50 percent).[1] In the middle of the economic crisis that had struck Argentina in the wake of the collapse of the Mexican peso in 1995, popular support for the minister of the economy was even more impressive. One polling institute found that Cavallo

1. "Menem's Rating Rises Despite Two Major Scandals," *Latin America Weekly Report,* December 12, 1991.

enjoyed almost 90 percent popular support for his policies in September 1995, and speculation ran high that he would succeed Menem as president.[2] The international financial markets shared this enthusiasm. In September 1992, the financial magazine *Euromoney* declared him "Finance Minister of the Year" and explained that he had managed to transform "Argentina's economy into one of the most promising sectors in Latin America."[3] The financial newspaper *Institutional Investor* echoed this assessment, labeling him Argentina's "master of reform," who had achieved not only stability but also growth and prosperity.[4] The *Wall Street Journal* referred to the Argentine "miracle" and explained that the country was experiencing a spectacular revival under the stewardship of Carlos Menem and Domingo Cavallo.[5] In the mid-1990s, some observers even suggested that thanks to Carlos Menem and Domingo Cavallo's successful reforms, the "Argentine Paradox" had been resolved once and for all. "Both the political and economic causes of the cyclical crises of Argentine political economy have been resolved for the foreseeable future. More important, the destructive dynamics that had so long existed between politics and economics, allowing problems in one to reinforce those in the other, has been broken."[6]

Only a few years later, Argentina was once again the "sick man of Latin America."[7] The economic and political crisis that Argentina experienced in 2001 and 2002 was arguably the worst since the country's independence. Over the course of two years, output fell by more than 15 percent, the Argentine peso lost three-quarters of its value, registered unemployment exceeded 25 percent, and more than half of the population of the once rich country had fallen below the poverty line.[8] The political situation was also chaotic. Argentina had five presidents over the course of two weeks in late 2001 and early 2002. The most significant of the interim presidents, Adolfo Rodríguez Saá, declared Argentina's default on close to US$150 billion in dollar-denominated obligations—the largest sovereign debt default in history—amid tumultuous celebrations in Congress just

2. "Why Argentines Cheer Man Who Hikes Taxes," *Christian Science Monitor*, September 26, 1995.

3. "Finance Minister of the Year: A Dramatic Difference," *Euromoney*, September 1992, 77.

4. "Argentina's Master of Reform—Economy Minister Domingo Cavallo's Program Has Done So Well, He's the Country's Most Popular Politician," *Institutional Investor*, May 1992.

5. "Argentine 'Miracle': Talk of Buenos Aires Is That Latest Revival in Economy Is Real," *Wall Street Journal*, September 11, 1992.

6. Erro, *Resolving the Argentine Paradox*, 223.

7. "The Slow Road to Reform," *Economist*, December 2, 2000.

8. The Argentine Instituto Nacional de Estadística y Censos de la República reported that in May 2002, 53 percent of the population lived below the poverty line. In October of the same year the figure reached an even higher level of 57.5 percent.

before Christmas 2001.[9] The crisis of 2001/2002 has resulted in a complete rein-
terpretation of the legacy of Menem and Cavallo in Argentina. Many observers
now believe that the Convertibility Plan was doomed to failure from the very
beginning.[10] Some even suggest that Cavallo had pursued a sinister plan to dis-
member the traditional Argentine economy and that the U.S. government and
the IMF had been at best accomplices and at worst major co-conspirators in
this plan.[11]

Seen in the historical context of economic policymaking under an almost
constant state of emergency, the decade of the 1990s displays some notable
departures but also important continuities with the political and economic
dynamics that had dominated Argentina since the 1970s. The Convertibility
Plan, which came into effect on April 1, 1991, succeeded in stopping hyperinflation and eliminating the persistent "culture of inflation."[12] Inflation fell rapidly from a hyperinflationary 1,300 percent in 1990 to the single digits in 1993.
The period 1991–2001 had the lowest average rate of inflation since the 1920s.
This was no small feat, since eliminating inflation had been something close to
the "holy grail" of Argentine economic policymaking for several decades during which dozens of ministers of the economy had attempted even more stabilization programs. All of them finally failed to eliminate inflation and instead
caused it to rise to higher levels than before. The achievement of defeating persistent inflation even survived the disintegration of convertibility. After the crisis of 2001/2002 many economists feared that Argentina would experience a
new spate of hyperinflation. However, subsequent governments took the utmost
care to keep this from happening. This supports the assertion that a decade of
price stability had altered the political and economic dynamics that had previously caused recurrent inflation. At the same time, the experience of hyperinflation in 1989–90 remained an important reference point, which served as a
warning to social actors not resume the distributional struggles of the 1970s
and 1980s.

Convertibility also achieved a second important goal, namely the overcoming of two decades of economic stagnation and decline. Between 1990 and 1998,

9. "Argentina in Crisis—Argentines Cheer Debt Default Decision; Payments Halted—Interim
President Announces that Savings Will Be Used to Finance Emergency," *Financial Times*, December 24, 2001.

10. Curia, *La trampa de la convertibilidad*; González Fraga, *Convertibility and the Argentine
Banking Crisis*; Schvarzer, *Convertibilidad y deuda externa*.

11. Arceo, "Hegemonía norteamericana"; Fuchs and Vélez, *Argentina de rodillas*; Galasso, *De la
Banca Baring al FMI* Minsburg and Antognazi, *Los guardianes del dinero*.

12. Smith, "State, Market, and Neoliberalism in Post-Transition Argentina," 50.

real per capita income rose by almost half. This fell short of Cavallo's bold predictions at the outset of his tenure when he promised that per capita income would more than double between 1991 and 1994 if the economic policies he proposed were faithfully implemented. Still, the period between 1991 and 1998 saw the strongest economic growth in Argentina since World War I. These observations make it difficult to dismiss convertibility as a mere fluke or even worse as an illusion built up to deceive the population, a view widely held in post-crisis Argentina.[13]

However, in many other aspects convertibility did not represent as radical a departure from the past as its protagonists had hoped.[14] In fact, it displayed many of the same flaws that had derailed previous stabilization attempts during the 1970s and 1980s. It created an overvalued peso similar to that of the *tablita* of Martínez de Hoz in the late 1970s.[15] Consequently, the mid-1990s saw a repetition of the period of *plata dulce* (sweet money) with well-to-do Argentines traveling to Miami and Europe on shopping trips and vacations. The real effective exchange rate of the peso was even higher in the summer of 2001 than in early 1981, just before the transition from de facto president Videla to Viola.[16] In both cases, the overvaluation critically contributed to a rapid buildup of foreign debt. On the one hand, the overvaluation reduced the competitiveness of Argentine producers and led to sharp deterioration of the trade balance. This occurred in 1979 and 1980 at the height of the *tablita* and again starting in 1992. On the other hand, the fixed exchange rate also created incentives to borrow in foreign currency. Interest rates on dollar-denominated debt were lower than on peso-denominated debt, and the convertibility system—like the *tablita* before—was perceived as an exchange-rate guarantee, which seemingly eliminated the risk involved in foreign exchange operations. Again, the buildup of foreign debt created a time bomb that exploded as soon as the fixed-exchange-rate system was abandoned.[17]

The debt dynamics of the 1990s displayed striking similarities to the late 1970s. However, since convertibility lasted much longer—more than ten years as compared to just over two in the case of the *tablita*—the consequences were even more damaging. Private foreign debt rose almost fourfold from US$3 billion

13. Kannenguiser, *La maldita herencia;* Tenembaum, *Enemigos.*

14. Domingo Cavallo, interview, Cambridge, Mass., April 8, 2004.

15. International Monetary Fund, *The IMF and Argentina, 1991–2001,* 3.

16. Mussa, *Argentina and the Fund,* 22.

17. Bordo, "Exchange Rate Regime Choice in Historical Perspective"; International Monetary Fund, Policy Development and Review Department, *Lessons from the Crisis in Argentina,* 34.

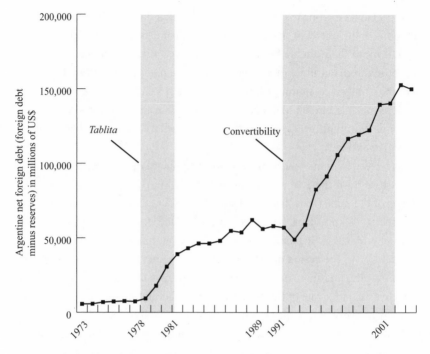

Fig. 6   Debt buildup during *tablita* and convertibility, 1973–2004

to US$12 billion during the period of the *tablita*. During the 1990s, by contrast, private foreign debt grew from a low of US$2 billion in 1990—the majority of private foreign debt had been nationalized during the previous decade—to more than US$30 billion in 2001.[18]

Public debt also skyrocketed, especially during Carlos Menem's second term in office. Fiscal policy remained the Achilles' heel of Argentine economic policymaking and significantly contributed to the rapid buildup of public foreign debt.[19] Public spending displayed a pattern similar to that of previous failed stabilization programs. The government initially succeeded in drastically reducing the fiscal deficit. In 1991, Argentina even posted a small fiscal surplus.[20] Even though part of the success was due to nonrecurring events such as privatizations or proceeds from the Brady Bond restructuring, many observers believed that Argentina had finally broken with its fiscally irresponsible past. However,

18. World Bank, World Development Indicator database for private, nonguaranteed debt (DoD, current U.S.$) (accessed March 18, 2005).
19. Mussa, *Argentina and the Fund,* 10.
20. Teijeiro, "Una vez más," 3.

it subsequently became obvious that the commitment to fiscal restraint was only superficial. As soon as improved conditions allowed for increased spending, the Menem administration and many provincial governments eagerly took advantage of this opportunity. Consequently, public foreign debt almost doubled from US$50 billion to more than US$90 billion between 1994 and 1999.[21] Despite solid economic growth, the debt to GDP ratio of the Argentine government rose from 29.2 to 41.4 percent, the most rapid growth since 1980.[22]

The Menem administration tried to hide the fiscal irresponsibility and the rapid buildup of debt because they feared that a large fiscal deficit might undermine investors' confidence, which they saw as crucial for the success of the program. They used various strategies to conceal the real expenditures. For example, revenues from the privatizations of public companies were counted as current income, while payments, which were realized with bonds and the capitalization of interest payments on outstanding debt, were not counted as current expenditure. Similarly, the central government failed to report deficits of provincial governments for which it would ultimately take responsibility. Mario Teijeiro calculated that the difference between the "official" and adjusted deficit amounted to more than US$75 billion over the period between 1991 and 2000 and that far from the rhetoric of orthodoxy of the Menem administration, the fiscal deficit amounted to between 4 and 6 percent of GDP throughout most of the 1990s.[23]

Similar to the 1970s, an external economic environment of low interest rates and abundant credit greatly facilitated fiscal irresponsibility and rising private consumption and investment. Interest rates on world financial markets fell sharply in the early 1990s. The London interbank interest rate (LIBOR) for loans of 180 days fell to just over 3 percent in 1992 from close to 9 percent in 1989 and 1990.[24] At the same time, following the various Brady deals, which had transformed large syndicated bank loans into tradable bonds, investors started regaining confidence in developing countries. The recent debt crisis suddenly seemed almost forgotten as countries that had been considered bankrupt just a couple of years earlier reinvented themselves as "emerging markets" and as such were valued customers for banks and an important destination for private foreign direct investment. In late 1991, the weekly magazine *Business Week* titled its

21. World Bank, World Development Indicator database for public and publicly guaranteed (PPG) debt (DoD, current U.S.$) (accessed March 18, 2005).

22. Mussa, *Argentina and the Fund.*

23. Teijeiro, "Una vez más."

24. The 180-day London Interbank Offered Rate, código 1K032, DataFIEL (accessed September 9, 2003).

analysis exuberantly, "From Bolsa to Bolsa, there's Plenty of Salsa."[25] Even the *Economist* observed that after a decade of disenchantment, investors were "falling in love again" with Latin American countries.[26] The optimism of the "emerging market" boom was reflected in much lower interest rate premiums that developing countries had to pay when they issued bonds on international financial markets.[27] Argentina benefited greatly from the optimistic investor climate. According to IMF estimates, it received US$100 billion in *net* capital inflows, including over US$60 billion in *gross* foreign direct investments.[28] However, at the same time as Argentina benefited from additional capital inflows, it also again exposed itself to the whim of international financial markets, which could reverse capital flows at the touch of a button.[29]

In a striking similarity to the crisis of the *tablita* in early 1981, international observers and financial markets did not waver in their support for the country when convertibility started to show serious strains in the second half of the 1990s. In 1996, Goldman, Sachs & Company sent a report to its clients titled "A Bravo New World," praising Menem for the successful stabilization of the economy and steadfast liberalization even in the face of contagion from the Mexican Crisis of 1994–95.[30] In early January 1998, the Union Bank of Switzerland argued in an analysis of the political and economic situation that Argentina's economy was in good shape. "Real GDP growth has been even more robust than expected, with increased lending activity fuelling a broader household recovery. Consumer price inflation remains benign, and few question the commitment of President Carlos Menem (or that of most political opponents) to the Convertibility Plan."[31]

The IMF also publicly supported Argentina as "exemplary" for how developing countries should manage their economies. At a press conference in October 1998, Michel Camdessus, managing director of the IMF at the time, stated, "Clearly, Argentina has a story to tell the world: a story which is about the importance of fiscal discipline, of structural change, and of monetary policy

25. "From Bolsa to Bolsa, There's Plenty of Salsa," *Business Week*, December 30, 1991.

26. "Falling in Love Again," *Economist*, August 22, 1992; "After a Decade, Bankers Say 'Adios' to Latin Debt Crisis," *ABA Banking Journal*, July 1992.

27. Powell, "Argentina's Avoidable Crisis," 4; Dominguez and Tesar, "International Borrowing and Macroeconomic Performance in Argentina," 39.

28. International Monetary Fund, *The IMF and Argentina, 1991–2001*, 11.

29. Guidotti, Sturzenegger, and Villar, "On the Consequences of Sudden Stops."

30. "Argentina Didn't Fall on Its Own; Wall Street Pushed Debt Till the Last," *Washington Post*, August 3, 2003.

31. "Argentina," *Union Bank of Switzerland New Horizon Economies*, January 1, 1998, 47.

rigorously maintained."[32] A week later, Carlos Menem had the rare privilege to follow Bill Clinton as the second speaker to address the annual meeting of the governors of the IMF and the World Bank in Washington, D.C. Menem visibly enjoyed the international recognition of his achievements. Without a hint of irony, he explained that Argentina had "restored our society's ethical values. . . . We definitely eradicated systemic corruption on the part of government employees' exercising arbitrary regulatory power." He attributed the "absolute economic miracle" to his political will to undertake the reforms and a broad social consensus in favor of deep structural reforms.[33]

However, the IMF's public support for Argentina was only a small part of their complicated interaction during this period. In fact, the behavior of the IMF during the 1990s resembled its behavior during the *tablita* of Minister of the Economy José Alfredo Martínez de Hoz between 1978 and 1981. The IMF was initially skeptical with respect to the sustainability of a fixed-exchange-rate regime. Once the program was in place, the IMF privately warned the Argentine authorities that fiscal and monetary policy needed to be tightly controlled. However, as long as international financial markets continued to lend money freely, the Argentine authorities had no need to follow the IMF's advice. This is also what happened during the last years of the Menem administration. Teresa Ter-Minassian, the deputy director of the Western Hemisphere Department of the IMF, started to worry about the sustainability of Argentina's fixed-exchange-rate regime in early 1997. Consequently, the IMF tried to pressure the Menem administration to reduce spending and better control the provinces, which were responsible for an increasing share of the public deficit. However, Menem had no reason to pay attention to these warning signals because international financial markets continued to trust Argentina's solvency and commitment to convertibility. The financial crises, which erupted around Asia in the fall of 1997 and the spread to Russia in 1998 further strengthened Menem's hand. The IMF publicly endorsed Argentina's economic policy because it needed to support one of the few remaining "success stories" of the Washington Consensus. A public rebuke might have precipitated a run on the peso just when the IMF was seeking to calm jittery world financial markets.[34]

32. Michel Camdessus, managing director, International Monetary Fund, press conference, October 1, 1998, 9:00 A.M., http://www.imf.org/external/np/tr/1998/TR981001.htm.

33. Carlos Saúl Menem, president of Argentina, "Statement to the 1998 Joint Annual Meetings of the Boards of Governors of the International Monetary Fund and the World Bank" (delivered at the fifty-third annual meeting of the Board of Governors, International Monetary Fund, Washington, D.C., October 6–8, 1998).

34. Blustein, *And the Money Kept Rolling In (and Out)*, 56.

The crises of 1981–82 and 2001–2 were both precipitated by a sharp reversal of the international situation. In the late 1970s, the combination of the second oil shock of 1979 and the "Volcker shock" of the same year sharply raised the cost of borrowing and eventually led to a reversal of capital flows. The late 1990s saw a similar series of external shocks that affected the Argentine economy. The most important of these were the rising value of the U.S. dollar, to which the peso was pegged under the convertibility regime and the crisis in Brazil in 1998–99, Argentina's most important trading partner, and the devaluation of its currency, the real.[35]

Convertibility also resembled earlier stabilization programs. The exchange-rate-based stabilization program was enacted a few months before crucial midterm elections at a moment when Menem's popularity was waning following his failure to stop the hyperinflation, the confiscatory BONEX Plan, and a series of corruption scandals.[36] The success of Cavallo's program not only ensured an important victory for the Peronists in 1991 but also created a political environment in which Menem could do what Alfonsín could not following the success of the Austral Plan: to change the constitution to allow himself to run for re-election. His ultimate goal was to create a permanent political legacy. The constitutional amendment required building a broad coalition, which—similar to Alfonsín's attempt at *concertación* in 1986–87—led to the adoption of policies that ended up undermining the very foundation of his legitimacy, namely the success of the stabilization program. Fiscal outlays almost doubled from 35 billion to 66 billion pesos between 1991 and 1994 as Menem tried to buy off different interest groups and win the support of the opposition Radical Party.[37] His strategy worked in the short term as he managed to convince his predecessor, Raúl Alfonsín, to sign the "Pact of Olivos," named after the Buenos Aires neighborhood where the presidential residence is located. This agreement opened the door for a bipartisan compromise to change the constitution in such a way as to allow for reelection of the president while giving the minority party a stronger position in the Senate.[38] The elections were set for mid-1995, and Menem won handsomely. Easy access to credit and the fear of the consequences of abandoning convertibility became important rallying points in the presidential elections. In 1995, Carlos Menem critically benefited from the

35. Powell, "Argentina's Avoidable Crisis," 3.
36. Smith, "State, Market, and Neoliberalism in Post-Transition Argentina," 63.
37. Teijeiro, "Una vez más," 3.
38. "Argentina Set to Cut President's Power, Permit Reelection," *Christian Science Monitor,* December 16, 1993; "A Happy Menem," *Economist,* April 2, 1994.

so-called *voto cuota*, the vote of middle-class Argentines who had purchased consumer goods with payment plans and favored a continuation of Menem's economic policies.[39] In early 1997, Carlos Menem started lobbying for another constitutional amendment to allow for a third consecutive term in office (the so-called *rereelección*) and used federal spending again as a means of garnering support. However, this time he was already too weak to rally even his own party. In addition, Menem started to lose popular support over corruption scandals, which led to the electoral defeat in congressional elections in October 1997.[40]

Yet the appeal of stability and predictability remained strong, especially among the Argentine middle class. This became particularly obvious during the presidential elections in 1999. Fernando De la Rúa campaigned on a pro-convertibility platform and used his lack of charisma as proof of his predictability. His opponent, the populist Peronist candidate Eduardo Duhalde, by contrast, had proposed modifications to the fixed-exchange-rate regime and called for a renegotiation of Argentina's foreign debt. De la Rúa's victory showed that large sectors of society were afraid of tinkering with the formula that had brought them stability for the first time in decades.[41] However, the support for convertibility was built on shaky foundations. The underlying social consensus relied on the memory of hyperinflation, which had united Argentines in the early 1990s. As the decade progressed, price stability was increasingly being taken for granted, and sectoral struggles over the distribution of costs and benefits of the policy reemerged. Pamela Starr accurately predicted in 1997, "The longer Argentina lives under the Cavallo Plan, the greater the likelihood that this disjuncture between the political and economic foundations of the Argentine miracle will destroy the cornerstone of that miracle—Argentina's currency board system."[42] This effect was accentuated by the fact that the fixed-exchange-rate system had severe drawbacks for the Argentine economy. With an overvalued peso, Argentine exports became increasingly uncompetitive on world markets, and the traditional domestic industry, which had been protected from international competition for decades, was ill-equipped to cope with the onslaught of cheap imports especially from Asian and neighboring MERCOSUR countries. The currency board also made it impossible to react to external shocks with a countercyclical monetary policy. This problem became especially obvious

39. "Argentines Vote for Continued Change," *New York Times*, May 24, 1995.
40. "La justicia electoral rechazó otro recurso en favor de la reelección," *Clarín*, April 7, 1998.
41. "SURVEY—ARGENTINA: Democracy Sends Down Deeper Roots: Growing Consensus on Economic Matters Has Followed a Historic Change in Power," *Financial Times*, December 15, 1999.
42. Starr, "Government Coalitions," 86.

during the crisis of 1995 when the currency board arrangement forced the Argentine authorities to react to the spillover from the Mexican Tequila Crisis with punishingly high interest rates, which resulted in a deep—albeit relatively brief—recession.[43] Still, the number of corporate bankruptcies reached unprecedented levels during the second half of the 1990s. Between 1995 and 2001, Argentina had on average more than two thousand bankruptcies per year, almost twice as many as during the peak moments of crisis in 1981 and 1987.[44] The social consequences were also far-reaching and persistent. Unemployment rose sharply from 7 percent in 1992 to a record 19 percent in 1995 to fall only slowly thereafter. It remained at a historically high 14 percent in 1999.[45]

Not unlike the case of the *tablita* in late 1980 and early 1981, with the passing of time, convertibility turned from a confidence-enhancing into a confidence-damaging factor.[46] With a significantly overvalued real exchange rate and high dollar-denominated public and private debt, international investors and Argentines alike became increasingly jittery when the economy started slowing down in 1998–99. Since an eventual break of the commitment to the peso-dollar parity would have terrible consequences and lead to a widespread collapse of the banking system as well as a default of the Argentine government on its sovereign debt, Argentines started to transfer their money abroad, and international investors began demanding higher interest rates from Argentine borrowers to compensate for the higher risk. These higher interest rate spreads (the "country risk" factor) raised financing costs for Argentine foreign debt and rendered the debt burden increasingly unsustainable, thus creating a vicious cycle.[47]

When Fernando De la Rúa replaced Carlos Menem as president in late 1999, Argentina entered another phase of economic emergency. In early December 1999, Lawrence Summers, U.S. secretary of the treasury, visited De la Rúa ahead of the official transition of power. While he publicly stated that "Argentina has a very manageable economic situation that has to be managed," the Clinton administration was intensely preoccupied that the large external debt together with a high fiscal deficit and a sharp recession could be a dangerous trap.[48] The incoming De la Rúa administration had to simultaneously restore investors'

43. Ganapolsky and Schmukler, "Crisis Management in Argentina."

44. Total number of bankruptcies, código 3J004, DataFiel (accessed July 23, 2005).

45. World Bank, World Development Indicators database for unemployment (% of total labor force) (accessed August 30, 2008).

46. International Monetary Fund, *Lessons from the Crisis in Argentina*, 4.

47. Perry and Serven, "Argentina's Macroeconomic Collapse," 5.

48. "U.S. Treasury Briefs Argentines on Pressing Economic Reform," *Wall Street Journal*, December 2, 1999.

confidence, eliminate the fiscal deficit, and stimulate the economy. These three elements were intimately linked. Regaining investors' confidence required returning the country to fiscal health and dynamic economic growth. At the same time, lack of confidence increased financing costs by driving up the risk premium Argentina had to pay on new loans. This made fiscal stabilization much harder to achieve. Between 1996 and 2000, the interest payments on Argentina foreign debt had risen from a manageable 2.3 percent to an unsustainable 4.1 percent of GDP.[49] To make matters worse, at least in the short term, fiscal austerity and economic growth also proved to be contradictory goals. During the years 2000 and 2001, the Argentine government tried to reduce the fiscal deficit by sharply increasing taxes and lowering expenditures. However, this resulted in a deepening economic slump, worsened the already high unemployment rate, and increased public opposition to the government. This further undermined investors' confidence, as they correctly perceived that an economic adjustment consistent with the maintenance of the pegged exchange rate would be increasingly politically impossible.[50] In late November 2000, the *Financial Times* columnist Martin Wolf argued that Argentina had entered a "debt trap," where "lack of confidence [had] become a self-fulfilling prophecy of doom."[51]

The period between late 2000 and the end of 2001 presented an eerily familiar picture of economic and political disintegration. Vice President Carlos "Chacho" Álvarez resigned in early October 2000 in protest over the payment of bribes to lawmakers in Congress in exchange for support of a controversial labor reform law. The IMF had urged Argentina to implement this labor law for a long time in the hope that it would create a more flexible labor market and improve Argentina's competitiveness.[52] Álvarez's resignation created an open rupture in the coalition between De la Rúa's UCR and Álvarez's Frepaso. By this time, it was clear that Argentina would not be able to solve the crisis on its own but rather needed massive international help to avoid a complete economic meltdown. This created an impossible situation for the IMF. On the one hand, the IMF grew increasingly disenchanted with the inability of the De la Rúa administration to reduce the fiscal deficit and restore confidence and economic

49. Economist Intelligence Unit database, CountryData, annual time series, Argentina (accessed July 20, 2005).

50. Mussa, *Argentina and the Fund*, 49.

51. Martin Wolf, "Argentina and the Debt Trap—If the Country Is to Avoid Default, It Must Find a Way to Reduce Its Reliance on Borrowing at Exorbitant Rates," *Financial Times*, November 22, 2000.

52. International Monetary Fund, *The IMF and Argentina, 1991–2001*, 32.

growth. Managing Director Horst Köhler was particularly skeptical that the economy could be jump-started under the convertibility system. Under the code name "Plan Gamma," the IMF staff therefore started secret contingency planning for a devaluation of the peso and a reduction of Argentina's debt burden through some involuntary debt restructuring.[53] At the same time, the IMF's room to maneuver was extremely limited. The Argentine government had repeatedly refused to even discuss the possibility of abandoning convertibility. The IMF staff's analysis also highlighted the grave consequences of a devaluation, especially for the Argentine banking system.[54] Since the crisis was largely caused by a lack of investors' confidence, the IMF was also understandably reluctant to undermine the struggling Argentine authorities by publicly criticizing their economic policies. Anything short of unconditional support, it was feared, could trigger the very panic everybody wanted to avoid.[55]

In an effort to break the gridlock and restore investors' confidence, the Argentine government, the IMF, and various other international financial institutions agreed on a massive preemptive stabilization program, the so-called *blindaje* (armor), in November 2000. It included a pledge to give Argentina up to US$20 billion and aimed at showing investors that De la Rúa enjoyed full international support and was completely committed to economic reform.[56] However, faced with problems implementing the commitments made to the IMF, Minister of the Economy José Luis Machinea resigned in early March 2001 to be replaced by Ricardo López Murphy, a conservative economist trained at the University of Chicago. López Murphy attempted to reduce the fiscal deficit with a shock program, which included a deeply unpopular reduction of spending on education.[57] Following intense popular protests and the resignations of the remaining Frepaso members of the cabinet on March 16, López Murphy stepped down after barely two weeks in office.[58]

Domingo Cavallo, who had installed convertibility under Carlos Menem, was now called upon by Fernando De la Rúa to save the system. He was widely perceived to be the only person with the ability to save the country from certain collapse. When he returned to the Ministry of the Economy in April 2001,

---

53. Blustein, *And the Money Kept Rolling In (and Out)*, 98.
54. International Monetary Fund, *The IMF and Argentina, 1991–2001*, 36.
55. Powell, "Argentina's Avoidable Crisis," 2.
56. Machinea, *La crisis de la deuda*, 63.
57. "De la Rúa decidió sacar el ajuste por decreto," *Clarín*, March 16, 2001.
58. "Aislado y sin apoyo, López Murphy se fue tres días después de anunciar su plan de ajuste," *Clarín*, March 20, 2001.

polls showed that between 50 and 70 percent of all Argentines supported Cavallo, while support for De la Rúa was below 30 percent.[59] However, instead of saving the country, Cavallo made the crisis even worse. In another case of "escalation of commitment" similar to Martínez de Hoz's desperate attempt to save the *tablita* in early 1981, Cavallo decided to risk everything for the maintenance of his economic legacy. Already the first month in office saw two measures that critically undermined confidence in the monetary and financial system. As a first step, Cavallo announced a modification of the Convertibility Law. Under the rules of the fixed peg to the U.S. dollar would give way to a peg to a currency basket consisting of euros and dollars with equal weight under the condition that the euro and dollar reached parity. He hoped that this would help improve Argentina's competitiveness at a time when the dollar's strength hurt Argentine exporters. However, the measure completely backfired. The change did not become effective because the euro did not reach parity with the dollar until the end of 2002. At the same time, it critically undermined the credibility of his commitment to the long-standing fixed exchange rate, which had been based on the simple formula that "a peso is a dollar, and a dollar is a peso." When withdrawals of deposits obliged banks to restrict credits to remain their liquidity, Cavallo tried to push the Central Bank to relax the reserve requirements. The president of the Central Bank, Pedro Pou, resisted, and Cavallo, feeling challenged in his authority to impose new measures at will, accused Pou of corruption and succeeded in having him removed from office. This shook the very foundations of Central Bank independence, which had been chiefly responsible for the price stability during the 1990s. At the same time, relaxing the reserve requirements weakened the once robust Argentine banking system and made it much more vulnerable to the looming crisis.[60]

In order to gain time, Cavallo announced a large voluntary debt restructuring, the so-called *megacanje*, in June. Argentine bonds with a face value of almost US$30 billion participated in this debt swap, which exchanged bonds with short maturities for those with longer maturities. This swap reduced the debt-service obligations in the short and medium term by more than US$12 billion. However, the price paid for the increased breathing space was steep. The implicit interest rate of the swap was a whopping 17 percent per year and sharply increased the present value of the total foreign debt.[61] When the fiscal deficit

---

59. "Argentina Invests Its Hopes in Economic 'Super Minister,'" *Washington Post*, April 20, 2001.
60. Healy, "Politics in a Tight Fix," 163.
61. International Monetary Fund, *Lessons from the Crisis in Argentina*, 60.

continued to widen and the country risk index continued to soar, Cavallo admitted that Argentina "had no more credit" and therefore needed to restrict its expenditure to the current tax receipts.[62] The "Zero Deficit Law," which he pushed through Congress in July, stipulated that fiscal outlays (especially wages) would adjust automatically in order to keep a balanced budget. This measure, though drastic, failed to either restore confidence or balance the budget. The country risk index continued to rise, and withdrawals of deposits continued to speed up.[63]

By mid-2001, Argentina was again at the brink of collapse. Cavallo's new measures had failed to restore confidence. At the same time, the political dynamics grew increasingly polarized and antagonistic. Protesters took to the streets almost every day, and trade unions frequently called for general strikes in opposition to new austerity measures. To make matters worse, the international community was now much less committed to rescuing Argentina from collapse than in previous years. The incoming George W. Bush administration favored a much more restrained approach to international crisis management than the Clinton administration had.[64] Secretary of the Treasury Paul O'Neill had gone on record advocating a hands-off approach to international financial crises and sharply criticized the previous strategy as the IMF riding "in on its horse and throw[ing] money at everybody and the private sector people get[ing] to take their money out."[65] He made it clear that Argentina could not expect a U.S.-sponsored bailout comparable to what President Clinton had assembled for Mexico in 1994. He explained that Argentina's problems were entirely of Argentina's own making: "They have been off and on in trouble for 70 years or more. . . . They don't have any export industry to speak of at all. And they like it that way. Nobody forced them to be what they are."[66] On another occasion he vowed not to use "the money of the plumbers and carpenters in the USA who make $50,000 a year" in order to rescue Argentina.[67]

Paul O'Neill's approach was consistent with conservative ideology, which had sharply criticized the IMF during the previous decade. Proponents of this ideology argued that IMF-sponsored rescue programs to countries in financial

62. "Austerity, or Bust," *Economist*, July 19, 2001.
63. Perry and Serven, "Argentina's Macroeconomic Collapse," 23.
64. Helleiner, "Strange Story of Bush," 960.
65. "O'Neill Formula: Aid to Brazil but No Open Hand," *International Herald Tribune*, July 25, 2001.
66. "Emerging Markets: How the Bug Can Spread," *Economist*, July 19, 2001.
67. Paul O'Neill, interview with Robert Novak and Al Hunt, CNN, August 18, 2001.

distress had severe negative consequences because they induced investors to take excessive risk in the belief they would get bailed out the next time crisis struck.[68] The policy recommendations of the Meltzer Commission, which were published in May 2001, called on the IMF to stop providing an "implicit . . . guarantee for large emerging market sovereign borrowers." It concluded, "Only default and the losses that follow will create the incentives to deter speculative flows in the capital markets and impose measured borrowing and serious reform on emerging government."[69] Anne Krueger, first deputy managing director of the IMF and a staunch conservative, followed a similar line of reasoning when she publicly speculated about the development of bankruptcy-like procedures for insolvent sovereign borrowers.[70]

Despite the Bush administration's reluctance, the IMF granted Argentina an additional US$8 billion package at the end of August. It stipulated that Argentina should not only eliminate its fiscal deficit but also conduct an orderly debt restructuring. At this point, however, confidence in Cavallo and De la Rúa's ability to control events had already evaporated. Critics in the United States believed that the IMF was throwing good money after bad. Michael Mussa, former chief economist of the IMF, publicly likened the IMF program to "refinancing the Titanic after it hit the iceberg."[71] The domestic crisis of confidence in the government's ability to defend convertibility was reinforced by calls by important economists for a devaluation of the peso.[72] All these voices may have given political leaders and the Argentine public at large the impression that Washington implicitly condoned a default or at least considered it easier to bear than the tough adjustment program implemented by Cavallo and De la Rúa.

With the elections in November 2001, the country entered another phase of political and economic emergency. With former president Raúl Alfonsín, who belonged to the same party as De la Rúa, publicly speaking out against the maintenance of convertibility and even Cavallo's party, Accion por la República, opposing the unpopular government, the opposition achieved a resounding victory at the polls.[73] As a result, the last days of November saw a full-scale bank run. While interbank interest rates soared above 500 percent as banks

68. International Financial Institution Advisory Commission, *Report.*
69. Meltzer and Lerrick, "Beyond IMF Bailouts."
70. Krueger, "Sovereign Debt Restructuring."
71. Michael Mussa, "Fantasy in Argentina," *Financial Times,* November 12, 2001.
72. Ricardo Hausmann, "A Way out for Argentina," *Financial Times,* October 30, 2001.
73. "Cavallo's Party Loses Its Allies," *Latin American Regional Reports: Southern Cone,* September 4, 2001.

struggled to meet withdrawals, Cavallo tried to calm the population. In a televised news conference on November 30, he blamed "irresponsible people talking about devaluation" for the panic and reaffirmed that "people's savings are safe."[74] However, the very next day Cavallo announced that Argentines would not be able to withdraw more than 250 pesos per week from their bank accounts. This measure, quickly dubbed the *corralito,* was the spark that lit the social powder keg and precipitated the downfall of De la Rúa and the breakdown of convertibility. People reacted with outrage to what they perceived to be outright confiscation. Large numbers of demonstrators took to the streets banging pots and pans, and angry crowds looted the supermarkets in the suburbs. Others took even more desperate measures. A father of two shot himself dead in front of running cameras after recounting his family's economic woes.[75] The IMF was equally disenchanted and convinced that nothing could save Argentina anymore. On Monday, December 3, Managing Director Horst Köhler ordered the IMF mission, which was negotiating in Buenos Aires, to return to Washington immediately. Despite De la Rúa's and Cavallo's pleas, the IMF announced shortly thereafter that further Argentine drawings had been suspended indefinitely.[76]

The next few weeks resembled the final stages of Isabel Perón's presidency in March 1976 and the final weeks of Raúl Alfonsín's after the election in May 1989. While President De la Rúa lost the support of even his own party, the struggle over the future shape of the Argentine economic order following devaluation and default burst into the open. Heavily indebted businesses intensely lobbied for the conversion of dollar-denominated debt into pesos (the "pesification"), while Argentine banks called for a compulsory conversion of dollar-denominated deposits. They were particularly afraid that without such a mandatory conversion, subsidiaries of foreign-owned banks would be the only ones to survive the crisis because they could count on the support of their parent institutions.[77] Amid growing street violence, De la Rúa declared martial law on December 19, severely limiting civil liberties. However, confrontations with police continued to escalate and resulted in the death of sixteen demonstrators. Domingo Cavallo and Fernando De la Rúa resigned the following day, leaving the country in political anarchy. Argentina had no fewer than five presidents over the course of two weeks in late 2001 and early 2002. The most significant

---

74. "Argentina Appeals for Calm as Bank Withdrawals Rise," *Financial Times,* December 1, 2001.
75. "Father of Two in Suicide Protest at Argentina's Plummeting Economy," *Independent,* December 4, 2001.
76. Blustein, *And the Money Kept Rolling In (and Out),* xxii.
77. Horacio Liendo (h), interview, Buenos Aires, December 4, 2003.

of the interim presidents, Adolfo Rodríguez Saá, declared Argentina's default on close to US$150 billion in dollar-denominated obligations on December 23.[78]

On January 1, 2002, Eduardo Duhalde was the fifth president to be elected by Congress. Duhalde, who had lost the presidential election in 1999 because he failed to fully support convertibility, was now the one responsible for dismantling its remains. On January 5 and 6, the two chambers of Congress passed the "Economic Emergency Law" in extended emergency sessions while continued bank holidays brought the country to a virtual standstill. The law stipulated a devaluation of the peso and an asymmetric pesification of dollar-denominated debts and deposits. Dollar-denominated debts were converted into pesos at parity, and deposits were converted at an exchange rate of 1.4 pesos per dollar.[79] Banks were initially seen as the main losers of the scheme because their liabilities increased by 40 percent while their assets remained constant in pesos. The government, however, promised to compensate the banks for the losses with newly issued bonds backed by new taxes on exports and oil extraction.[80]

It was more than a little ironic that this scheme, which ended Cavallo's legacy, resembled his youthful efforts some two decades earlier. The new minister of the economy, Jorge Remes Lenicov, under intense pressure from large Argentine business groups, had agreed to the asymmetric pesification as a means of helping heavily indebted businesses, whose debt burden shrank dramatically as the peso fell against the dollar and inflation started to climb. Argentine savers who had continued to trust the banking system were once again the real victims of an economic emergency measure. While their savings were trapped in the *corralito* and could not be withdrawn, the peso fell to more than 4 to 1 against the dollar during the second half of 2002 while inflation picked up sharply. Savers who failed to withdraw their deposits with the help of court action or illegal schemes propagated by shady exchange houses soon saw their life savings reduced to a small fraction of their former value.[81]

The treatment of Argentina's external debt, by contrast, represented a genuine departure from previous crises. Even during the worst economic and political crises, Argentina had always tried to avoid an open break with international investors. This was the case during the run-up to the military coup in 1976, the

78. "Argentina in Crisis—Argentines Cheer Debt Default Decision; Payments Halted—Interim President Announces That Savings Will Be Used to Finance Emergency," *Financial Times*, December 24, 2001.

79. "Diputados aprobó la devaluación y el pase de las deudas a pesos," *Clarín*, January 6, 2002.

80. "Fixing the Rate, Not the Problem," *Economist*, January 11, 2002.

81. Rodríguez Diez, *Historia secreta*, 89.

South Atlantic War in early 1982, the height of the debt crisis in 1983–84, and the hyperinflation in 1989–90. Following the declaration of default in late December 2001 and the devaluation of the peso in early January 2002, by contrast, Argentina took a much tougher stance in the negotiations with international creditors, private and official alike. Negotiations with the IMF dragged on for years with Argentina progressively gaining the upper hand while constantly reminding the Washington-based institution that it had to accept a large part of the responsibility for the crisis.[82] After arduous negotiations, foreign bondholders finally agreed to an unprecedented "haircut" on their claims against Argentina. They would be paid only 35 cents on the dollar for more than US$80 billion of government bonds on which Argentina had defaulted in December 2001. This operation reduced Argentina's public debt by more than a third, from almost US$190 billion to US$120 billion. Yet it still remains uncomfortably high.[83]

Argentina also continued to follow the decades-old pattern of blaming the crisis on the previous economic and political model, and discarding it wholesale in favor of something close to the opposite. The crisis of 2001 started a new cycle of populist and antiglobalization policies. Duhalde and his successor in the presidency, the former governor of Santa Cruz, Néstor Kirchner, were not only determined to solve the crisis at hand but also to erase the legacy of Carlos Menem and Domingo Cavallo, whom they blamed for all the ills of the country. They sharply attacked the IMF and international banks for their role in destroying the Argentine economy and vowed to eradicate the legacy of a decade of *neoliberalismo*. In practical terms, this included a rejection of market-oriented economic reform and integration into the world economy, two concepts championed by Menem and Cavallo during the 1990s. Instead, they proposed the nationalization of previously privatized industries, price controls on utilities and public services, and a more active involvement of the state in the economy.[84] They also abandoned Menem's efforts to develop a more pragmatic foreign policy, which had included a close alignment—the so-called carnal relations—with the United States and constructive relations with Western Europe, epitomized by the reestablishment of diplomatic relations with the United Kingdom almost a decade after the end of hostilities in the South Atlantic. Instead, Duhalde and Kirchner chose to embrace Fidel Castro and align Argentina politically and

---

82. "Argentina and the IMF: Which Is the Victim?" *Economist*, March 4, 2004.
83. "Argentina's Debt Restructuring: A Victory by Default?" *Economist*, March 3, 2005.
84. "Argentina: Under-utilised," *Economist*, January 27, 2005.

economically with Venezuela under its populist and virulently anti-American president Hugo Chavez.[85]

The political and economic history of Argentina since the early 1990s suggests that the Argentine paradox is far from resolved. Severe crises such as the hyperinflation in 1989–90 and the economic collapse in 2001–2 temporarily succeeded in generating a new social consensus with respect to the country's basic economic and political orientation. However, the consensus is a fragile one. Unlike neighboring Chile and Brazil, where politicians of different ideologies appear to agree on the broad outlines of a national project, Argentina's social consensus is defined in purely negative terms: each administration blames all the country's problems on its predecessor. This is a recipe for continued political, social, and economic instability. If history can serve as a guide, the present social consensus around the demonization of the IMF and the United States and the rejection of globalization and "neoliberalismo" is unlikely to outlast the next crisis.

85. Castañeda, "Latin America's Left Turn."

CONCLUSION:
THE COST OF PARALYSIS

Argentina was one of the success stories of the first wave of globalization at the end of the nineteenth century. The architecture in Buenos Aires still attests to the riches that the country accumulated during the Belle Époque, when Argentines enjoyed one of the highest standards of living in the world—higher than that of Germany and Japan and much higher than that of Spain and Italy. The sense of optimism was boundless. In 1905, a visitor to Argentina commented, "In spite of its enormous advance which the Republic has made within the last ten years, the most cautious critic would not hesitate to aver that Argentina has but just entered upon the threshold of her greatness."[1] How different was the perception of Argentina at the turn of the twenty-first century. In early 2002, two eminent economists noted in the *Financial Times*, "The truth is that Argentina is bankrupt—economically, politically and socially. Its institutions are dysfunctional, its government disreputable, its social cohesion unstuck."[2] Despite the rapid economic recovery since then,

---

1. Martin, *Through Five Republics (of South America)*, 2.
2. Ricardo Caballero and Rudiger Dornbusch, "Argentina Cannot Be Trusted," *Financial Times*, March 8, 2002.

Argentina's long-term economic performance has been disappointing even compared to neighboring Brazil and Chile.

This study showed that it is no coincidence that Argentina's greatest economic success occurred during the first globalization under the gold standard at the end of the nineteenth century and its longest and most persistent decline started at the outset of the second globalization in the 1970s. One of the fundamental differences between the two episodes was that Argentina had a social and political consensus over how to respond to the international environment during the first globalization, but not during the second. During the Belle Époque, creating a consensus was much easier because the country was ruled by a small, mostly landholding aristocracy whose interests were best served by integrating the country fully in the world economy. Foreign investment in infrastructure and basic industry allowed for rapid economic expansion and the opening of new agricultural frontiers. This process was far from smooth and was accompanied by a series of severe economic crises, most notably the Baring Crisis of 1891. However, rapidly expanding agricultural exports helped service the growing debt and pay for imports of manufactured goods.[3] On the eve of World War I, per capita income in Argentina was almost four times higher than four decades earlier.

A century later, international financial markets were again awash in capital, and trade liberalization offered opportunities for countries to invest, export, and grow; however, Argentina was unable to take full advantage of these opportunities because its political system had changed radically since the heyday of the export-led economic boom of the late nineteenth century. Because no social class or economic interest group was strong enough to impose its vision of Argentina's future, it was easy for any two or more groups to join forces and derail another group's economic program. Consequently, starting in the early 1970s, Argentina became trapped in a permanent political struggle over the future course of the economy. Governments—both civilian and military—oscillated between protectionism and interventionism on the one hand and economic liberalization and opening on the other. Each economic and political crisis was met by a sharp reversal of previous economic policies. The result was a steady erosion of trust in any government's ability to keep its commitments. The long-term costs of the political deadlock were staggering. Between the early 1970s and the late 1980s real per capita GDP *fell* while Argentina assumed a

3. Cortés Conde, "Growth of the Argentine Economy."

foreign debt that exceeded US$60 billion. Only the now-discredited Convertibility Plan was able to generate an—albeit transitory—new social consensus. The origins of the deadlock over economic policy date back to two fundamental developments during the first half of the twentieth century, the political inclusion of popular sectors during the 1910s and 1920s and the discrediting of economic liberalism during the Great Depression and World War II in the 1930s and 1940s. The result was an increasing political polarization of the country combined with the emergence of a new antiliberal political and economic consensus.[4] The political and social polarization led political leaders in power to impose their political and economic model at the expense of the political enemy, who was portrayed as a traitor to the national cause and an utter incompetent. Juan Domingo Perón famously stated, "Al amigo todo, al enemigo ni justicia" [Everything for a friend, not even justice for an enemy].[5] Anti-Peronism was no less radical in its rhetoric and actions during the subsequent decades; not only did his successors ban Perón's Justicialist Party, the government of de facto president Pedro E. Aramburu even banned the very mention of his name.

The conflictual nature and the "winner takes all" attitude of Argentine society obscured a broad antiliberal consensus, which only started to unravel in the 1970s: Both Peronists and anti-Peronists distrusted democratic institutions and tried to manipulate them for their own advantage when in power while plotting against the existing order when in opposition. Furthermore, despite sharply divergent rhetoric, both Peronists and anti-Peronists also deeply distrusted free market capitalism. Important sectors of society, including Peronist trade unions, industrialists producing for the domestic market, and the armed forces, which controlled a large sector of Argentine heavy industry, believed that Argentina needed a strong presence of the state in the economy.[6] Consequently, both military and civilian governments supported the economic and political model based on a corporatist system of interest representation with state-led, inward-oriented economic policies.

The consensus started to unravel in the late 1960s and early 1970s. The changing world economy was one important contributing factor of the crisis. The breakdown of the Bretton Woods System and the Oil Shock of 1973 undermined confidence in the United States and in Western capitalism. At the same

---

4. Mallon and Sourrouille, *La política económica en una sociedad conflictiva.*
5. Perón, *Actualización política y doctrinaria.*
6. Malloy, "Authoritarianism and Corporatism in Latin America," 11.

time, the liberalization of world financial markets offered opportunities to over-come some of the existing constraints on borrowing and investment. The post-war model of state capitalism was also under ideological attack from both the Left and the Right during the 1970s. Populist and Marxist movements, which had become increasingly mobilized and radicalized in the wake of the Cuban Revolution, called for a break with the capitalist system.[7] They were inspired by Egyptian president Gamal Abdel Nasser's "Third World" strategy and called for a struggle against "Western imperialism" and for "economic modernization." They argued that this objective could be achieved with the help of more state intervention in the economy and that diversion of trade from the traditional markets in industrial countries to other developing countries could help devel-oping countries assert their economic independence.[8] Economic liberals also attacked the postwar consensus. Inspired by anti-Keynesian economists in the United States and Europe, they argued that government interventions during the postwar years had led to massive economic misallocations. One Argentine economist called Argentina's economic system "socialism without a plan and capitalism without a market."[9] The only solution, in their opinion, was to dis-mantle the corporatist state and return to the outward-oriented economic model of the late nineteenth century.

Neither of the two opponents of the postwar economic order could muster enough support to replace it with a new one. As a consequence, Argentina be-came trapped in a permanent struggle over how to adapt to the new challenges of the 1970s and 1980s. This strategic indecision was exacerbated by an almost uninterrupted series of economic and political crises, which led governments to adopt short-term and often contradictory economic measures in a desper-ate effort to gain breathing space. Between 1973 and 1991, Argentina had no fewer than thirteen presidents (including de facto and interim presidents), and the transitions generally occurred in a haphazard manner with no regard to previously established timetables and without cooperation between the out-going and incoming administrations. The turnover in the Ministry of the Econ-omy was even more staggering. Within a span of eighteen years, Argentina had no fewer than twenty-one ministers of the economy. Isabel Perón holds the sad record of having six ministers of the economy in only twenty months in office.

7. Drake, *Labor Movements and Dictatorships*, 6.

8. Juan Domingo Perón, "Modelo Argentino para el proyecto nacional," in *Obras completas*, 27:348; Subsistema Relaciones Internacionales, "Análisis de la situación estratégica regional y mun-dial," 4 (cited in full in Chap. 1, note 14).

9. Sturzenegger, *Mercado, plan, crecimiento, estabilización en Argentina*.

The political and economic instability was also reflected in rates of inflation, which were extraordinary even for a country like Argentina, which had been accustomed to high inflation throughout the postwar period.

While Argentina's neighbors Brazil and Chile faced similar challenges during the 1970s and 1980s, they never suffered from the same political paralysis. In Brazil, the military was consistently committed to a developmentalist national project and adjusted their economic policy in response to the changing international environment. In Chile, by contrast, the military government of Augusto Pinochet was unencumbered by the corporatist legacy, which weighed heavily on their counterparts in Argentina and Brazil. The largely apolitical nature of the military establishment also facilitated Pinochet's monopolization of power for more than sixteen years, a feat no Argentine or Brazilian dictator accomplished during the twentieth century. Consequently, Pinochet was able to implement a much more consistent program of market-oriented economic reform even during moments of severe economic crisis. By the time Pinochet left office in early 1990, he had effectively established a new economic consensus, which his democratic successors largely embraced.

The dramatic differences between military governments in Argentina, Brazil, and Chile strongly suggests that social and political structures in each country mattered more than the "incompetence" or hidden malicious intent of a particular economic team, as some observers have asserted.[10] In fact, this study showed that new ministers of the economy generally reacted rationally to the crisis at hand. Each time, the incoming economic team implemented stabilization programs aimed at avoiding a further deterioration of the crisis and stabilizing the power of the government, which required the protection of the interests of powerful groups. However, measures that were politically expedient and helped stabilize the economy in the short term frequently had important unintended consequences that aggravated economic problems and made necessary increasingly extreme emergency measures. Worse still, as political opponents and economic actors anticipated the pernicious effects of the short-term measures, the government's attempt to manipulate the economy for short-term gain created an explosive political and economic situation. Political groups in opposition started to block economic measures and tried to extract compromises and concessions. This was the case even during the period of most severe political repression, when the government had to face the passive resistance of

---

10. Arceo, "Hegemonía norteamericana"; Beveraggi Allende, *El vaciamiento económico de Argentina;* Fuchs and Vélez, *Argentina de rodillas;* Majul, *Por qué cayó Alfonsín.*

important sectors of society. This took the form of foot dragging on the part of a bureaucracy that steadfastly resisted attempts to streamline the public sector and refused to implement economic measures. Industrial workers used "weapons of the weak,"[11] such as sabotage and work slowdowns, known as "trabajo con tristeza" (work with sorrow) to express their discontent and force concessions. Businesses also had ample possibilities to express their grievances outside normal political channels by resorting, for example, to work stoppages, contraband, and invoicing tricks on exports in order to avoid handing over foreign exchange to the government.

Only during four periods were governments able to establish a semblance of stability which allowed for long-term planning: (1) the initial Social Pact of José Ber Gelbard under the presidency of Juan Domingo Perón, from 1973 to 1974; (2) a period of three years during the tenure of José A. Martínez de Hoz, between 1977 and early 1980; (3) the first two years of the Plan Austral during the presidency of Raúl Alfonsín, from July 1985 until mid-1987; and (4) the first eight years of the Convertibility Plan, from 1991 to 1998.

How did they manage to break the vicious circle of economic and political instability, and why did they ultimately fail to achieve stability? This study shows that the most important element was confidence in the administration based on the credibility of the economic team and its proposed measures. This begs the question of how this credibility can be established. The study highlights the importance of particular actors for the unfolding events. Ministers of the economy enjoyed considerable discretionary power to shape economic policymaking during critical junctures. In moments of crisis, the ruling group would often choose a minister of the economy based on his potential to restore market confidence. This was the case even if he did not completely share their economic ideology or fully represent their particular economic interests.[12] Once in power, the minister could use the explicit or implicit threat of resignation, which might destroy the very confidence he claimed to have built, to push through measures that ran counter to the interests of the group that had brought him to power.[13] However, the reliance on the "confidence factor" also led to the paradoxical result that ministers of the economy were strongest in times of crisis and lost power once the situation improved. This was the case with José Martínez

---

11. Scott, *Weapons of the Weak*.
12. See, for example, Schneider, "Material Bases of Technocracy."
13. For the case of José A. Martínez de Hoz, see, for example, Schvarzer, *Martínez de Hoz*.

de Hoz, Juan Sourrouille, Domingo Cavallo, and even Roberto Lavagna following the crisis in 2001.[14]

The second critical element for the creation of confidence was the existence
of political legitimacy. In each of the four periods, the government initially
enjoyed a strong—albeit not necessarily democratic—mandate, and in each
case it promised to implement a long-term program that would ensure not
only economic stabilization but also growth and development. The economic
measures enacted at the outset of each of the four periods of relative stability
were similar in so far as they not only attempted to create confidence but also
vitally depended on it for their success. The Social Pact with "voluntary" re-
straints on wage and price increases only worked as long as each actor believed
that everyone was adhering to it. As soon as discipline started to break down,
trade unions had incentives to call for higher wages and businesses to cheat on
price controls. A fixed or quasi-fixed exchange rate such as during the *tablita,*
the Austral Plan, and the Convertibility Plan only generated stability as long as
actors believed that the exchange-rate mechanism would be maintained. As
soon as confidence waned, there was a strong incentive to transfer money out
of the country in the form of "capital flight" in order to avoid the costs of
devaluation. The failure of the economic management finally also undermined
the legitimacy of the government, which in many cases led to a hasty or unconstitutional departure of the head of state and his economic team.

An additional problem plagued all of the stabilization programs implemented during this period. The government had strong incentives to renege on
its promises after convincing the public that these promises were unbreakable.
In a system of price and wage controls, governments often found it politically
expedient to grant price or wage increases to particularly powerful constituencies. After adopting an exchange-rate-based stabilization program backed by
the explicit promise to reduce the fiscal deficit and to stop financing expenditures with the printing press, governments often found it almost impossible to
resist the temptation to break the promise as soon as stability was achieved and
political pressure to stimulate the economy mounted.[15]

How could a government convince investors that it would not renege on its
commitments? Economic theory suggests that a government can achieve superior results by tying its hands and following strict rules instead of allowing for

14. "After Lavagna, an Uncertain Tilt Towards Populism," *Economist,* December 1, 2005.

15. The problem that a commitment might not be credible because the government has incentives to renege on it later is widely known as "time inconsistency." Calvo, "On the Time Consistency";
Calvo and Obstfeld, "Optimal Time-Consistent Fiscal Policy"; Fischer, "Dynamic Inconsistency."

discretionary measures.[16] This study showed that this solution might not be viable in a highly conflictual society with limited respect for institutions. Subsequent governments did not feel bound by legal commitments and decided to break the "rules of the game," violating individual property rights without hesitation during periods of economic and political emergency.

The consequences of a long sequence of unstable governments imposing short-term measures under what we might call "logic of emergency economics" were far-reaching because they critically undermined the institutional structure of the country. Douglass North famously pointed out that "it is not transport costs but the costs of transacting that are the key obstacles that prevent economies and societies from realizing well-being."[17] The destruction of trust in a government sharply raises transaction costs as companies learn to spend more money on bribes, political lobbying, and political consultants who specialize in second-guessing the government because they realize that anticipating economic measures is more profitable than productive investment and being on the wrong side of the next emergency measure can mean bankruptcy.[18]

The lack of credibility of subsequent governments' commitment to uphold property rights created an important obstacle to long-term growth. As Mancur Olson argued, successful economic development critically depends on the protection of property rights. This requires a state that is strong enough to protect its citizens from predators, and at the same time is restrained enough not to become a predator itself.[19] In Argentina, instead of protecting property rights, the state became what Carlos Escudé has called a "parasitic state," from which citizens needed to seek refuge either by asking for special favors from the ruling elite or by transferring wealth abroad.[20]

The repeated destruction of property rights prepared the ground for a system of "crony capitalism" in Argentina that haunts the country today.[21] Once economic agents no longer trusted the government commitment to uphold property rights, they became hesitant to save and invest in the country. As Stephen Haber explains, cronyism offers a second-best solution to the commitment problem. The government grants a privileged group of investors special advantages

16. Kydland and Prescott, "Rules Rather than Discretion"; Minford, "Time-Inconsistency, Democracy, and Optimal Contingent Rules."
17. North, "Institutions and Economic Growth," 1320.
18. Arriazu, Leone, and López Murphy, *Políticas macroeconómicas y endeudamiento privado*, 33.
19. Olson, *Power and Prosperity*,196.
20. Escudé, *El estado parasitario.*
21. For the most recent corruption scandals, see "Corruption in Argentina: More Brouhaha for the Government," *Economist,* July 11, 2007.

in return for a share of the profits. In this way, members of the ruling political elite benefit from the economic well-being of this group of investors and have no incentives to violate the latter's property rights.[22]

This system of crony capitalism has severe drawbacks that can partly explain Argentina's political and economic turmoil during the past two decades. It leads to misallocation of resources into sectors that enjoy particular protection through the government. Income inequality is also bound to rise between economically powerful groups with access to the government and the rest of society. Since the commitment to the protection of property rights is based on personal contacts and not on the rule of law as in countries with limited government, it is also much weaker. A change in government—either through elections or unconstitutional means—destroys the commitment to the protection of property rights. This became evident most recently during the crisis of 2001–2, where after the resignation of President Fernando De la Rúa and his minister of the economy, Domingo Cavallo, subsequent governments no longer felt bound to protect property rights, which had previously been called inviolable. Investors who anticipate this possibility will have shorter time horizons and are more likely to invest in financial assets that can be withdrawn at the slightest hint of a political crisis, rather than in physical capital such as factories or infrastructure, which have longer maturities and might be subject to confiscation.[23]

The failure of convertibility to achieve permanent stability, the chaotic political and economic transition in 2001/2002, and the high degree of corruption in Argentina at the turn of the twenty-first century are all consequences of two decades of policymaking based on the desire to avoid an imminent crisis even at the cost of a worse crisis in the future. If history can serve us as a guide, the critical test for Cristina Fernández de Kirchner, Néstor Kirchner's wife and successor in the Casa Rosada, is going to come as soon as growth slows down and sectoral interests start fighting again over scarce resources. Kirchner's public image might very well follow the same path of other Argentine politicians who achieved temporary economic stability and growth: the transformation from a savior-like figure to the devil incarnate.

22. Haber, *Crony Capitalism,* xv.
23. Ibid., xvi.

BIBLIOGRAPHY

Acuña, Carlos. "Politics and Economics in the Argentina of the Nineties (Or, Why the Future No Longer Is What It Used to Be)." In *Democracy, Markets, and Structural Reform in Latin America: Argentina, Bolivia, Brazil, Chile, and Mexico,* ed. William C. Smith, Carlos Acuña, and Eduardo Gamarra, 31–73. New Brunswick, N.J.: Transaction Publishers, 1994.

Acuña, Marcelo Luis. *Alfonsín y el poder económico: El fracaso de la concertación y los pactos corporativos entre 1983 y 1989.* Buenos Aires: Corregidor, 1995.

Adelman, Jeremy, and Miguel Angel Centeno. "Between Liberalism and Neoliberalism: Law's Dilemma in Latin America." In *Global Prescriptions: The Production, Exportation, and Importation of a New Legal Orthodoxy,* ed. Yves Dezalay and Bryant G. Garth. Ann Arbor: University of Michigan Press, 2002.

Akerlof, George A., and Paul M. Romer. "Looting: The Economic Underworld of Bankruptcy for Profit." *Brookings Papers on Economic Activity,* no. 3 (1993).

Alemann, Roberto T. "La política económica durante el conflicto austral: Un testimonio." *Anales de la Academia Nacional de Ciencias Económicas* (Buenos Aires) 27 (1982): 7–38.

Arceo, Enrique. "Hegemonía norteamericana, internacionalización financiera y productiva y nuevo pacto colonial." In *La guerra infinita: Hegemonía y terror mundial,* ed. Ana Esther and Emir Sader. Buenos Aires: CLACSO, 2002.

Argentina. Comisión Rattenbach. *Informe Rattenbach: El drama de Malvinas.* Buenos Aires: Ediciones Espártaco, 1988.

Argentina. Instituto Nacional de Estadística y Censos de la República. *La pobreza urbana en la Argentina.* Buenos Aires: República Argentina, Presidencia de la Nación, 1990.

Argentina. Junta militar. *Documentos básicos y bases políticas de las fuerzas armadas para el Proceso de Reorganización Nacional.* Buenos Aires: Junta Militar, 1980.

Arriagada Herrera, Genaro. *Pinochet: The Politics of Power.* Thematic Studies in Latin America. Boston: Allen & Unwin, 1988.

Arriazu, Ricardo Héctor, Alfredo M. Leone, and Ricardo Lopez Murphy. *Políticas macroeconómicas y endeudamiento privado: Aspectos empíricos.* Buenos Aires: GEL, 1987.

Ayres, Robert L. "The 'Social Pact' as Anti-Inflationary Policy: The Argentine Experience Since 1973." *World Politics* 28, no. 4 (1976): 473–501.

Azpiazu, Daniel, Eduardo M. Basualdo, and Miguel Khavisse. *El nuevo poder económico en la Argentina de los años 80.* Buenos Aires: Editorial Legasa, 1986.

Ballesteros, Jorge. *Actas de la Resolución causa No. 14.467 "Olmos, Alejandro S/dcia."* Buenos Aires: E-libro.net, 2000. http://www.e-libro.net/E-libro-viejo/gratis/ballesteros.pdf.

Banco Central de la República Argentina. *Memoria anual.* Buenos Aires: Banco Central de la República Argentina, various years.

Basualdo, Eduardo M., and Matías Kulfas. "Fuga de capitales y endeudamiento externa en la Argentina." *Revista Realidad Económica,* no. 173 (2000): 76–103.

Beveraggi Allende, Walter Manuel. *El vaciamiento económico de Argentina, orquestado por Martínez de Hoz.* Montevideo: Editorial Artigas, 1981.

Biglaiser, Glen. "The Internationalization of Chicago's Economics in Latin America." *Economic Development and Cultural Change* 50, no. 2 (2002): 269–86.

Bignone, Reynaldo B.A. *El último de facto II: Memoria y testimonio: Quince años después.* Buenos Aires: El Autor, 2000.

Blustein, Paul. *And the Money Kept Rolling In (and Out): Wall Street, the IMF, and the Bankrupting of Argentina.* New York: Public Affairs, 2005.

Bogdanowicz-Bindert, Christine A. "The Debt Crisis: The Baker Plan Revisited." *Journal of Interamerican Studies and World Affairs* 28, no. 3 (1986): 33–45.

Bordo, Michael D. "Exchange Rate Regime Choice in Historical Perspective." Paper presented at the Henry Thornton Lecture at the Cass Business School, City University, London, England, March 26, 2003.

Boughton, James M. *Silent Revolution: The International Monetary Fund, 1979–1989.* Washington, D.C.: International Monetary Fund, 2001.

Bouvard, Marguerite Guzman. *Revolutionizing Motherhood: The Mothers of the Plaza de Mayo.* Latin American Silhouettes. Wilmington, Del.: Scholarly Resources, 1994.

Bruno, Michael. *Crisis, Stabilization, and Economic Reform: Therapy by Consensus.* Oxford: Clarendon Press; Oxford University Press, 1993.

Bruno, Michael, and William Easterly. "Inflation's Children: Tales of Crises That Beget Reforms." *American Economic Review* 86, no. 2 (1996): 213–17.

Calvo, Guillermo. "Fractured Liberalism: Argentina Under Martínez de Hoz." *Economic Development and Cultural Change* 34, no. 3 (1986): 511–33.

———. "On the Time Consistency of Optimal Policy in a Monetary Economy." *Econometrica* 46, no. 6 (1978): 1411–28.

Calvo, Guillermo, and Maurice Obstfeld. "Optimal Time-Consistent Fiscal Policy with Finite Lifetimes." *Econometrica* 56, no. 2 (1988): 411–32.

Calvo, Guillermo, and Carmen Reinhart. "Fear of Floating." *Quarterly Journal of Economics* 117, no. 2 (2002): 379–408.

Campbell, John Coert, Guy de Carmoy, and Shin Ichi Kondo. *Energy, the Imperative for a Trilateral Approach: A Report of the Trilateral Task Force on the Political and International Implications of the Energy Crisis to the Executive Committee of the Trilateral Commission, Brussels, June 23–25, 1974.* New York: The Commission, 1974.

Canitrot, Adolfo. *Orden social y monetarismo.* Estudios CEDES, vol. 4, no. 7. Buenos Aires: Centro de Estudios de Estado y Sociedad, 1981.

Cardoso, Oscar R., R. Kirschbaum, and E. van der Kooy. *Falklands—the Secret Plot.* East Molesey, U.K.: Preston, 1987.

Castañeda, Jorge G. "Latin America's Left Turn." *Foreign Affairs* 85, no. 3 (2006).

Cavallo, Domingo. "Argentina and the IMF During the Two Bush Administrations." *International Finance* 7, no. 1 (2004): 137–50.

Cavallo, Domingo F., and Joaquin A. Cottani. "Argentina's Convertibility Plan and the IMF." *American Economic Review* 87, no. 2 (1997): 17–22.

Cavarozzi, Marcelo. "Beyond the Transitions to Democracy in Latin America." *Journal of Latin American Studies* 24, no. 3 (1992): 665–84.

Cellini, Cristina, and Susana Pombo. "Los cinco meses del Dr. Sigaut." *Estudios e Investigaciones,* no. 8 (1981): 22–24.

Centeno, Miguel Angel. "Between Rocky Democracies and Hard Markets: Dilemmas of the Double Transition." *Annual Review of Sociology* 20 (1994): 125–47.

————. "Redefiniendo la tecnocracia." *Desarrollo Económico* 37, no. 146 (1997): 215–40.

Citicorp. "Citicorp Reports." New York: Citicorp, 1982.

Coes, Donald V. *Macroeconomic Crises, Policies, and Growth in Brazil, 1964–90*. World Bank Comparative Macroeconomic Studies. Washington, D.C.: World Bank, 1995.

Cooper, Richard N. "Currency Devaluation in Developing Countries." *Essays in International Finance* 86 (1971).

Corbacho, Alejandro L., Andrés Cisneros, and Carlos Escudé. *Historia general de las relaciones exteriores de la República Argentina*. Buenos Aires: Grupo Editor Latinoamericano, 1998.

Corradi, Juan E. *The Fitful Republic: Economy, Society, and Politics in Argentina*. Latin American Perspectives series, no. 2. Boulder, Colo.: Westview Press, 1985.

Corrales, Javier. "Do Economic Crises Contribute to Economic Reform? Argentina and Venezuela in the 1990s." *Political Science Quarterly* 112, no. 4 (1997–98): 617–44.

Cortés Conde, Roberto. "The Growth of the Argentine Economy, 1870–1914." In *The Cambridge History of Latin America*, ed. Leslie Bethell. Cambridge: Cambridge University Press, 1984.

Crozier, Michel, Samuel P. Huntington, and J. Oji Watanuki. *The Crisis of Democracy: Report on the Governability of Democracies to the Trilateral Commission*. The Triangle Papers, no. 8. New York: New York University Press, 1975.

Curia, Eduardo. *La trampa de la convertibilidad*. Buenos Aires: Ediciones Realidad Argentina, 1999.

Damill, Mario, and Roberto Frenkel. *Hiperinflación en Argentina: 1989–1990*. Documentos CEDES, no. 62. Buenos Aires: Centro de Estudios de Estado y Sociedad, 1990.

————. *Malos tiempos: La economía Argentina en la década del los Ochenta*. Documentos CEDES, no. 46. Buenos Aires: Centro de Estudios de Estado y Sociedad, 1990.

Davis, Sonny B. *A Brotherhood of Arms: Brazil–United States Military Relations, 1945–1977*. Niwot: University Press of Colorado, 1996.

De Pablo, Juan Carlos. *Política económica argentina: Materiales para el desarrollo del tema según el método de los casos*. Buenos Aires: Ediciones Macchi, 1984.

De Pablo, Juan Carlos, and Roberto T. Alemann. *La economía que yo hice*. 3rd ed. 2 vols. Buenos Aires: Ediciones El Cronista Comercial, 1986.

De Vries, Margaret Garritsen. *The International Monetary Fund, 1972–1978: Cooperation on Trial*. 3 vols. Washington, D.C.: The Fund, 1985.

Della Paolera, Gerardo, Maria Alejandra Irigoin, and Carlos G. Bózzoli. "Passing the Buck: Monetary and Fiscal Policies." In *A New Economic History of Argentina*, ed. Gerardo Della Paolera and Alan M. Taylor. Cambridge: Cambridge University Press, 2003.

Della Paolera, Gerardo, and Alan M. Taylor, ed. *A New Economic History of Argentina*. Cambridge: Cambridge University Press, 2003.

————. *Straining at the Anchor: The Argentine Currency Board and the Search for Macroeconomic Stability, 1880–1935*. NBER Series on Long-term Factors in Economic Development. Chicago: University of Chicago Press, 2001.

Di Tella, Guido. "Argentina's Economy Under a Labour-Based Government, 1973–76." In *The Political Economy of Argentina, 1946–83*, ed. Guido Di Tella and Rudiger Dornbusch. Basingstoke: Macmillan in association with St Anthony's College, Oxford, 1989.

————. *Argentina Under Perón, 1973–76: The Nation's Experience with a Labour-Based Government*. New York: St. Martin's Press, 1983.

Di Tella, Guido, and Luis Justo. *Perón-Perón, 1973–1976.* Buenos Aires: Editorial Sudamericana, 1983.

Di Tella, Guido, and Carlos Rodríguez Braun. *Argentina, 1946–83: The Economic Ministers Speak.* New York: St. Martin's Press, 1990.

Díaz Alejandro, Carlos F. *Essays on the Economic History of the Argentine Republic.* New Haven: Yale University Press, 1970.

———. "Latin America in the 1930s." In *Latin America in the 1930s: The Role of the Periphery in World Crisis,* ed. Rosemary Thorp. New York: St. Martin's Press, 1984.

———. "Latin American Debt: I Don't Think We Are in Kansas Anymore." *Brookings Papers on Economic Activity,* no. 2 (1984): 335–403.

———. "Stop-Go Cycles and Inflation During the Postwar Period." In *Essays on the Economic History of the Argentine Republic,* ed. Carlos F. Díaz Alejandro. New Haven: Yale University Press, 1970.

Dominguez, Kathryn M.E., and Linda L. Tesar. "International Borrowing and Macroeconomic Performance in Argentina." NBER Working Paper, no. 11353. National Bureau of Economic Research, Cambridge, Mass., May 2005.

Dornbusch, Rudiger. "Argentina Since Martínez De Hoz." NBER Working Paper, no. 1466. National Bureau of Economic Research, Cambridge, Mass., 1984.

———. "Stopping Hyperinflation: Lessons from the German Experience of the 1920s." NBER Working Paper, no. 1675. National Bureau of Economic Research, Cambridge, Mass., 1985.

———. "The World Debt Problem: 1980–1984 and Beyond." In *Dollars, Debts, and Deficits,* ed. Rudiger Dornbusch, 131–50. Leuven: Leuven University Press, 1986.

Dornbusch, Rudiger, and Mario Henrique Simonsen. "Inflation Stabilization with Incomes Policy Support: A Review of the Experience in Argentina, Brazil and Israel." MIT and National Bureau of Economic Research, Cambridge; EPGE Fundação Getulio Vargas, 1987.

Drake, Paul W. *Labor Movements and Dictatorships: The Southern Cone in Comparative Perspective.* Baltimore: Johns Hopkins University Press, 1996.

Drazen, Allan, and Vittorio Grilli. "The Benefit of Crises for Economic Reforms." *American Economic Review* 83, no. 3 (1993): 598–607.

Eichengreen, Barry J. "Institutions and Economic Growth: Europe After World War II." In *Economic Growth in Europe Since 1945,* ed. N. F. R. Crafts and Gianni Toniolo. Cambridge: Cambridge University Press, 1996.

Epstein, Edward C. "Recent Stabilization Programs in Argentina, 1973–86." *World Development* 15, no. 8 (1987): 991–1005.

Erro, Davide G. *Resolving the Argentine Paradox: Politics and Development, 1966–1992.* Boulder, Colo.: Lynne Rienner, 1993.

Escudé, Carlos. *El estado parasitario: Argentina, ciclos de vaciamiento, clase política delictiva y colapso de la política exterior.* Buenos Aires: Lumiére, 2005.

Feitlowitz, Marguerite. *A Lexicon of Terror: Argentina and the Legacies of Torture.* New York: Oxford University Press, 1998.

Feldman, David Lewis. "The United States Role in the Malvinas Crisis, 1982: Misguidance and Misperception in Argentina's Decision to Go to War." *Journal of Interamerican Studies and World Affairs* 27, no. 2 (1985): 1–22.

Fernández, Roque B. "La crisis financiera argentina: 1980–1982." Working Paper 35. Centro de Estudios Macroeconómicos de Argentina, Buenos Aires, October 1982.

———. *What Have Populists Learned from Hyperinflation?* Working Paper 12. Centro de Estudios Macroeconómicos de Argentina, Buenos Aires, 1990.

Ffrench-Davis, Ricardo, and Ernesto Tironi. "El nuevo escenario económico internacional." In *Orden económico internacional y desarrollo*, ed. Carlos F. Diaz Alejandro, Ricardo Ffrench-Davis, and Ernesto Tironi. Santiago: Corporación de investigaciones económicas para latinoamérica (CIEPLAN), 1978.

Fischer, Stanley. "Dynamic Inconsistency, Cooperation, and the Benevolent Dissembling Government." *Journal of Economic Dynamics and Control* 2 (1980): 93–107.

Fishlow, Albert. "Flying Down to Rio: Perspectives on U.S.-Brazilian Relations." *Foreign Affairs* 57, no. 2 (1978).

———. "Latin American Adjustment to the Oil Shocks of 1973 and 1979." In *Latin American Political Economy: Financial Crisis and Political Change*, ed. Jonathan Hartlyn and Samuel A. Morley, 54–84. Boulder, Colo.: Westview Press, 1986.

Flecha de Lima, Paulo-Tarso. "Liberalism Versus Nationalism: The Prodevelopment Ideology in Recent Brazilian Political History (1930–1997)." *Presidential Studies Quarterly* 29, no. 2 (1999): 370–88.

Fontana, Andrés Miguel. "Political Decision Making by a Military Corporation: Argentina, 1976–1983." Ph.D. diss., University of Texas, Austin, 1987.

Frank, Andre Gunder. *Capitalism and Underdevelopment in Latin America: Historical Studies of Chile and Brazil.* New York: Monthly Review Press, 1967.

Frenkel, Roberto, and Jose Maria Fanelli. "Argentina y el FMI en la última decada." In *El FMI, el Banco Mundial y la crisis latinoamericana*, ed. Sistema Económico Latinoamericano (SELA), 105–61. Mexico City: Siglo Veintiuno, 1986.

Fuchs, Jaime, and José Carlos Vélez. *Argentina de rodillas: Terrorismo económico de Martínez de Hoz a Cavallo.* Buenos Aires: Tribuna Latinoamericana, 2001.

Fundación de Investigaciones Económicas Latinoamericanas (Buenos Aires, Argentina), and Consejo Empresario Argentino. *El Gasto público en la Argentina, 1960–1988.* Buenos Aires: Fundación de Investigaciones Económicas Latinoamericanas, Consejo Empresario Argentino, 1991.

Galasso, Norberto. *De la Banca Baring al FMI: Historia de la deuda externa Argentina.* Buenos Aires: Colihue, 2003.

Ganapolsky, Eduardo, and Sergio Schmukler. "Crisis Management in Argentina During the 1994–95 Mexican Crisis: How Did Markets React?" World Bank Working Paper. World Bank, Washington, D.C., 2001.

Gatica, Jaime. *Deindustrialization in Chile.* Boulder, Colo.: Westview Press, 1989.

Geddes, Barbara. "The Politics of Economic Liberalization." *Latin American Research Review* 30, no. 2 (1995): 195–214.

Gerchunoff, Pablo, and Lucas Llach. *El ciclo de la ilusión y el desencanto: Un siglo de políticas económicas argentinas.* Buenos Aires: Compañía Editora Espasa Calpe Argentina, 1998.

Goldwert, Marvin. *Democracy, Militarism, and Nationalism in Argentina, 1930–1966: An Interpretation.* Latin American Monographs. Austin: University of Texas Press, 1972.

———. "The Rise of Modern Militarism in Argentina." *Hispanic American Historical Review* 48, no. 2 (1968): 189–2005.

González Fraga, Javier. *Convertibility and the Argentine Banking Crisis.* Buenos Aires: Universidad Católica, 2002.

Grant, Michael. *The Fall of the Roman Empire: A Reappraisal.* Radnor, Pa.: Annenberg School Press, 1976.

Grinspun, Bernardo. *La evolución de la economía Argentina desde Diciembre de 1983 a Septiembre de 1989.* Buenos Aires: Ediciones Radicales, 1989.

———. "Intenciones de política económica." In *La economía que yo hice,* ed. Juan Carlos De Pablo and Roberto T. Alemann. Buenos Aires: Ediciones El Cronista Comercial, 1986.

Guidotti, Pablo E., Federico Sturzenegger, and Agustín Villar. "On the Consequences of Sudden Stops." Mimeograph. Department of Economics, Universidad Torcuato di Tella, Buenos Aires, 2003.

Haber, Stephen H. *Crony Capitalism and Economic Growth in Latin America: Theory and Evidence.* Stanford, Calif.: Hoover Institution Press, 2002.

Haggard, Stephan, and Robert R. Kaufman. "The Political Economy of Democratic Transition." *Comparative Politics* 29, no. 3 (1997): 263–83.

Hayek, Friedrich August von. *The Constitution of Liberty.* Chicago: University of Chicago Press, 1960.

Healy, Conor Nicholas. "Politics in a Tight Fix: The Role of Politics in Determining the Sustainability of Hard Exchange Rate Regimes." Ph.D. diss., Princeton University, 2006.

Helleiner, Eric. "The Strange Story of Bush and the Argentine Debt Crisis." *Third World Quarterly* 26, no. 6 (2005): 951–69.

Heymann, Daniel. "The Austral Plan." *American Economic Review* 77, no. 2 (1987): 284–87.

———. "From Sharp Disinflation to Hyperinflation, Twice: The Argentine Experience, 1985–1989." In *Lessons of Economic Stabilization and Its Aftermath: The Argentine Experience, 1985–1989,* ed. Michael Bruno, Stanley Fischer et al. Cambridge: MIT Press, 1991.

Hirschman, Albert O. "The Political Economy of Import-Substituting Industrialization in Latin America." *Quarterly Journal of Economics* 82, no. 1 (1968): 1–32.

———. "The Political Economy of Latin American Development: Seven Exercises in Retrospection." *Latin American Research Review* 22, no. 3 (1987): 7–36.

Huneeus, Carlos. "Technocrats and Politicians in the Democratic Politics of Argentina (1983–95)." In *The Politics of Expertise in Latin America,* ed. Miguel Angel Centeno and Patricio Silva. New York: St. Martin's Press, 1988.

Huser, Herbert C. *Argentine Civil-Military Relations from Alfonsín to Menem.* Washington, D.C.: National Defense University Press, 2002.

Instituto de Estudios Latinoamericanos (Argentina). *Argentina 1984: Partido Peronista: Proclamas y manifiestos de sus líneas internas.* Buenos Aires: Instituto de Estudios Latinoamericanos, 1984.

International Monetary Fund. *Annual Report.* Washington, D.C.: International Monetary Fund, 2003.

———. *World Economic Outlook: A Survey by the Staff of the International Monetary Fund.* Washington, D.C.: International Monetary Fund Publication Services, 1981.

International Monetary Fund, Independent Evaluation Office. *The IMF and Argentina, 1991–2001.* Washington, D.C.: International Monetary Fund Publication Services, 2004.

International Monetary Fund, Policy Development and Review Department. *Lessons from the Crisis in Argentina.* Washington, D.C.: International Monetary Fund, 2003.

James, Harold. *The End of Globalization: Lessons from the Great Depression.* Cambridge: Harvard University Press, 2001.

———. *International Monetary Cooperation Since Bretton Woods.* Washington, D.C.: International Monetary Fund; New York: Oxford University Press, 1996.

Kannenguiser, Martín. *La maldita herencia: Una historia de la deuda y su impacto en la economía argentina: 1976–2003.* Buenos Aires: Editorial Sudamericana, 2003.

Kapur, Devesh, John Prior Lewis, and Richard Charles Webb. *The World Bank: Its First Half Century.* 2 vols. Washington, D.C.: Brookings Institution, 1997.

Kaufman, Robert R. "Democratic and Authoritarian Responses to the Debt Issue: Argentina, Brazil, and Mexico." *International Organization* 39, no. 3 (1985): 473–503.

Kiguel, Miguel A., and Pablo Andrés Neumeyer. "Inflation and Seigniorage in Argentina." Working Paper 289, Country Economics Department, The World Bank, October 1985.

Kindleberger, Charles Poor. *Europe's Postwar Growth: The Role of Labor Supply.* Cambridge: Harvard University Press, 1967.

Kirkpatrick, Jeane. "Dictatorships and Double Standards." *Commentary* 68, no. 5 (1979).

Kornbluh, Peter. *The Pinochet File: A Declassified Dossier on Atrocity and Accountability.* New York: New Press, 2003.

Kraft, Joseph. *The Mexican Rescue.* New York: Group of Thirty, 1984.

Krueger, Anne O. "Debt, Capital Flows, and LDC Growth." *American Economic Review* 77, no. 2 (1987): 159–64.

———. "A New Approach to Sovereign Debt Restructuring." Paper presented at the Indian Council for Research on International Economic Relations, Delhi, India, December 20, 2001.

Kydland, Finn E., and Edward C. Prescott. "Rules Rather than Discretion: The Inconsistency of Optimal Plans." *Journal of Political Economy* 85, no. 3 (1977): 473–92.

Larraquy, Marcelo, Katherine Cortés Guerrieri, Guido Bilbao, María José Grillo, and Daniel Guebel. *López Rega: La biografía.* Buenos Aires: Sudamericana, 2004.

Levy, Walter J. "Oil Power." *Foreign Affairs* 49, no. 4 (1971).

Lewis, Colin M., and Nissa Torrents. *Argentina in the Crisis Years, 1983–1990: From Alfonsín to Menem.* London: Institute of Latin American Studies, 1993.

Lewis, Paul H. *The Crisis of Argentine Capitalism.* Chapel Hill: University of North Carolina Press, 1990.

———. *Guerrillas and Generals: The "Dirty War" in Argentina.* Westport, Conn.: Praeger, 2002.

Lewis, W. Arthur. "Economic Development with Unlimited Supplies of Labour." *Manchester School Economic and Social Studies* 22 (1954).

———. *The Evolution of the International Economic Order.* Princeton: Research Program in Development Studies, Woodrow Wilson School, Princeton University, 1977.

Lipson, Charles. "Bankers' Dilemmas: Private Cooperation in Rescheduling Sovereign Debts." In *Cooperation Under Anarchy,* ed. Kenneth A. Oye. Princeton: Princeton University Press, 1986.

———. "The International Organization of Third World Debt." *International Organization* 35, no. 4 (1981): 603–31.

Lissakers, Karin. *Banks, Borrowers, and the Establishment: A Revisionist Account of the International Debt Crisis.* New York: BasicBooks, 1991.

Llach, Juan J. "La naturaleza institucional e internacional de las hiperestabilizaciones. El caso de Alemania desde 1923 y algunas lecciones para la Argentina de 1985." *Desarrollo Económico* 26, no. 104 (1987): 527–60.

Lomax, David F. *The Developing Country Debt Crisis.* London: Macmillan, 1986.

López, Ernesto. "Gasto militar en la Argentina: 1970–1986." In *Defensa y democracia, un debate entre civiles y militares,* ed. Gustavo Druetta, Eduardo Estevez, and Ernesto López. Buenos Aires: Puntosur, 1990.

Machinea, José Luis. *La crisis de la deuda, el financiamiento internacional y la partici- pación del sector privado, financiamiento del desarrollo.* Santiago de Chile: CEPAL, Secretaría Ejecutiva, 2002.

——. "Stabilization Under Alfonsín." In *Argentina in the Crisis Years, 1983–1990: From Alfonsín to Menem,* ed. Colin M. Lewis and Nissa Torrents. London: Institute of Latin American Studies, 1993.

——. *Stabilization Under Alfonsín's Government: A Frustrated Attempt.* Documentos CEDES, no. 42. Buenos Aires: Centro de Estudios de Estado y Sociedad, 1990.

——. "The Use of the Exchange Rate as an Anti-inflationary Instrument in a Stabi- lization-Liberalization Attempt: The Southern Cone Experiment." Ph.D. diss., University of Minnesota, 1983.

Machinea, José Luis, and Juan Sommer. *El manejo de la deuda externa en condiciones de crisis de balanza de pagos: La moratoria 1988–89.* Documentos CEDES, no. 59. Buenos Aires: Centro de Estudios de Estado y Sociedad, 1990.

Mack, Carlos. *Der Falkland (Malvinas)-Konflikt: Eine Konstellationsanalyse des britisch- argentinischen Konfliktes unter besonderer Berücksichtigung der argentinischen Entscheidung zur Invasion.* Frankfurt am Main: Lang, 1992.

Maier, Charles S. *In Search of Stability: Explorations in Historical Political Economy.* Cam- bridge Studies in Modern Political Economies. Cambridge: Cambridge Univer- sity Press, 1987.

Mainwaring, Scott. "Democracy in Brazil and the Southern Cone: Achievements and Prob- lems." *Journal of Interamerican Studies and World Affairs* 37, no. 1 (1995): 113–79.

Majul, Luis. *Por qué cayó Alfonsín: El nuevo terrorismo económico: Los personajes, las conexiones, las claves secretas.* Buenos Aires: Editorial Sudamericana, 1990.

Mallon, Richard D., and Juan V. Sourrouille. *Economic Policymaking in a Conflict Soci- ety: The Argentine Case.* Cambridge: Harvard University Press, 1975.

——. *La política económica en una sociedad conflictiva: El caso argentino.* Biblioteca de economía política. Buenos Aires: Amorrortu editores, 1973.

Malloy, James M. "Authoritarianism and Corporatism in Latin America: The Modal Pattern." In *Authoritarianism and Corporatism in Latin America,* ed. James M. Malloy, 3–19. Pittsburgh: University of Pittsburgh Press, 1977.

——. "The Politics of Transition in Latin America." In *Authoritarians and Democrats: Regime Transition in Latin America,* ed. James M. Malloy and Mitchell A. Selig- son. Pittsburgh: University of Pittsburgh Press, 1987.

Manzetti, Luigi. *The International Monetary Fund and Economic Stabilization: The Argen- tine Case.* New York: Praeger, 1991.

——. "Political Manipulations and Market Reforms Failures." *World Politics* 55, no. 3 (2003): 315–60.

Martin, Maria Haydée, Alberto S.J. de Paula, and Ramón Gutiérrez. *Los ingenieros mil- itares y sus precursores en el desarrollo argentino.* 2 vols. Buenos Aires: Fabrica- ciones Militares, 1976.

Martin, Percy F. *Through Five Republics (of South America): A Critical Description of Argen- tina, Brazil, Chile, Uruguay, and Venezuela in 1905.* New York: Dodd Mead, 1906.

Martínez de Hoz, José Alfredo. *Bases para una Argentina moderna, 1976–80.* Buenos Aires: N.p., 1981.

——. *Quince años después.* Buenos Aires: Emecé Editores, 1991.

Meadows, Dennis, and the Club of Rome. *The Limits to Growth: A Report for the Club of Rome's Project on the Predicament of Mankind.* New York: Universe Books, 1972.

Meltzer, Allan, and Adam Lerrick. "Beyond IMF Bailouts: Default Without Disruption." Working Paper. Gailliot Center for Public Policy, Carnegie Mellon University, Pittsburgh, May 2001.

Mendelsohn, Stefan, and the Group of Thirty. Study Group on Capital Movement and the Growth of International Indebtedness. *The Outlook for International Bank Lending: A Survey of Opinion Among Leading International Bankers.* New York: The Group, 1981.

Miller, Richard Bradford. *Citicorp: The Story of a Bank in Crisis.* New York: McGraw-Hill, 1993.

Minford, Patrick. "Time-Inconsistency, Democracy, and Optimal Contingent Rules." *Oxford Economic Papers* 47, no. 2 (1995): 195–210.

Ministerio de Economía y Producción. "Evolución reciente de la economía Argentina y perspectivas de sostenibilidad: Un enfoque comparado." Análisis 4. Buenos Aires: Ministerio de Economía y Producción, September 2005.

Minsburg, Naúm, and Irma Antognazi. *Los guardianes del dinero: Las políticas del FMI en la Argentina.* Buenos Aires: Editorial Norma, 2003.

Müller, Alberto E.G., and Martín G. Rapetti. "Un quiebre olvidado: La política económica de Martínez de Hoz." In *Actas de la XXXV Reunión Anual de la Asociación Argentina de Economía Política.* Córdoba: La Asociación Argentina de Economía Política, 2000.

Munck, Ronaldo. "Introduction: A Thin Democracy." *Latin American Perspectives* 24, no. 6 (1997): 4–21.

———. "The 'Modern' Military Dictatorship in Latin America: The Case of Argentina (1976–1982)." *Latin American Perspectives* 12, no. 4 (1985): 41–74.

Mussa, Michael. *Argentina and the Fund: From Triumph to Tragedy.* Washington, D.C.: Institute for International Economics, 2002.

N'Haux, Enrique M. *Menem-Cavallo: El poder mediterráneo.* Buenos Aires: Corregidor, 1993.

North, Douglass Cecil. "Institutions and Economic Growth: An Historical Introduction." *World Development* 17, no. 9 (1989): 1319–32.

O'Brien, Philip J. "Authoritarianism and the New Orthodoxy: The Political Economy of the Chilean Regime, 1973–1982." In *Generals in Retreat: The Crisis of Military Rule in Latin America,* ed. Philip J. O'Brien and Paul A. Cammack, 144–83. Manchester: Manchester University Press, 1985.

———. "The Debt Cannot Be Paid: Castro and the Latin American Debt." *Bulletin of Latin American Research* 5 (1986): 41–63.

O'Donnell, Guillermo A. *Bureaucratic Authoritarianism: Argentina, 1966–1973, in Comparative Perspective.* Berkeley and Los Angeles: University of California Press, 1986.

———. "External Debt: Why Don't Our Governments Do the Obvious?" *CEPAL Review* 27 (1985): 27–33.

———. "Reflections on the Patterns of Change in the Bureaucratic-Authoritarian State." *Latin American Research Review* 13, no. 1 (1978): 3–38.

Olson, Mancur. *Power and Prosperity: Outgrowing Communist and Capitalist Dictatorships.* New York: Basic Books, 2000.

———. *The Rise and Decline of Nations: Economic Growth, Stagflation, and Social Rigidities.* New Haven: Yale University Press, 1982.

Oxhorn, Philip, and Graciela Ducatenzeiler. *What Kind of Democracy? What Kind of Market? Latin America in the Age of Neoliberalism.* University Park: Pennsylvania State University Press, 1998.

Padilla del Bosque, Rodolfo. "Estimación de la fuga de capitales bajo diversas metologías para los casos de Argentina, Brasil, Mexico y Venezuela. Análisis de sus posibles causas y efectos." Working Paper. Centro de Investigaciones Económicas Instituto Torcuato di Tella, Buenos Aires, 1991.

Parker, Phyllis R. *Brazil and the Quiet Intervention, 1964.* Austin: University of Texas Press, 1979.

Pereira, Luiz Bresser, and Yoshiaki Nakano. *The Theory of Inertial Inflation: The Foundation of Economic Reform in Brazil and Argentina.* Translated from the Portuguese by Colleen Reeks. Boulder, Colo.: Lynne Rienner, 1987.

Perón, Juan Domingo. *Actualización política y doctrinaria para la toma del poder.* Madrid: El Movimiento, 1971.

————. *Obras completas.* 27 vols. Buenos Aires: Proyecto Hernandarias, 1984.

Perry, Guillermo, and Luis Serven. "Argentina's Macroeconomic Collapse: Causes and Lessons." Draft chapter for "Managing Economic Volatility and Crises: A Practitioner's Guide," ed. Joshua Aizenman and Brian Pinto. March 2004. http://www1 .worldbank.org/economicpolicy/documents/mv/pgchapter11.pdf.

Pinheiro, Letícia. "O pragmatismo responsável no arquivo do presidente Geisel." In *Dossiê Geisel,* ed. Celso Castro, Maria Celina Soares d Araújo, and Alzira Alves de Abreu, 75–88. Rio de Janeiro: Fundação Getulio Vargas Editora, 2002.

Polonsky, Mariángeles. "Estructura del comercio exterior argentino del año 2006." *Revista del CEI: Comercio exterior e integración,* no. 8 (2007).

Potash, Robert A. *The Army and Politics in Argentina.* Stanford: Stanford University Press, 1969.

————. "The Changing Role of the Military in Argentina." *Journal of Interamerican Studies* 3, no. 4 (1961): 571–78.

Powell, Andrew. "Argentina's Avoidable Crisis: Bad Luck, Bad Economics, Bad Politics, Bad Advice." *Brookings Trade Forum,* 2002.

Pozzi, Pablo A. "Argentina, 1976–1982: Labour Leadership and Military Government." *Journal of Latin American Studies* 20, no. 1 (1988): 111–38.

Prebisch, Raúl. *Towards a Dynamic Development Policy for Latin America.* New York: United Nations, 1963.

Ramamurti, Ravi. "The Impact of Privatization on the Latin American Debt Problem." *Journal of Interamerican Studies and World Affairs* 34, no. 2 (1992): 93–125.

Ramos, Joseph. "The Economics of Hyperstagflation." *Journal of Economic Development* 7, no. 4 (1980): 467–88.

Rapoport, Mario. *Historia económica, política y social de la Argentina (1880–2000).* Buenos Aires: Ediciones Macchi, 2000.

Restivo, Néstor, and Raúl Dellatorre. *El Rodrigazo, 30 años después: Un ajuste que cambió al país, Claves para todos.* Buenos Aires: Capital Intelectual, 2005.

Robben, Antonius C.G.M. *Political Violence and Trauma in Argentina.* The Ethnography of Political Violence. Philadelphia: University of Pennsylvania Press, 2005.

Rodríguez, Carlos A. "Commentarios a la segunda parte." In *Inflación y estabilización: La experiencia de Israel, Argentina, Brasil, Bolivia y Mexico,* ed. Michael Bruno and Jose Maria Fanelli. Mexico City: Fondo de Cultura Económica, 1988.

Rodríguez Diez, Alejandro. *Historia secreta: Devaluación y pesificación.* Buenos Aires: Bifronte, 2003.

Rostow, W. W. *The Stages of Economic Growth, a Non-Communist Manifesto.* Cambridge: Cambridge University Press, 1960.

Rouquié, Alain. "El poder militar en la Argentina de hoy: Cambio y continuidad." In *El poder militar en la Argentina (1976–1981),* ed. Peter Waldmann and Ernesto Garzón Valdés, 65–76. Frankfurt am Main: Verlag Klaus Dieter Vervuert, 1982.

Schamis, Hector E. "Reconceptualizing Latin American Authoritarianism in the 1970s: From Bureaucratic-Authoritarianism to Neoconservatism." *Comparative Politics* 23, no. 2 (1991): 201–20.

Schneider, Ben Ross. "The Material Bases of Technocracy: Investor Confidence and Neoliberalism in Latin America." In *The Politics of Expertise in Latin America,* ed. Miguel Angel Centeno and Patricio Silva. New York: St. Martin's Press, 1998.

Schuker, Stephen A. *American "Reparations" to Germany, 1919–33: Implications for the Third-World Debt Crisis.* Princeton: International Finance Section, Department of Economics, Princeton University, 1988.

Schvarzer, Jorge. *Argentina, 1976–81: El endeudamiento externo como pivote de la especulación financiera.* Buenos Aires: Centro de Investigaciones Sociales sobre el Estado y la Administración, 1983.

———. *Convertibilidad y deuda externa.* 2nd ed. Buenos Aires: EUDEBA, 2003.

———. *Implantación de un modelo económico: La experiencia Argentina entre 1975 y el 2000.* Buenos Aires: A-Z Editoria, 2000.

———. *Martínez de Hoz: La lógica política de la política económica.* Buenos Aires: Centro de Investigaciones Sociales sobre el Estado y la Administración (CISEA), 1983.

———. *Un modelo sin retorno: Dificultades y perspectivas de la economía Argentina.* Buenos Aires: Centro de Investigaciones Sociales sobre el Estado y la Administración, 1990.

Scott, James C. *Weapons of the Weak: Everyday Forms of Peasant Resistance.* New Haven: Yale University Press, 1985.

Sheahan, John. *Patterns of Development in Latin America: Poverty, Repression, and Economic Strategy.* Princeton: Princeton University Press, 1987.

Shonfield, Andrew. *Modern Capitalism: The Changing Balance of Public and Private Power.* London: Oxford University Press, 1968.

Sigmund, Paul E. *The United States and Democracy in Chile.* Baltimore: Johns Hopkins University Press, 1993.

Silva, Eduardo. "Capitalist Coalitions, the State, and Neoliberal Economic Restructuring: Chile, 1973–88." *World Politics* 45, no. 4 (1993): 526–59.

Singer, Hans Walter. "The Distribution of Gains Between Investing and Borrowing Countries." *American Economic Review* 40, no. 2 (May 1950): 473–85.

Skidmore, Thomas E. "The Politics of Economic Stabilization in Postwar Latin America." In *Authoritarianism and Corporatism in Latin America,* ed. James M. Malloy. Pittsburgh: University of Pittsburgh Press, 1977.

———. *The Politics of Military Rule in Brazil, 1964–85.* New York: Oxford University Press, 1988.

Smith, William C. *Authoritarianism and the Crisis of the Argentine Political Economy.* Stanford: Stanford University Press, 1989.

———. "Heterodox Shocks and the Political Economy of Democratic Transition in

Argentina and Brazil." In *Lost Promises: Debt, Austerity, and Development in Latin America*, ed. William L. Canak, 138–66. Boulder, Colo.: Westview Press, 1989.

———. "State, Market, and Neoliberalism in Post-Transition Argentina: The Menem Experiment." *Journal of Interamerican Studies and World Affairs* 33, no. 4 (1991): 45–82.

Solanet, Manuel. *Notas sobre la guerra de Malvinas*. Buenos Aires: Grafikar Sociedad de Impresores, 2004.

Solomon, Robert. "The Debt of Developing Countries: Another Look." *Brookings Papers on Economic Activity*, no. 2 (1981): 593–607.

———. "'The Elephant in the Boat?' The United States and the World Economy." *Foreign Affairs* 60, no. 3 (1982): 573–92.

Sourrouille, Juan V., Bernardo P. Kosacoff, and Jorge Lucángeli. *Transnacionalización y política económica en la Argentina*. Buenos Aires: Bibliotecas Universitarias Centro Editor de América Latina, Centro de Economía Transnacional, 1985.

Sourrouille, Juan V., and Jorge Lucángeli. *Política económica y procesos de desarrollo: La experiencia argentina entre 1976 y 1981*. Estudios e informes de la CEPAL 27. Santiago: United Nations, 1983.

Starr, Pamela K. "Government Coalitions and the Viability of Currency Boards: Argentina Under the Cavallo Plan." *Journal of Interamerican Studies and World Affairs* 39, no. 2 (1997): 83–133.

Stein, Ernesto H., and Jorge M. Streb. "Political Stabilization Cycles in High-Inflation Economies." *Journal of Development Economics* 56, no. 1 (1998): 159–80.

Stigler, G. J. "A Theory of Oligopoly." *Journal of Political Economy* 72 (1964): 44–61.

Stiles, Kendall W. "Argentina's Bargaining with the IMF." *Journal of Interamerican Studies and World Affairs* 29, no. 3 (1987): 55–85.

———. *Negotiating Debt: The IMF Lending Process*. Boulder, Colo.: Westview Press, 1991.

Sturzenegger, Adolfo. *Mercado, plan, crecimiento, estabilización en Argentina*. Buenos Aires: Banco Central de la República Argentina, 1984.

Sturzenegger, Federico. "Description of a Populist Experience: Argentina, 1973–1976." In *The Macroeconomics of Populism in Latin America*, ed. Rudiger Dornbusch and Sebastian Edwards. Chicago: University of Chicago Press, 1991.

Tanzi, Vito. "Rationalizing the Government Budget—Or Why Fiscal Policy Is so Difficult." In *Economic Policy Reform: The Second Stage*, ed. Anne O. Krueger. Chicago: University of Chicago Press, 2000.

Taylor, Alan M. "On the Costs of Inward-Looking Development: Price Distortions, Growth, and Divergence in Latin America." *Journal of Economic History* 58, no. 1 (1998).

Teijeiro, Mario. "Una vez más, la política fiscal." Working Paper. Centro de Estudios Públicos, Buenos Aires, June 2001.

Tenembaum, Ernesto. *Enemigos: Argentina y el FMI: La apasionante Discusión entre un periodista y uno de los hombres clave del Fondo en los noventa*. Ed. Colección Biografías y Documentos. Buenos Aires: Editorial Norma, 2004.

Thompson, Andres. *"Think Tanks" en la Argentina: Conocimiento, instituciones y política*. Documentos CEDES, Serie Organizaciones no Gubernamentales y Filantropía, no. 102. Buenos Aires: Centro de Estudios de Estado y Sociedad, 1994.

Torre, Juan Carlos. "Conflict and Cooperation in Governing the Economic Emergency: The Alfonsín Years." In *Argentina in the Crisis Years, 1983–1990: From Alfonsín to Menem*, ed. Colin M. Lewis and Nissa Torrents. London: Institute of Latin American Studies, 1993.

———. *Los sindicatos en el gobierno, 1973–1976.* Biblioteca política argentina 30. Buenos Aires: Centro Editor de América Latina, 1983.

Torres, José Luis. *La década infame.* Buenos Aires: Editorial de Formación "Patria," 1945.

Tulchin, Joseph S., and Augusto Varas. *From Dictatorship to Democracy: Rebuilding Political Consensus in Chile.* Woodrow Wilson Center Current Studies on Latin America. Boulder, Colo.: Lynne Rienner, 1991.

Túrolo, Carlos M. *De Isabel a Videla: Los pliegues del poder.* Buenos Aires: Editorial Sudamericana, 1996.

United States Arms Control and Disarmament Agency. *World Military Expenditures and Arms Transfers, 1973–1983.* Ann Arbor, Mich.: Inter-University Consortium for Political and Social Research, 1986.

U.S. Congress, Senate. Committee on Banking, Housing, and Urban Affairs. *Final Report of the International Financial Institution Advisory Commission: Hearing Before the Committee on Banking, Housing, and Urban Affairs.* 106th Cong., 2nd sess., March 9, 2000.

Vacs, Aldo C. "A Delicate Balance: Confrontation and Cooperation Between Argentina and the United States in the 1980s." *Journal of Interamerican Studies and World Affairs* 31, no. 4 (1989): 23–59.

Valdés, Juan Gabriel. *Pinochet's Economists: The Chicago School in Chile.* Historical Perspectives on Modern Economics. Cambridge: Cambridge University Press, 1995.

Valenzuela, Arturo. "The Military in Power: The Consolidation of One-Man Rule in Chile." In *The Struggle for Democracy in Chile, 1982–1990,* ed. Paul W. Drake and Ivan Jaksic. Lincoln: University of Nebraska Press, 1991.

Verbitsky, Horacio. *Ezeiza, espejo de la Argentina.* Buenos Aires: Planeta, 1995.

Viola, Eduardo, and Scott Mainwaring. "Transitions to Democracy: Brazil and Argentina in the 1980s." *Journal of International Affairs* 38 (1985): 193–219.

Volcker, Paul A., and Toyoo Gyohten. *Changing Fortunes: The World's Money and the Threat to American Leadership.* New York: Times Books, 1992.

Whyte, Glen, Alan M. Saks, and Sterling Hook. "When Success Breeds Failure: The Role of Self-Efficacy in Escalating Commitment to a Losing Course of Action." *Journal of Organizational Behavior* 18, no. 5 (1997): 415–32.

Winch, Donald. "Keynes, Keynesianism, and State Intervention." In *The Political Power of Economic Ideas: Keynesianism Across Nations,* ed. Peter A. Hall, 107–27. Princeton: Princeton University Press, 1989.

World Bank. *Argentina: Economic Memorandum.* Washington, D.C.: World Bank, 1985.

———. *Argentina: Reforms for Price Stability and Growth: A World Bank Country Study.* Washington, D.C.: World Bank, 1990.

———. *Argentina's Privatization Program: Experience, Issues, and Lessons.* Washington, D.C.: World Bank, 1993.

———. "World Development Indicators." Washington, D.C.: World Bank, various years.

Zlotogwiazda, Marcelo, and Luis Balaguer. *Citibank vs. Argentina: Historia de un país en bancarrota.* Buenos Aires: Editorial Sudamericana, 2003.

ARCHIVES AND PUBLISHED RECORDS

Archives of the International Monetary Fund, Washington, D.C.
Archivo de la Cámara de Diputados, Buenos Aires

Archivos del Ministerio de Relaciones Exteriores y Culto de la República Argentina, Buenos Aires

Arquivo Antônio Azeredo da Silveira, Fundação Getulio Vargas, Rio de Janeiro

Arquivo Ernesto Geisel, Fundação Getulio Vargas, Rio de Janeiro

Arquivo Marcílio Marques Moreira, Fundação Getulio Vargas, Rio de Janeiro

Arquivo Paulo Nogueira Batista, Fundação Getulio Vargas, Rio de Janeiro

Arthur F. Burns Papers, Gerald R. Ford Presidential Library, Ann Arbor, Mich.

Jimmy Carter Library, Atlanta, Ga.

Collection of ephemera from the Argentine national elections, 1989, Princeton University Library.

Gerald R. Ford Presidential Library, Ann Arbor, Mich.

Robert Hill Papers, Dartmouth College, Hanover, N.H.

"Olmos, Alejandro vs. José A. Martínez de Hoz," Tribunales de Commodoro Py, Buenos Aires

Ronald Reagan Presidential Library, Simi Valley, Calif.

Donald Regan Papers, Treasury Department, 1975–1992, Library of Congress, Washington, D.C.

David Rockefeller Collection, JPMorganChase Archives, New York, N.Y.

William Simon Papers, Lafayette College, Easton, Pa.

U.S. GOVERNMENT PUBLIC DOCUMENTS

Board of Governors of the Federal Reserve System. Available at http://federalreserve.gov/monetarypolicy/fomc_historical.htm.

Central Intelligence Agency, FOIA Released Documents

National Security Council. Accessible through the Declassified Documents Reference System (DDRS).

U.S. Department of State, State Argentina Declassification Project (1975–84)

U.S. Department of State, FOIA Released Documents

INDEX